Water in the Hispanic Southwest

Michael C. Meyer

Water in the Hispanic Southwest

A Social and Legal History, 1550–1850

With a New Afterword by the Author

The University of Arizona Press   Tucson

About the Author

Michael C. Meyer's longstanding interest in Mexican and Latin American history has taken the form of writing, editing, teaching, and research. Director of the Latin American Area Center at the University of Arizona since 1974, he has written and edited ten books on the history of Mexico and Latin America, including *The Course of Mexican History,* coauthored with William L. Sherman. In 1980 Dr. Meyer became a director of PROFMEX, the Consortium of United States Research Programs for Mexico. His interest in water law in the history of the Southwest stemmed from his involvement as an expert witness in the longstanding water rights case of the *State of New Mexico vs. R. Lee Aamodt.* Dr. Meyer served as editor of the *Hispanic American Historical Review* for five years, and became senior editor of *The Americas* in 1977 and member of the board of advisers of the *Arizona Journal of International and Comparative Law* in 1982.

First paperbound printing 1996
THE UNIVERSITY OF ARIZONA PRESS

Copyright © 1984
The Arizona Board of Regents
All Rights Reserved

This book was set in 10/12 VIP Baskerville.
Manufactured in the U.S.A.
⊛ This book is printed on acid-free, archival-quality paper.

Library of Congress Cataloging in Publication Data

Meyer, Michael C.
    Water in the Hispanic Southwest.

    Bibliography: p.
    Includes index.
    1. Water-rights—Southwest, New—History.
2. Water—Law and legislation—Southwest, New—History.
3. Water—Southwest, New—History.   I. Title.
KF5569.M49   1984   346.7904'691   83-24276
                          347.9064691
ISBN 0-8165-0825-9
ISBN 0-8165-1595-6 (pbk.)

To Goldalee, Scott, Debra, and Sharon

Contents

Preface

For thousands of years the philosophies, religions, and mythologies of mankind have concerned themselves with water—with its regenerative qualities and its destructive potential. From stories of the Creation and the Flood, permeating a score of cultures, to philosophical musings spanning centuries, water has played a pivotal role in determining how man views himself and his fellow man, and how he tries to cope with his physical and spiritual environment.

In the ancient world, water was one of those few determinants of life that actually defined the most fundamental kind of social doctrine. As water was subjected to some measure of human control and the first victories over aridity were scored, agriculture became a mainstay of human existence and man moved tenuously along the road to civilization. It was no accident that the first civilized communities developed in the Tigris and Euphrates river valleys, where irrigation provided for a food surplus and ultimately made urban life possible.

Water helped ancient man learn those first difficult lessons about the rights of others and responsibility to a larger society. Even the most rudimentary irrigation system required organization, discipline, cooperation, and a measure of social cohesion. Mutual need begets mutual aid. Notions of sharing, of equity, of compromise, and of the common good first floated precariously on this liquid foundation to be later cemented in philosophical thought and codified law. Philosophically, judicially, and even ecologically man began to cope with the timeless quandaries of water: too little or too much, too dirty or too salty, too inaccessible, too stagnant, too hot or too cold. It is not surprising that a substance so basic to all sources of life should have permeated philosophical, scientific, and religious thought. It became part of the moral and mental legacy parents passed on to their children. The suffering innate to a shriveled landscape or the abundance conveyed by the green of thriving crops was understood more in terms of water than any other requirements of plant reproduction. By the time the Europeans arrived in the New World, both the Spaniards and the American Indians had long-accepted value systems which incorporated attitudes toward water into basic dogma, not easily susceptible to dispute.

Because water availability or scarcity is paramount to much of the argumentation which follows, it was necessary to determine with some accuracy wet and dry years in the Southwest from roughly 1550 to 1850. Part of the process was cumbersome in the extreme, but rewarding nevertheless. During the course of my research in Spanish, Mexican, and southwestern archives, I took special note of any reference to weather generally, and precipitation specifically. Although over a thousand of such references were uncovered, I still found myself with vast chronological and geographical gaps. Dendrochronology came to my rescue. The Laboratory of Tree-Ring Research at the University of Arizona has published chronologies for almost two hundred locations in the Mexican north and the United States Southwest, making it possible to chart wet and dry years in northern New Spain for many centuries. Some of the data cover a period of more than a thousand years, but in almost all of the cases the beginning chronologies antedate the arrival of the Spaniards in the sixteenth century. They make it possible to approximate actual rainfall for some two hundred sites for every year from 1500 to the present.

Can historians have sufficient faith in these chronologies to apply them with assurance to their own research? The answer is unequivocally yes. Comparisons of the tree-ring analyses with the documentary evidence uncovered in the archives provide the kind of statistically valid independent verification that historians would love to have for other kinds of data. The comparisons give one tremendous confidence in the reliability of the dendrochronologies. In very few cases is there any discrepancy at all. If a government official, a soldier, or a clergyman reports to a superior that a drought has enveloped his area, or that the rains during the year have been more generous than usual, this information will almost always be reflected in the dendrochronologies for the same area at the same time. In those cases where minor variance occurs, one is often tempted to place greater faith in the chronologies than in the historical evidence. An official reporting that his region has experienced six years of severe drought might be exaggerating, speaking metaphorically, or simply displaying a bad memory. If the dendrochronologies in this case establish four very dry years, preceded by a wet one and another dry one, the tree-ring analysis is probably the more reliable source. Throughout this study, in the absence of specific documentary citations, references to wet or dry years are supported by the dendrochronological evidence.[1]

The chapters which follow are grouped into two major sections. Part I treats the influence of water on the development of the north, with special attention given to inter- and intra-racial conflict. Part II is concerned with conflict resolution and the adaptation of Spanish and Mexican jurisprudence and the respective judicial systems to the many unanticipated controversies that water produced. Neither part is designed to establish that the history of the Southwest is simply a product of water availability. The purpose is more modest, that of uncovering the role of water in the series of historical processes which gave the Hispanic Southwest its unique regional character.

I have eschewed the early temptation of one historically trained to present the major themes in a strict chronological fashion in the belief that in this case such organization not only leads to unnecessary repetition but, more importantly, tends to dissipate the overriding continuities of the water history of the Southwest. During the preparation of several early drafts I became increasingly convinced that traditional periodization does not lend itself to the study of the interaction of physical and human reality when technological change is most noticeable for its absence and when the highest levels of governmental authority are largely uninformed about and unresponsive to local needs. Rainfall in northern New Spain was not captured or put to beneficial use because a commandant general was appointed for the Provincias Internas. The Yaqui and Mayo rivers did not run full or scant because Father Hidalgo issued the Grito de Dolores. The irrigation networks in Tucson and San Antonio did not hold or break because José María Morelos was captured and executed. Crops did not prosper or wither in the Río Grande valley because Agustín de Iturbide conceived the Plan de Iguala, and the mines did not flood in

---

1. Data are available for Arizona, New Mexico, Texas, California, Baja California, Sonora, Chihuahua, Coahuila, and Durango. The four volumes published to date are Linda G. Drew (ed.), *Tree-Ring Chronologies of Western America* (Tucson: Laboratory of Tree-Ring Research, 1972), Linda G. Drew, *Tree-Ring Chronologies of Western America* (Tucson: Laboratory of Tree-Ring Research, 1975), Linda G. Drew, *Tree-Ring Chronologies for Dendroclimatic Analysis* (Tucson: Laboratory of Tree-Ring Research, 1976), and Jeffrey S. Dean and William J. Robinson, *Expanded Tree-Ring Chronologies for the Southwestern United States* (Tucson: Laboratory of Tree-Ring Research, 1978).

Baja California because Antonio López de Santa Anna sold the Mesilla Valley to the United States.

These truisms aside, not even an event as politically momentous as Mexican independence from Spain exerted much influence on conflict resolution, as the local judicial systems remained largely impervious to the change of sovereignty. With the passage of time the names and titles of officials changed, lines of reporting authority were altered, territories were realigned with new designations and new officialdoms, Indians were denied and subsequently granted citizenship, but in spite of all of the historiographical clamor about these changes their substantive import was negligible with respect to water. When individual citizens appeared before local magistrates to contest water allocations, they found that Mexican independence had not subverted Spanish judicial principle or procedure.

Perhaps the best example of the change in form, but not in substance, is the procedure used to obtain a land grant, with or without a water right attached. Throughout the entire colonial period the process was long, cumbersome, and litigious. It culminated in a formal act of possession. The individual acquiring title would go out to the land in question, accompanied by an appropriate royal official, would pull up some grass, turn over a small amount of soil, throw a few stones, and cry out: "Long live the King. Long live the Spanish Kingdom." After independence the entire complicated procedure remained almost identical, except in the act of possession the grantee, accompanied by the proper official, would pull up some grass, turn over a small amount of soil, throw a few stones, and cry out: "Long live the President. Long live the Mexican nation." In his study of the Southwest during the Mexican period David Weber has postulated that the judicial system remained Spanish with but few modifications.[2] He is certainly correct. Except in the most superficial sense the continuities were not broken by Mexican independence.

As in any undertaking of this kind, one incurs debts as he proceeds. It is a pleasure to acknowledge them while retaining responsibility for anything that might have gone wrong. Lawyer and Pecos historian Em Hall whetted my interest in the topic, not knowing that it would consume me for the next five years. William Taylor, with whom I

2. David J. Weber, *The Mexican Frontier, 1821-1846: The American Southwest Under Mexico* (Albuquerque: University of New Mexico Press, 1982), p. 38.

sparred in court in the water case of the *State of New Mexico versus R. Lee Aamodt et al.,* convinced me on several occasions of the folly of my ways and, in the interest of documentary rigor, prompted me to buttress other arguments. Archivists Rosario Parra of the Archivo General de Indias in Seville and Alejandra Moreno of the Archivo General de la Nación in Mexico City gave free and easy access to the huge corpus of documentation in their respective repositories. Susan Deeds helped in the process of converting a nineteenth- and twentieth-century historian into a colonialist. When paleographic frustrations set in, William Sherman was generous with his time. Murdo MacLeod's extensive bibliographic and historiographic knowledge in many fields repeatedly came to my aid when I needed to pursue a matter others might have considered esoteric. John Super, long interested in the agricultural history of colonial Spanish America, not only gave important documentary citations but also shared pertinent microfilm with me. Richard Greenleaf, Kieran McCarty, Mardith Schuetz, Paul Vanderwood, and Michael Murphy did the same. Charles Polzer made available to me his mammoth and unprecedented documentary guide, even before it was intended to be used by the historical public. In Mexico City colleagues at the Instituto de Investigaciones Históricas of the Universidad Nacional Autónoma de México, and especially Miguel León-Portilla, Roberto Moreno, Ignacio del Rio, and Sergio Ortega, spent hours with me in the refinement of my approach. Marilyn Bradian never allowed the tedium of typing successive drafts to compromise her good humor. To each, I am grateful.

MICHAEL C. MEYER

PART I

Water and Society

CHAPTER 1

Water, Culture, and Tradition

The northern frontier of New Spain, stretching more than 2,000 miles from east to west and almost 1,500 miles from south to north, occupied more than 960,000 square miles,[1] an area considerably larger than western Europe, and housed scores of Indian groups, many of whom spoke languages unintelligible to one another (fig. 1.1, page 6). A region so huge and diverse offered a formidable challenge to any self-appointed group of conquerors. The first Spaniards in the Southwest, like those elsewhere in the vast dominions of the Spanish empire in America, sought to establish a homogeneous society, rooted in Spanish tradition and secured by an unquestioning allegiance to both the Crown and the Roman Catholic Church. In the span of several centuries much was accomplished, some for the good and some for the bad, but the cultural homogeneity never emerged. Even in the face of physical subjugation, the native American tradition was far too strong in this area to yield readily to total absorption by a conquering race.

There can be no doubt that acculturation left a particularly telling imprint on the formation of the southwestern ethos. Cultural syncretism and biological fusion combined to bring about a new society, indebted to but distinct from the component parts that sired and nurtured it. Whether the result of force, applied by the stronger

---

1. The figure combines the total area of the four United States states to the north of the international boundary and the six Mexican states to the south. This area closely approximates the region covered in this study.

group, or the result of grudging acceptance, acculturation has an
importance that cannot be denied. But that process occurred everywhere in Spain's overseas possessions and does not explain why, at the
time of the United States conquest in 1848, the region was already so
different from the Central Valley of Mexico, the Yucatecan-
Guatemalan area, the Magdalena River valley of Colombia, or the
Bolivian *altiplano*. Without question the Indian admixture to the
emerging mestizo society is a prime factor which made the nineteenth-century resident of Taos so different from the Venezuelan of
the Orinoco or the Texan distinct from the Yucatecan. It is possible
too, but not yet established, that the Spaniards who were attracted to
northern New Spain were differently motivated than those who went
elsewhere. But perhaps there is an even more basic explanation.

Acculturation is not an all-encompassing phenomenon. Even in its
broadest conception it is insufficiently holistic as it concerns itself only
with the interactions of humans and does not address human adaptation to and manipulation of a delicate ecosystem. This process, which
might be thought of as *ecolturation*, also helped mold the contours of
southwestern society.

Human interaction with the ecosystem in northern New Spain was
not simply a matter of being wise to the ways of the desert. Certainly
the experienced southwestern dweller could find sufficient liquid
sustenance in the prickly pear (*Opuntia engelmannii*) or the barrel
cactus (*Ferocactus wislinzeni*) to stave off temporary thirst, but such
cunning tells us little about how concern with aridity conditioned a
world view.

At one level of abstraction the ecolturative process was concerned
with turning brown to green and green to brown without ever denying
the inherent beauty of either. Like acculturation it pitted two potentially antagonistic forces and sought at least a modicum of accommodation from each. There was constant give and take, and even
when one yielded peacefully to the other a certain price had to be
paid.

Because abundant plant life could thrive only with an adequate
water source, desert greenbelts stretched along streams and arroyos
long before the first humans happened on the scene. It was not
moisture alone which first altered the desert kaleidoscope. The same
water source which permitted germination of the mesquite or palo
verde seed served as a magnet to bird and animal life. Animal drop-
pings added nutriments to the soil and, in the process, propelled the
greening of the pencil-thin desert belts. But it was only with the arrival
of humans in the Southwest, perhaps some 50,000 years ago, that

ecolturation added a new dimension to the evolutionary change of the southwestern environment.

Like plant and animal life, the first human inhabitants of the desert were drawn to the same greenbelts. After thousands of years of trial and error, man's manipulation of water sources began to change the landscape. Irrigation was perhaps the most far-reaching early result of man's quest for security. As water was channeled out of natural streams and into adjacent fields, the elongated greenbelts became wider. The desert fought back with its own defensive mechanisms. Water diverted from its natural course, no matter how crudely, left downstream oases drier and less attractive to exploitation. Brown began to reclaim its heritage from green. Plant and animal life staked out claims to new areas, and the natural process began anew. But in those areas where ecolturation had already occurred there could be no turning back of the clock. The specific changes brought about by the new man-land relationship were subjected to subsequent mutations but seldom, if ever, could the ecosystem recover its pristine state. Once disturbed, the natural harmonies of the desert could not be entirely restored. By assimilating the natural environment to human needs, ecolturation had left its indelible imprint on the land, the flora, the fauna, and the human inhabitants of the Southwest. As the natural and man-made environments coalesced, a "mestizo" or miscegenated ecosystem emerged.

The goal of ecolturation was to blend competing forces into a new natural harmony in which the desert would yield to domestication and ultimately become a garden. But the process was infinitely complex, and innocent miscalculation as well as irrational manipulation occurred repeatedly, often to the detriment of both man and land. Violent resistance to ecolturation marked the history of the Southwest. Just as acculturation pressures often culminated in Indian rebellion against Spanish control, the natural forces of the desert also had ways of responding to thoughtless attempts at ecolturation. Bleeding an irrigation ditch off a main water source, constructing a dam, or even building a bridge across a normally placid stream could leave weakened banks ready to collapse under the brunt of the first sudden storm. Devastating floods resulted in tremendous loss of life and property but also wreaked havoc with the surrounding natural environment.

Those Spaniards who ventured north from Mexico City, Guadalajara and Zacatecas found a physical and cultural environment quite unlike that discovered by the vast majority of their New World countrymen. The one physical reality that overshadowed all others was

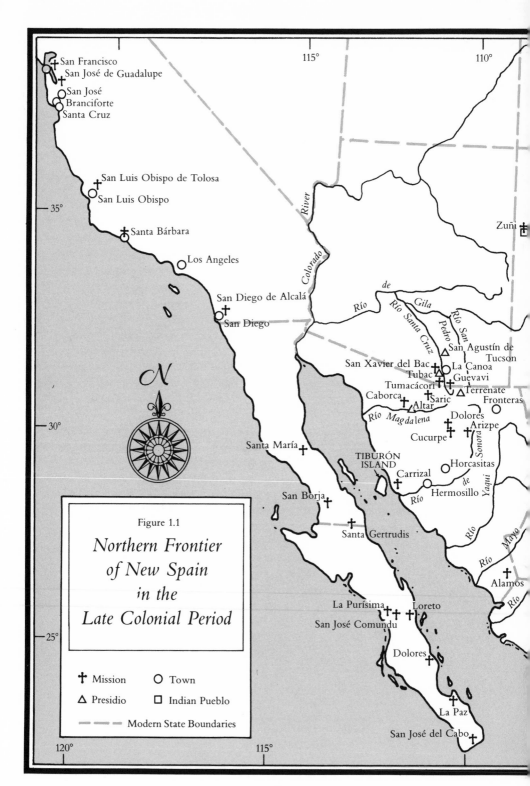

San Francisco
San José de Guadalupe
San José
Branciforte
Santa Cruz

San Luis Obispo de Tolosa
San Luis Obispo

Santa Bárbara

Los Angeles

San Diego de Alcalá
San Diego

115°

110°

Zuñi

Colorado River

de

Río   Gila

Río San Pedro

Río Santa Cruz

San Agustín de
Tucson
San Xavier del Bac
Tubac   La Canoa
Tumacácori   Guevavi
Caborca   Saric
Altar   Terrenate
Río Magdalena   Fronteras

Santa María

TIBURÓN
ISLAND

Carrizal

San Borja

Santa Gertrudis

Dolores
Arizpe
Cucurpe

Horcasitas

Hermosillo

Río

Río Sonora
de
Río Yaqui

Río

Alamos

Río Mayo

La Purísima   Loreto
San José Comundu

Dolores

La Paz

San José del Cabo

Figure 1.1

*Northern Frontier
of New Spain
in the
Late Colonial Period*

✝ Mission   O Town

△ Presidio   □ Indian Pueblo

— — — Modern State Boundaries

120°

115°

35°

30°

25°

6

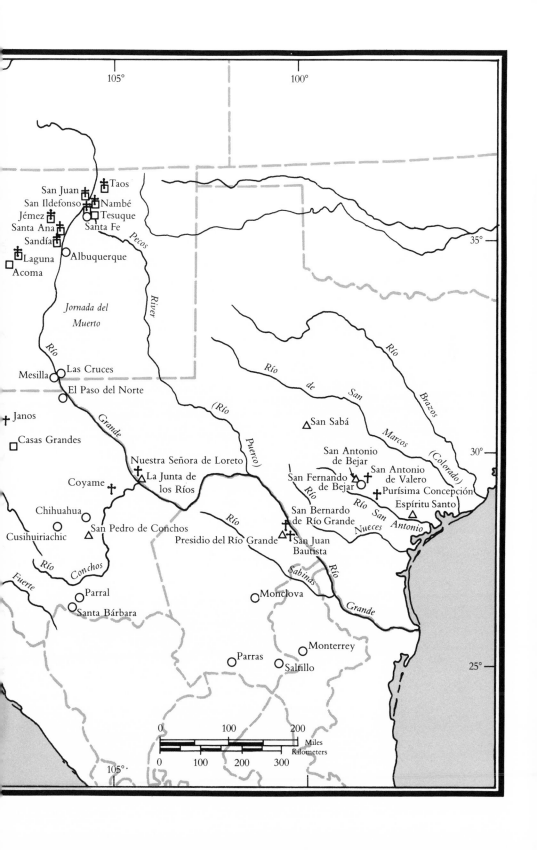

105°   100°

San Juan
Taos
San Ildefonso Nambé
Jémez Tesuque
Santa Ana Santa Fe
Sandía
Laguna Albuquerque
Acoma

Pecos

River

Jornada del
Muerto

Río

Mesilla Las Cruces
El Paso del Norte

35°

Janos

Casas Grandes

Grande

(Río

Puerco)

San Sabá

30°

San Antonio
de Bejar
San Antonio
de Valero
San Fernando
de Bejar Purísima Concepción
Espíritu Santo

Nuestra Señora de Loreto
Coyame La Junta de
los Ríos

Río
de
San

Marcos

Brazos

(Colorado)

Río

Chihuahua
Cusihuiriachic San Pedro de Conchos

Río

Río
Fuerte Conchos

San Bernardo
de Río Grande
Presidio del Río Grande San Juan
Bautista

Río
San

Antonio

Nueces

Parral
Santa Bárbara

Sabinas

Río

Grande

Monclova

25°

Parras Monterrey
Saltillo

105°

0   100   200
Miles
Kilometers
0   100   200   300

aridity, and the one cultural reality of similar magnitude was human adaptation to it. Without this adaptation survival in the Southwest would have been impossible. With it, ecolturation was inevitable.

As the only weapon in the constant battle against aridity, water exerted a tremendous influence on the history of the Mexican north or the Greater Southwest. It actuated and dominated an amazing variety of social and economic relationships. It dictated growth patterns, precipitated conflict, influenced the form of governmental institutions, and helped define how different social and ethnic groups related to one another. But some of the processes were more subtle. Human identity in this arid zone could not be defined in an ecological vacuum. As water became recognized widely as the prime determinant of the ecolturation process, it came to occupy a unique place in the southwestern psyche. Because of its cardinal role in the daily struggle for survival it was also afforded a telling reverence in southwestern religion, mythology, and lore.

If water was a major factor in shaping the contours of southwestern society, why is it that we know so little about it? Although the historiography of Spanish American colonial land tenure is rich,[2] relatively little is known about the historical relationship of land to water anywhere in Spain's huge American empire. The explanation for the paucity of water historiography is attributable to a series of interrelated factors. The highest-level Indian culture groups in the New World were almost invariably found in areas that were well-watered. This was not an accident. Either they constructed their civilizations in these areas because water was available, or the availability of water made possible the development of their civilizations. The Spaniards were attracted first to these same areas not only because of the availability of water but also because the native populations clustered there offered bodies to be worked and souls to be saved. The most important early contacts between Europeans and Indians, in both the Andean highlands of South America and the Central Valley of Mexico, thus occurred in areas where water was relatively plentiful.

It was only when the Spaniards began moving out into the periphery, for the most part in the second half of the seventeenth century, that they began venturing into areas where water was at a premium and therefore hotly contested. In New Spain this development oc-

---

2. Of the many valuable studies on the subject, only the following two fully appreciate the crucial role of water: Charles Harris III, *A Mexican Family Empire: The Latifundio of the Sánchez-Navarros, 1766–1867* (Austin: University of Texas Press, 1976), and William B. Taylor, *Landlord and Peasant in Colonial Oaxaca* (Stanford: Stanford University Press, 1972).

curred most obviously when the Spaniards began to penetrate the northern reaches of the viceroyalty—Sonora, Arizona, Baja and Alta California, Chihuahua, New Mexico, Coahuila, Nuevo León, and Texas. These are areas that traditionally have not commanded great interest in the historical scholarship, and much of the historical literature that has emerged relies on previous studies in central Mexico as models. If the issue of land tenure dominated historical thought to the south, its ostensible importance remained unchallenged in the north, even in light of the fact that anyone who has lived in an arid zone understands the potential menace of the desert and knows that land without water is often worthless. Indeed, it may be more of a liability than an asset.

Postulating the importance of water in the history of the desert Southwest does not mean to suggest a predetermined environmentalism. Geography does not create history. Furthermore, I hold no brief for water determinism. Ecolturation in fact represents the very antithesis of a deterministic environmentalism, as it addresses not simply the influence of the physical environment on man but rather the reciprocity of influences between the two. Ecolturation theory must rest on the foundation that neither man nor the environment is completely passive. While it readily accepts that scientific discovery, political decisions, social organization, and, most importantly, the application of new technology, can change the influence of nature, it insists that unintended and unanticipated natural reactions in turn influence the society which precipitated the original change.

By the end of the fifteenth century, when Europeans set out to find a sea route to India and instead chanced upon a new continent, hundreds of American Indian tribes had long learned to venerate water and to propitiate the deities who sent or withheld it. The most elaborate New World water cult was that of the Maya in southern Mexico and northern Central Mexico. No fewer than twenty Maya deities concerned themselves with matters of water, and in the Yucatan Peninsula alone some sixty villages had names associated with some manifestation of water. To pay homage to Chaac, the most powerful God of Rain, the Maya of Chichén-Itzá practiced human sacrifice. In the early morning, victims (men, women, and children) were cast into a great *cenote* or sacred well along with jewels and other valuable possessions. If they lived until noon, they were removed to relay messages from Chaac concerning the rainfall to be anticipated during the coming months. If they died, at least the Chaac had been appeased.[3]

If the Chaac rain cult in Yucatan marked the culmination of water worship in ancient Mexico, other tribes too saw in rain deities a powerful force determining agricultural cycles and the life process itself. The Lacandones of Chiapas drew the line at human sacrifice but did offer chickens and other small animals to their god of rain. In the Central Valley a variety of Nahuatl-speaking tribes, and ultimately the Aztecs, venerated Tlaloc, the God of Rain or Lord of the Waters. He was so important to Aztec religion that he shared with Huitzilopotchtli the place of honor in the Gran Templo de Tenochtitlán. The Zapotecs of Oaxaca called him Cocijo, and the Tononacs named him Tajin. To the Mixtecs, he was Tzahui, while in the far north the ceremonies of water devotion were directed by the Papago to Siiwani, and by the Comanches to the Thunderbird, by the Pueblos of San Juan to Tan-yi-ojua, and by the Queres to Tzitz-cha-yan. The Mayo Indians of Sonora celebrated as sacred the waters from the Río Mayo,[4] and the Zuni of western New Mexico believed that the Kachina gods resided in the Zuni River.[5]

The earliest European description of Zuni religion comes from the diary of Francisco Vásquez de Coronado. After capturing the Zuni village of Hawikuh in the summer of 1540, he recorded: "So far as I can find out, these Indians worship water, because they say it makes the maize grow and sustains their life, and the only other reason they know is that their ancestors did the same."[6] What Coronado did not learn was that one of the priesthoods of Zuni ceremonialism was the

3. The most thorough and perceptive discussion of the Maya water cult is found in Renan Irigoyen, *Bajo el signo de Chaac* (Mérida, Yucatan: Editorial Zamna, 1970), pp. 17–57.

4. See H. B. Nicholson, "Los Principales Dioses Meso-Americanos," in Centro de Investigaciones Antropológicas de México, *Esplendor del México Antiguo* 2 vols. (Mexico: Editorial del Valle de México, 1976), I, 161–178; Joseph W. Whitecotton, *The Zapotecs: Princes, Priests and Peasants* (Norman: University of Oklahoma Press, 1977), p. 169; Ruth M. Underhill, *Papago Indian Religion* (New York: Columbia University Press, 1946) pp. 13, 212–213; W. W. Newcomb, Jr., *The Indians of Texas: From Pre-Hispanic to Modern Times* (Austin: University of Texas Press, 1961), pp. 190–191. There is some evidence to suggest that the baby Jaguar of the Olmecs was also a rain god. See, for example, Olivia Vlahos, *New World Beginnings: Indian Cultures in the Americas* (New York: The Viking Press, 1970), p. 237; Muriel Porter Weaver, *The Aztecs, Maya and their Predecessors: Archaeology of Mesoamerica* (New York: Seminar Press, 1972), p. 56; Charles H. Lange, et al. (eds.), *The Southwestern Journals of Adolph F. Bandelier, 1885–1888* (Albuquerque: University of New Mexico Press, 1975), p. 83; N. Ross Crumine, *The Mayo Indians of Sonora: A People Who Refuse to Die* (Tucson: University of Arizona Press, 1977), p. 116.

5. Karl A. Wittfogel and Esther S. Goldfrank, "Some Aspects of Pueblo Mythology and Society," *Journal of American Folklore* 56 (January-March, 1943), 25.

6. Quoted in Herbert Eugene Bolton, *Coronado: Knight of Pueblo and Plains* (Albuquerque: University of New Mexico Press, 1964), p. 131.

Rain Priesthood.[7] Forty years later in the Río Grande valley Hernán Gallegos, the chronicler of the Sánchez Chamuscado expedition, witnessed a *mitote*, the Pueblo Indian rain dance. It included flagellation of the chief religious leader to help bring on the rains. After the dancing, which lasted the entire day, Gallegos recorded the final step in the impressive hydro-religious practice.

> As soon as the mitote has concluded, the flayed lord makes an offering of a certain number of sticks, adorned with many plumes, so that the people may place them in the cornfields and water-holes; for they worship and offer sacrifices at these holes. The natives do this, they say, because then they will never lack water.[8]

Venerated in different ways and occupying different positions in the elaborate pantheon of New World deities, the rain god, rain lord, or rain magician throughout the western hemisphere controlled clouds, springs, lightning and thunder, wells and, of course, rain. Even if occasionally capricious, he was the giver of life and a force not to be needlessly offended.

Not all North American Indians were agricultural at the time of the first European contact. The Seri and the Mescalero and Chiricahua Apache, for example, did not engage in agriculture; they subsisted on hunting, gathering, and fishing. Irrigation was practically unknown in Texas prior to the arrival of the Spanish. But the vast majority of North American Indian tribes had practiced some form of agriculture for centuries. The Papago of the Pimería Alta had scarcely reduced agriculture to a science but did plant and sow maize, beans, and squash along floodplains; during the rainy season by blocking arroyos with crude brush dams, they were able to channel water into their fields. They lived a seminomadic life during the remainder of the year and subsisted by exploiting the flora and fauna. The absence of a permanent and reliable source of water kept them on the borderline between living a sedentary or nonsedentary existence.[9] The more highly developed northern culture groups had depended heavily on agriculture in the struggle for survival. Some made use of

7. Zuni religion is discussed in Ruth L. Bunzel, "Introduction to Zuni Ceremonialism," *Bureau of American Ethnology Annual Report* 47 (1932), 474–487. She is incorrect, however, in her suggestion that the Spaniards introduced irrigation to the Zuni pueblos.

8. "Gallegos Relation of the Chamuscado-Rodríguez Expedition." In George P. Hammond and Agapito Rey (eds.), *The Rediscovery of New Mexico, 1580–1594* (Albuquerque: University of New Mexico Press, 1966), p. 101.

9. Bernard L. Fontana, *Of Earth and Little Rain: The Papago Indians* (Flagstaff, Arizona: Northland Press, 1981), pp. 19 and 37.

irrigation, at times casual (such as the floodplain irrigation of the Pima of Arizona or the Chihuahua Mogollones), but occasionally elaborate in conception and superlative in scope.

Five or six hundred years before the arrival of the Spaniards, the Anasazi of the Pueblo III or Classic Pueblo Period (roughly 1000 A.D. to 1300 A.D.) initiated various programs of water control on the northern fringes of the Southwest. On Chapin Mesa at Mesa Verde in southwestern Colorado they built check dams and an irrigation ditch more than four miles in length.[10] At Chaco Canyon, in northwest New Mexico, the Anasazi constructed both check dams and diversion dams, the latter requiring canals and headgates. This system of water control permitted support of a Chaco population numbering almost 10,000 persons.[11] At about the same time, the Hohokam of central and southern Arizona, using only wooden digging sticks and a variety of stone axes, built more than 125 miles of irrigation canals in the lower Salt River valley (fig. 1.2). The canals, which were operating by 700 A.D. and reached their maximum size some 600 years later, made possible the cultivation of corn, beans, and squash in a harsh desert environment. These ditches, up to thirty feet wide and ten feet deep, were designed to prevent loss of water through seepage; the bottoms of the canals were hard, suggesting the possibility of some kind of plastering with adobe (fig. 1.3).[12] Because the agricultural fields were located on terraces higher than the water sources, it was necessary to locate the diversion headgates far upstream.[13] The gradients were carefully designed, as Hohokam agriculturalists knew that too slow a rate of flow encouraged excessive evaporation in the canals and too fast a rate induced erosion of the banks.[14] The system must have worked well. The paucity of animal remains uncovered by modern

10. Frank Reeve, *New Mexico: Land of Many Cultures* (Boulder, Colorado: Pruitt Publishing Company, 1969), p. 42; Arthur H. Rohn, "Prehistoric Soil and Water Conservation on Chapin Mesa, Southwestern Colorado," *American Antiquity* 28 (April, 1963), 441–447.

11. R. Gwinn Vivian, "Conservation and Diversion: Water Control Systems in the Anasazi Southwest," in Theodore E. Downing and McGuire Gibson (eds.), *Irrigation's Impact on Society* (Tucson: University of Arizona Press, 1974), p. 104.

12. F. W. Hodge, "Pre-historic Irrigation in Arizona," *American Anthropologist* 6 (July, 1893), 325; H. M. Wormington, *Prehistoric Indians of the Southwest* (Denver: The Denver Museum of Natural History, 1951), p. 125; Emil W. Haury, "Arizona's Ancient Irrigation Builders," *Natural History* 54 (September 1945), 300–310.

13. Robert A. Hackenburg, "Ecosystemic Channeling: Cultural Ecology from the Viewpoint of Aerial Photography," in Evon Z. Vogt (ed.), *Aerial Photography in Anthropological Field Research* (Cambridge: Harvard University Press, 1974), p. 33.

14. Richard B. Woodbury and John Q. Ressler, "Effects of Environmental and Cultural Limitations upon Hohokam Agriculture, Southern Arizona," *University of Utah Anthropological Papers* 62 (December, 1962), 49.

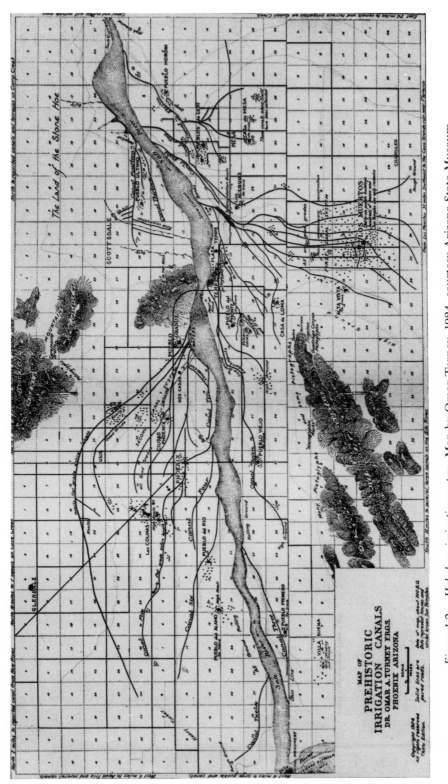

Figure 1.2   Hohokam irrigation system. Map by Omar Turney, 1924, courtesy Arizona State Museum

Figure 1.3   Hohokam canal, dating from 800 to 1000 A.D., with a hard bottom. Photograph by Helga Teiwes, courtesy Arizona State Museum

archaeologists in the immediate area suggests a heavy reliance on agriculture. Systematic manipulations of water reached northern Chihuahua as well. As the result of Anasazi influence, Casas Grandes in the twelfth century had a functioning aqueduct of stone-lined canals, reservoirs, and a fifteen-meter well within the city itself.[15]

At the time of the European discovery of the New World, it was the Pueblos of New Mexico, descendants of the Anasazi, who led all other southwestern tribes in the harnessing of water. Irrigation systems, including terraces and reservoirs, had flourished along the upper Río Grande valley since about 1400, permitting the cultivation of maize, squash, beans, melons, cotton, and chile. The irrigation techniques were not elaborate, but they served their purpose well and drew the attention and admiration of those first Spaniards who set foot in New Mexico in the sixteenth century.[16] Castaño de Sosa, describing the irrigation canals in the Tewa Pueblos in 1591, called them "incredible to anyone who had not seen them with his own eyes."[17]

The influences of irrigation practices on cultural development, even in a region as relatively homogeneous as that of the Pueblos, is far reaching. At the time of the first Spanish contacts, irrigation in the eastern pueblos of the Río Grande valley was much more intensive than that of the western pueblos (Zuni and Hopi), located in areas where there were few permanently flowing streams. The work of digging and maintaining complicated networks of ditches was physically demanding and, as a result, the men were the agriculturalists in the Río Grande valley. In the western pueblos, where irrigation was not as basic to cultivation, women worked with the men during the agricultural cycle. The differentiation in sexual roles in agriculture carried over to other aspects of Pueblo society. In the west, where women worked in the fields, they were also much more likely to own property, to participate actively in the ceremonial life of the tribe, and to initiate courtship relationships than their female counterparts along the Río Grande.[18] While it would be a gross exaggeration to suggest

15. Florence C. Lister and Robert H. Lister, *Chihuahua: Storehouse of Storms* (Albuquerque: University of New Mexico Press, 1966), p. 8.

16. Pueblo Indian irrigation practices are described in James Anthony Vlasich, "Pueblo Indian Agriculture, Irrigation and Water Rights," (University of Utah dissertation, 1980), pp. 13–51.

17. "Castaño de Sosa's 'Memoria.'" In Hammond and Rey, *The Rediscovery of New Mexico*, p. 282.

18. This thesis, controversial in the anthropological literature, was first developed in Wittfogel and Goldfrank, "Some Aspects of Pueblo Mythology," pp. 17–30. Accepting the Wittfogel-Goldfrank thesis, but applying it to clan structure rather than sexual roles, is Edward P. Dozier, "The Pueblos of the South-Western United States," *The Journal of the Royal Anthropological Institute of Great Britain and Ireland* 90 (1960), 146–160. Fred Plog finds the thesis suggestive but by no means conclusive. See his "The

the development of a matriarchal society in the west, as opposed to a patriarchal one in the east, there is strong evidence that comprehensive irrigation in the east prompted the development of a culture more dominated by males.

Differences in water availability also accounted for the development of different religious practices in the two Pueblo areas. Because the western pueblos could not count on a reliable water supply, Hopi, Zuni, Acoma, and Laguna religion encompassed many more magical rites in the spiritual appeal for water. On the other hand, although magical rites are not absent among the Río Grande pueblos, they receive much less emphasis. The eastern pueblos coped with water uncertainty in a more practical way by expending all available energy in the construction and maintenance of the irrigation network.[19]

Because the Indian population in northern Mexico and the Southwest had access to only rudimentary technology in the pre-conquest period, water exerted inordinate influence on both life patterns and social relationships. Population density in any area of the north was largely the product of water availability, as was the seasonal movement of many tribes. Water shortages sometimes precipitated the fragmentation of tribes and, in the case of the Cahuilla of southern California and Baja California, the eventual formation of new, ceremonially independent groups.[20] Adaptation to aridity consistently challenged human ingenuity and conditioned the most novel responses. The first Spaniards to visit Gran Quivira on the Chupadero Mesa of New Mexico were shocked to learn that the Indian population preserved their own urine to dampen the earth for the construction of walls.[21]

Farther to the south, in the region of Mexico's high aboriginal cultures, the influences of water might have been just as subtle, but they were also more obvious. In Yucatán, Oaxaca, and the Central Valley of Mexico complicated water systems flourished. Sophisticated irrigation agriculture allowed the food surplus which, in turn, made the development of urban civilization possible.[22] Throughout the con-

Keresan Bridge: An Ecological and Archaeological Account," in Charles L. Redman, Mary Jane Berman, et al. (eds.), *Social Archeology: Beyond Subsistence and Dating* (New York: Academic Press, 1978), pp. 349-372.

19. Santa Clara pueblo anthropologist Edward P. Dozier posited this thesis in his *The Pueblo Indians of North America* (New York: Holt, Rinehart and Winston, 1970), p. 133.

20. Sidney W. Mintz, "The Role of Water in Julian Steward's Cultural Ecology," *Journal of the Steward Anthropological Society* 11 (Fall, 1979), 22–25.

21. Joseph H. Toulouse, Jr., "Early Water Systems at Gran Quivira National Monument," *American Antiquity* 10 (April, 1945), 363.

22. The early contentions of Alfred Kroeber and Carl Sauer that irrigation was unimportant in pre-conquest Mexico have been convincingly disproven. See Angel Palerm and Eric Wolf, *Agricultura y civilización en Mesoamérica* (Mexico: Sep Setentas, 1972), pp. 30–64.

stellation of civilizations in central and southern Mexico one could find diversion and check dams, dikes, canals, sluices, aqueducts, deep wells, reservoirs, tanks, and irrigation ditches with technologically advanced headgates and lateral channels. It was in the lake country of the Central Valley that irrigation reached unprecedented heights. It was irrigation absurdly but brilliantly in reverse. Rather than channel the water over the land, the Aztecs and their neighbors floated land over the water. The *chinampas*, or "Floating Gardens," were built by alternating layers of mud with straw and various aquatic plants in the form of high rafts. Built out into the lakes, they probably did not do much floating, as they were anchored with tree roots. With rich soil placed on the top and with no shortage of moisture and humidity, the chinampas were extremely fertile and helped support a large population cluster in the Central Valley of Mexico.[23]

There is no agreement among anthropologists concerning the New World origins of irrigation—whether it developed by diffusion or by independent invention. A strong case for local, independent invention was made by anthropologist Julian Steward, who found tremendous variation in irrigation techniques. In contrast to the unique chinampa agriculture of Mexico's central lake country, Steward observed that the California Paiute Indians practiced irrigation without agriculture—that they irrigated hillsides to stimulate the growth of wild seeds and roots in imitation of the kind of moisture which was found naturally in the lower altitudes of the same area.[24] Other independent inventions were not unlikely, but they do not invalidate the reasonable speculation that countless groups simply borrowed the idea from neighbors who themselves had borrowed it from neighbors.

Why did some northern Indians not engage in irrigation agriculture while others tried to convert the desert into garden? The Seri, the Mescalero Apache, and countless other hunters, gatherers, and fishermen were certainly capable of constructing irrigation canals. It was not that the idea never occurred to them, as they not only were in close proximity to sedentary agriculturalists but undoubtedly observed how these irrigation systems worked on countless occasions. But they made a conscious decision not to follow this course. In his brilliant study of water, power, and the hydraulic society Karl A. Wittfogel addresses just this question and concludes that the decision reflects the cultural values each group attaches to freedom.

23. Chinampa agriculture is discussed in Eric Wolf, *Sons of the Shaking Earth*, (Chicago: University of Chicago Press, 1962), pp. 74–76, and Michael D. Coe, *Mexico: Ancient People and Places* (New York: Frederick A. Praeger, 1962), pp. 58–59 and 69–70.
24. Mintz, "The Role of Water in Julian Steward's Cultural Ecology," pp. 19–20.

> Man pursues recognized advantage. Whenever internal or
> external causes suggest a change in technology . . . he compares
> the merits of the existing situation with the advantages—and
> disadvantages—that may accrue from the contemplated change.
> Special effort is required to attain the new objective; and this
> effort may involve not only increased work and shift from pleasant
> to unpleasant operations but also social and cultural adjustments,
> including a more or less serious loss of personal and political
> independence.[25]

Irrigation implies not only a sedentary existence but subjection to
more stringent measures of social control. For some northern tribes
the attendant loss of freedom did not adequately compensate for the
greater security that irrigation agriculture promised.

Water disputes undoubtedly occurred in pre-conquest America,
especially in the desert regions. Harnessing water for productive
purposes required the cooperative effort of many, but subsequent
allocation schemes were a source of potential conflict. The kinds of
disputes which occurred are largely unknown, because neither the
archaeological record nor the standard ethnohistorical sources are
responsive on this score. From what is known of American Indian
ownership patterns, it seems unlikely that water was considered private property to be bought or sold or traded.[26] Its centripetal position
in Indian religion reinforces this hypothesis. This does not suggest,
however, that it was not a part of the power structure in Indian
America. But, when water was summoned to the pursuit of political or
military goals, it is likely that this action was tribal or communal, rather
than individual.

Ecolturation began in the Southwest when man first learned to
manipulate his environment. The contention of some that primitive
man caused no drain on the earth's bounty is patently absurd. But
spread thinly over a vast expanse of territory, with only rudimentary
technology, and belonging to a series of cultures not remarkably
consumptive, man did not have a great impact. An acutely perceptive
and rational reverence for the natural environment, molded in tradition and reinforced by religion, further minimized the negative repercussions of ecolturation. However, the struggle between man and
nature had begun, and it left an imprint on both.[27]

25. Karl A. Wittfogel, *Oriental Despotism: A Comparative Study of Total Power* (New
Haven: Yale University Press, 1957), p. 16.
26. For example, land and water ownership among the Aztecs did not extend to
commoners. They were allowed use of land and water but did not exercise domain.
See Carlos H. Alba, *Estudio comparado entre el derecho azteco y el derecho positivo mexicano*
(Mexico: Instituto Indigenista Interamericano, 1944), pp. 40–41.
27. Henry F. Dobyns has posited that Sonora desert Apache used fire to drive game,

The early hunters and fishermen scarcely altered the delicate desert ecosystem, as the fauna of the ancient Southwest was more than sufficient to withstand the basic food requirements of man. Adaptation to the environment was more important than domination of it, and most primitive religions sanctioned a code that permitted the killing of only that which was necessary to sustain life. Jémez Pueblo educator Joe Sando explained the Indian relationship with the ecosystem well: "They came face to face with nature, but did not exploit her. They became a part of the ecological balance instead of abusing and finally destroying it."[28]

As the native American evolved from a nomadic hunter, gatherer, and fisherman into a sedentary agriculturalist, as he sought to enhance the habitability of a hostile environment, a modest ecolturative change began. Irrigation farming, even in its crudest form, set in motion ecological chain reactions. Plants were introduced into habitats where they could not have sustained themselves previously. Terracing changed the natural flow of streams, and man-made water diversions modified the natural vegetation, changed the organic matter in the soil, and began to alter the migratory patterns of birds and animals.

The arrival of the Spaniards in the Southwest occasioned major modifications in man-land relationships. The Spaniards attached different kinds of values to the earth's natural resources, and they had developed the technology to implement their own perspective. With the introduction of a new concept of private ownership, the nature of water conflict changed drastically. Of equal importance, the modest ecological disequilibrium which had followed on the heels of the first human settlement intensified. Building a new, large irrigation ditch could result in more than a casual change of the surrounding landscape. Depending on the quality of the soil, a large canal over a period of years could erode into a deep *barranca*, or canyon, not only permanently altering the topography but rendering itself useless for irrigation purposes and requiring the opening of still new lands.

The Spaniards who first came into contact with the water traditions of America at the beginning of the sixteenth century had developed their own notions about the relationship of water, religion, and

---

and, in the process, devastated the desert ecosystem. The evidence comes primarily from a single document and is scarcely conclusive. Moreover, it does not address the question of the extent of the practice through time or space or the possibility of a documentary aberration. See Dobyns, *From Fire to Blood: Historic Human Destruction of Sonoran Riverine Oases* (Socorro, New Mexico, Ballena Press, 1981), pp. 1–43 passim.
28. Joe S. Sando, *The Pueblo Indians* (San Francisco: The Indian Historical Press, 1976), pp. 18–19.

society. Some of the Hispanic legacy was compatible with the native tradition; some of it was not. The attempt to harmonize divergent understanding of the role of water occasioned much acrimony in the centuries that followed.

Because so much of the Iberian Peninsula is arid, and because sun radiation is great, water always carried high priority in the ancient and medieval kingdoms that would eventually become Spain. Fountains, of which Spaniards have always been fond, were long considered a symbol of prosperity because the water that gushed from them was so often in short supply. It is not unlikely that water caused more lawsuits in Spanish history than did land.[29] The huge Roman aqueduct in Segovia, constructed in the first century B.C., and the intricate Moorish irrigation system at the Alhambra in Granada offer a different kind of testimony to the importance of water in Spain's long struggle to become a nation-state.

The extent of Arabic influence on Spanish culture provokes historiographical controversy of gargantuan proportions. Those Spanish historians wishing to degenerate the Moorish occupation argue against a lasting Moorish legacy to Spanish civilization. Among other rejected cultural influences, irrigation practices play a major role in the dispute. Other historians find the similarities of irrigation techniques in Iberia and North Africa so persuasive that the Moorish legacy is offered as incontrovertible. Without attempting here to enter into that debate, suffice it to say that in the relationship of water to language, the Arabic legacy to Spanish civilization is difficult to deny. A short list of Spanish water terms with Arabic derivation would have to include *aljibe* (reservoir, from the Arabic *al-yubb*), *albanal* (drain or canal, from the Arabic *al-ball'a), alema* (allotment or irrigation water, from the Arabic *al-amma), alberca* (pool or pond, from the Arabic *al-birka), alamin* (irrigation judge, from the Arabic *al-amin), acequia* (irrigation ditch, from the Arabic *as-saquiya), almoceda* (irrigation right for certain days, from the Arabic *al-musda*), and *alfarda* (irrigation tax, from the Arabic *al-farda*).[30]

When vague notions of water gave way to a fixed system for its use and control, it was not Moorish influence alone that prevailed. Extensive irrigation in southern Spain had antedated the Moorish invasion of the eighth century. The judicial system that came forth

29. Elena de La Souchere, *An Explanation of Spain.* (New York: Vantage Books, 1965), p. 16.
30. Real Academia de España. *Diccionario de la lengua española* (19th ed., Madrid: Editorial Espasa-Calpe, S.A., 1970), passim.

after the fall of the Roman Empire was a composite of Roman, Germanic, and Moorish law. In the thirteenth century King Alfonso X, *El Sabio,* ordered the famous codification of Spanish law that was given form in *Las siete partidas*. For the first time, water law was codified.[31]

In spite of a strong Iberian tradition of the commonality of land and water, these resources tended to become instruments of power through privatization as their importance became engrained in the increasingly acquisitive psychology of the Spaniards.[32] It was not difficult for one to exercise dominance over a neighbor by controlling a water source. Feudal lords could enhance their suzerainty, local officials their authority, the kings their imperiality by skillful manipulation and taxation (either in currency or in kind) of this most basic resource. Water was used repeatedly in Spanish history to bargain, to raise funds, to apply subtle pressure, and to haughtily coerce.[33] During the long centuries of the Reconquest against the Moors, during that monumental struggle between Islam and the West, grants of land and water were used to encourage settlement in frontier areas recently recaptured. Water in Spain was thus not only a fundamental source of life, it was an exploitable natural resource to be used to propel a desired course of action and to be employed as a weapon against real or imagined enemies. The Spaniards clearly recognized and utilized water as a source of power.

It was historically inevitable that in the clash of cultures which followed on the heels of the Spanish conquest of America water would play a major role. For the first time Indians were instructed by example in what must have seemed a string of absurdities. Man was not a part of nature but was somehow set apart from it to use it. His goal was not to adapt peacefully to his habitat but to dominate and change it. Water was suddenly a source of private wealth, of capital, of rent, of income, and most importantly, of human power over one's fellow man. Observing the Indian reverence for nature, a few Spaniards became environmentalists by contagion, but most remained slaves of their Iberian cultural baggage. Just as in so many other matters which followed the Spanish conquest, different needs, differ-

31. *Las siete partidas del sabio rey don Alfonso* 4 vols. (Madrid, 1789).

32. The process of privatization of common property in Extremadura is discussed in David E. Vassberg, "Concerning Pigs, the Pizarros and the Agro-Pastoral Background of the Conquerors of Peru," *Latin American Research Review* 13 (1978), pp. 54–55.

33. Robert Ignatius Burns, "Irrigation Taxes in Early Mudejar Valencia: The Problems of Alfarda," *Speculum* 44 (October, 1969), 560–567.

ent uses, and different value systems were centers of contention in
the matter of water. In the second half of the sixteenth century, as
Spaniards began to venture into the arid zones of North America,
bringing with them new crops, new dietary predilections, new technol-
ogies, and new economic systems, water controversies assumed major
proportions. And not incidentally, in the process ecoluturation acceler-
ated the momentum of natural change.

Except for eastern Texas, the Mexican north which Spaniards first
encountered in the sixteenth century was generally arid or semi-arid,
but occasionally extremely arid. The availability of water spelled the
difference between desolation and abundance with countless grada-
tions in between. This vast desert region had been occupied continuously for several thousand years, but the population density was low,
perhaps less than two persons per square mile, in the middle of the
sixteenth century. Aridity increased as one moved west from Texas
and Coahuila to New Mexico and Chihuahua, and then to Arizona
and Sonora and southern California and Baja California. With the
exception of the higher elevations and coastal zones of the north,
evaporation was usually high and humidity generally low. The topography and natural vegetation certainly reminded those first Spaniards of southern Spain. They were not surprised that the sun could
blister the landscape and crack the soil. They fully understood the
meaning of moisture deficiency and knew that the critical challenges
of aridity conditioned the development of a special kind of human
society. They were not shocked to learn that the labor of controlling
water and putting it to beneficial use could occupy much of the
working day in the constant struggle to wrest bounty from the parched
landscape.

The northern frontier of New Spain—this new desert into which
they ventured—was much more varied than its counterpart in An-
dalucia and Castile. It had a wider range of altitudes, soils, animal life,
drought-resistant vegetation, and even more capricious cycles of annual rainfall. The mountains were more rugged and towering, and
the barrancas or canyons more impenetrable. Erosion and sedimentation bequeathed a physiography at once both harsh and captivating—
frightening, yet alluring. The rainy season extended from July to
September, but few areas of the desert received more than twelve or
thirteen inches of precipitation per year. In the drier parts, years of
less than seven or eight inches were not uncommon. The mountains of
this northern land captured most of the moisture carried by prevailing Pacific and Gulf of Mexico winds, and left the valleys parched for
most of the year. The winter mountain snow cover was almost always

insufficient to provide the lower elevations with a reliable source of water, except during the early spring thaw.[34]

With a few major exceptions (the Río Grande, the Colorado, the Fuerte, the Yaqui, and the Gila being among the most notable), the water sources which the Spaniards dignified with the word "Río" were scarcely rivers at all. Not even the largest (the Río Grande) proved valuable for transportation and commerce, either before or after the Spanish conquest. Although scientific evidence suggests forcefully that they carried a larger flow then than now,[35] most rivers were not perennial; they ran only part of the year, trying their best to carry off the excess of a sudden summer rain or capturing the runoff from an exceptional winter snow cover in the surrounding mountains. The more common pattern was for the water that reached them to sink quickly into the sandy bed and within a few miles to disappear forever from human sight. On occasion, however, they ran partly on the surface, then underground, protected from the evaporative powers of the environment, to be forced to the surface again by the geological structure of a given area.

If these northern rivers did not always carry sufficient water to reflect the glaring desert sun, they nevertheless proved amazingly magnetic, drawing in the surrounding animal life and providing the modicum of moisture required for a better-than-average desert flora. It was along these same "rivers," arroyos, and quixotic streams that most Indian populations adapted to desert life. The alluvial plains, ranging in width from a few feet to several miles, were rich, and an unreliable source of water, although taxing to human ingenuity, was better than none at all. Here, too, would be built Spanish towns, missions, and presidios. As the two groups were forced by physical and historical circumstance into closer and closer contact, precious water soon came to dominate the varied contests for power and survival.

34. An excellent description of the physical environment of northwestern New Spain is found in Roger Dunbier, *The Sonora Desert: Its Geography, Economy and People* (Tucson: University of Arizona, 1970), passim.

35. For this point, see Henry F. Dobyns, *Spanish Colonial Tucson: A Demographic History* (Tucson: University of Arizona Press, 1976), p. 73.

CHAPTER 2

Water and the Settlement
of the North

Spaniards first intruded into the desert Southwest in the third decade of the sixteenth century, with permanent settlement still seventy-five to a hundred years away. The first Spanish visitor to the region, Alvar Núñez Cabeza de Vaca, found himself there quite by accident after suffering a shipwreck in the Gulf of Mexico, but the reports he made on his return to Mexico City stimulated interest and exploration in the decades which followed. In 1542 a much more systematic expedition under the command of Francisco Vásquez de Coronado explored Sonora, Arizona, and New Mexico. Spanish seamen under Hernando de Alarcón and Juan Rodríguez Cabrillo sailed along the California coasts at approximately the same time. The first serious penetration of Chihuahua was delayed until the 1560s, the same time that Spanish slavers also moved into Texas.

Just before the turn of the century, three northern outposts were founded: the city of Monterrey in the Nuevo Reyno de León (1596), the soon-to-be-abandoned village of San Juan in the upper Río Grande valley of New Mexico (1598), and La Paz in the southern reaches of the Baja California peninsula (1596). Within a hundred years the map of the Hispanic Southwest looked quite different. Spanish towns, missions, and presidios were scattered over much of the northern frontier: Santa Fe and El Paso in the New Mexico territory; Saltillo and Monclova in Coahuila; Tumacácori, Guevavi, and San Xavier del Bac in Arizona; Horcasitas, Dolores, Cucurpe, Pitic, Arizpe, and Fronteras in Sonora; Parral, Conchos, Casas Grandes, and Janos in Chihuahua; and Loreto in the Baja California peninsula.

As Spanish settlement of northern New Spain began in earnest in the seventeenth century, the availability of water limited many options and thus in large measure molded the kind of society that developed on the frontier. It determined the original paths of exploration and the foundation and settlement of new towns.[1] Overland expeditions to California were delayed for many years because desert aridity was so threatening.[2] During the initial period of exploration, as well as during later reconnaissance, few disappointments surpassed the discovery of an abundant desert water source whose water "was of bad quality and of an even worse smell and taste"[3] or "so noxious that animals died after drinking it."[4] Disappointment of the same magnitude was occasioned by the desert *mirage*, a phenomenon best described by Josiah Gregg, a Missouri merchant who traded in New Mexico in the 1820s:

> The thirsty wayfarer, after jogging for hours under burning sky, at length espies a pond—yes it must be water—it looks too natural for him to be mistaken. He quickens his pace, enjoying in anticipation the pleasure of a refreshing draught: but lo! as he approaches, it recedes or entirely disappears; and when upon its apparent site, he is ready to doubt his own vision—he finds a parched plain under his feet. It is not until he has been thus a dozen times deceived, that he is willing to relinquish the pursuit: and then perhaps, when he really does see a pond, he will pass it unexamined, for fear of another disappointment.[5]

1. The first large Spanish expedition into the arid Southwest was that of Francisco Vásquez de Coronado in 1540 and 1541. As it moved north from the present state of Jalisco into Sinaloa, Sonora, Arizona, and New Mexico, it followed the river valleys whenever possible. On those occasions when it was impossible to move along the rivers, the troops suffered tremendously from lack of water. The objectives of Coronado's lieutenant, García López de Cárdenas, on his famous trip to the Grand Canyon, were not met because the expedition had to be aborted for lack of water. See Bolton, *Coronado*, pp. 141–142, and A. Grove Day, *Coronado's Quest: The Discovery of the Southwestern States* (Berkeley: University of California Press, 1964), pp. 144–145.

2. Lorenzo Cancio to Viceroy Marqués de Cruillas, May 14, 1765, Archivo General de la Nación, Ramo de Provincias Internas, Vol. 86, Expediente 1. Hereafter cited as AGN with appropriate information.

Spelling and accentuation in the Spanish manuscript sources is both antiquated and inconsistent. Proper names incorporated into the text have been modernized, but citational notes and direct quotes have been left in their original form.

3. Diario que formo oi 24 de Febrero de 1768 ... de orden del Senor Gov^{or} Dn Juan de Pineda, AGN, Historia, Vol. 24, Exp. 9.

4. Descripción topográfica de las misiones de propaganda fide de nuestra Señora de Guadalupe de Zacatecas la Sierra Madre, *Documentos de la historia de México* (Mexico: Imprenta de Vicente García Torres, 1856), IV, 4. Hereafter cited as DHM with appropriate information.

5. Josiah Gregg, *Commerce of the Prairies* (New York: Bobbs-Merrill, 1970), p. 37.

If subsequent travelers at least had some idea of what to expect in the deserts of the north, those first Spaniards did not. Leaders of exploratory expeditions invariably made copious notes in their diaries on water availability and quality in an effort to properly instruct their superiors on the advisability of contemplated settlement.[6] When Blas Fernández y Somera traversed the entire lower California peninsula in 1766, a journey which lasted a month, he made twenty-five separate entries on water in his report.[7] But water availability was meaningful only if it was also accessible. A river course that traversed a sandstone or limestone bed for thousands of years often left high banks. It is obvious that the water from the Colorado River at the Grand Canyon cannot be used to irrigate the broad, flat plains on either side of the Canyon. Reduced in magnitude a thousand times, the same basic problem plagued countless other sections of important water sources in the northern desert. Spanish explorers soon learned to consider not only water availability but also water accessibility when reporting to superiors on possible settlement sites. In the third quarter of the eighteenth century, for example, Luis Casorla wrote to the Governor of Texas that he had uncovered a desirable location along the Río Brazos. Among his reasons for recommending it was the fact that "the river is almost at the same level as the surrounding land."[8] The message was important, as a number of previous attempts to open irrigation networks in Texas had failed because of the impossibility of raising the water to the level of the fields.[9]

Travel in the north was unusually difficult. Whenever possible, those Spaniards who first crossed the hostile environs of the northern desert followed rivers, because they had learned by experience that watering holes between the rivers were not only far apart, but some-times unreliable. But rivers did not always lead to the intended desti-

6. As examples see Diario de la Campaña executada de orden del Exmo Señor Marqués de Casafuerte por Dn. Joseph Berrosteran, Capitan del Presidio de Conchos . . . en el año de 1729. Archivo General de Indias, Audiencia de Guadalajara 513. Hereafter cited as AGI with appropriate information. Diario de la Campaña de orden del Exmo Señor Conde de Revilla Gigedo en el Año de 1747 por el Governador de Coahuila Don Pedro de Ravago, AGI, Audiencia de Guadalajara, 513; Diario del Capitan Dn Juan Bautista de Anza, June 26, 1774, AGI, Audiencia de Guadalajara, 418.

7. Blas Fernández y Somera, "Diario del Viage que se hizo en la Provincia de California. . . 1776," cited in *Noticias y documentos acerca de las Californias, 1764–1795* (Madrid: José Porrua Turanzas, 1959), p. 20 ff.

8. Luis Casorla to Barrón de Ripperdá, Nov. 1, 1772, AGI, Audiencia de Guadalajara, 513.

9. Betty Eakle Dobkins, *The Spanish Element in Texas Water Law* (Austin: University of Texas Press, 1959), pp. 104–106.

nation, and it was necessary to cope as best one could. When travelers began to run low on water, the expedition would be halted and three or four men would be sent out to search for a watering hole. In this way the majority would not expend needless energy and, in the process, increase their water consumption.[10] After one particularly difficult journey in the Sonora desert in 1765, Lorenzo Cancio reported to the viceroy in Mexico City that if he would be properly rewarded for suffering heat and thirst, he would be highly decorated.[11] Travelers repeatedly blamed delays in arrivals and failures to carry out assignments on the lack of water, a condition which had an especially severe impact on pack and transport animals.[12] Water for human consumption and for preparing food could be carried along, but pasture and water for the horses, mules, and oxen had to be uncovered along the way. When they were not, orders even as important as reporting on the mines under direct instruction of the Crown could not be obeyed.[13]

Even if a river valley was available, following its course was not always the most expeditious means of getting from point *A* to point *B*. The trek between Santa Fe and El Paso, an important link in the Chihuahua–New Mexico trade, affords one example. The entire distance can be covered along the Río Grande. But south of Socorro and north of present-day Las Cruces the river meanders off far to the west, to later move east again and ultimately reach El Paso. Rather than following the huge bend and being carried far out of the way, travelers, whether moving north or south, preferred to place themselves at the mercy of an incredibly hostile environment. They continued directly across a broad *bolson*, a hundred miles of lava flows, sand dunes, alkali flats, scant vegetation, little animal life, and seldom any water. Many paid the supreme price, and the area became known as the Jornada del Muerto. By the eighteenth century the Jornada was

10. Luis Vélez de las Cuebas Cabeza de Vaca to Don Joseph de González, Feb. 20, 1740, AGN, Californias, Vol. 38, Exp. 4.

11. Lorenzo Cancio to Viceroy Marqués de Cruillas, June 17, 1765, AGN, Provincias Internas, Vol. 86, Exp. 1.

12. See, for example, Diario de las visitas a las misiones. . .hecha por José Manuel Ruiz, Sep. 28, 1798, Archivo Histórico de Baja California Sur, Leg. 1, Doc. 342. Hereafter cited as AHBCS with appropriate information. Other examples are contained in Javier Aguilar to Governador Felipe Goycochea, Aug. 7, 1806, AHBCS, Leg. 1, Doc. 469, and Diario de los Viages de Mar y Tierra Hechos al Norte de California. . .por Dirección del Ilustríssimo Señor d. Joseph de Gálvez. . . . Oct. 24, 1770, AGI, Audiencia de Guadalajara, 418.

13. Pedro Corbalan to Viceroy Antonio Maria Bucareli y Ursua, May 14, 1773, AGN, Provincias Internas, Vol. 91, Exp. 1.

notorious, but Spanish travelers had learned to cope with the lack of water. A 1760 description instructs us on the special preparations:

> On that day we came to the Jornada del Muerto. To prepare for it a detour is made to seek the river at a place called San Diego. The night is spent there. Everything necessary is made ready. . . . It's about half a league from the river. Barrels are brought for the purpose. These are filled with water for the people. On the morning of the thirteenth [May 13, 1760] the horses were taken to the river to drink. Somewhat later, all the food for the journey was prepared, and at half past seven we left that part with considerable speed, stopping only to change horses. During this interval we ate what there was, and we traveled in this fashion until eight-thirty at night. . . . On the fourteenth day of May . . . we made an early start. We reached the river at eleven-thirty. The livestock were so thirsty that they ran to reach the water. After this fashion were the thirty leagues of this difficult stage traveled.[14]

Decisions on a new town, if they were carefully conceived, invariably took the water supply into consideration, because it was well known that the reliability of the water source was prerequisite to the permanence of the settlement. If the decision to found a new town was positive, the original ordinances of the community would generally specify how the available water was to be apportioned. In 1573 King Philip II issued extensive ordinances on the founding of new towns, and they dictated, among other things, how cropland and water were to be distributed.[15] Subsequent legislation amplified the 1573 ordinances and specified that prior to individual water allocations the town itself should secure its needs.[16]

Although these regulations for the founding of towns were to have general applicability throughout the Spanish empire, in practice there was great variation as new communities came to dot the desert landscape of northern New Spain. On some occasions water allocations were vague, stipulating only that water necessary for irrigation was to be distributed. When Santa Fe, New Mexico, was established, for example, the Alcaldes Ordinarios and Regidores were instructed to

---

14. Eleanor B. Adams (ed.), *Bishop Tamaron's Visitation of New Mexico, 1760* (Albuquerque: Historical Society of New Mexico, 1954), pp. 41–42.

15. "Ordenanzas de su Magestad para los nuevos descubrimientos, conquistas y pacificaciones, Julio de 1573," in *Colección de documentos inéditos relativos al descubrimiento, conquista y organización de las antiguas posesiones de América y Oceania,* 42 vols. (Madrid: n.p., 1864–1884), XVI, 142–187.

16. Ynstrucción práctica que hande obserbar los comisionados para el repartimiento de tierras en los pueblos de los quatro ríos de Sinaloa, Fuerte, Mayo y Hiaqui . . . Jan. 25, 1771, AGN, Historia, Vol. 16, Exp. 8.

specify for each settler "two *solares* [of 159.51 acres each] for the house
and garden, two *suertes* [of 52.88 acres each] for an orchard, two
suertes for a vineyard and olive grove, and four additional *cavallerías*
[of 106 acres each] *and for the irrigation of them, the necessary water*"
[emphasis mine].[17] Similarly vague was the founding document for
the town of San Juan Nepomuceno in Chihuahua, which instructed
that "House lots, lands and waters will be distributed equally giving to
each the suerte that he can sow and cultivate for his comfortable
existence. . . . "[18] A more common pattern was for the founding document to specify that the available water was to be shared equally by the
settlers, that special care be taken to assure those downstream of their
allotment, and that surplus water left in the ditches be returned to the
generating source.[19] The latter concept, while theoretically admirable
from the point of view of conservation, in practice left much to be
desired. Clean water diverted from a natural stream was often returned to that stream polluted with salts, chemicals, garbage, and
human wastes. Not all communities obeyed the law, but, as figure 2.1
shows, the presidio of Tubac did. The acequia took water from the
Río de Tubac (today the Río Santa Cruz) and returned any excess
water to the same river.

The vagaries and inconsistencies of water provisions in founding
documents complicated the administration of justice in northern New
Spain. It was necessary to bring prevailing concepts together and to
issue a definitive statement on how water should be divided when new
towns were founded. An opportunity presented itself at the time of
the founding of Pitic (or Hermosillo), Sonora. The founding ordinance for that community not only laid the basis for the future water
history of that town, but proved to be the single most revealing water
document of the eighteenth century in northern New Spain (fig. 2.2).

The Plan de Pitic, dated 1789, enacted under the General Com-
mandancy of Jacobo Ugarte y Loyola and signed in Chihuahua by
Juan Gasiot y Miralles, has been the subject of considerable historiographical and legal controversy.[20] This founding document for the

17. "Ynstrucción a Peralta por Vi-Rey," March 30, 1709, cited in *New Mexico Historical
Review* 4 (April, 1929), p. 180.
18. Vando de Don Teodoro de Croix, Nov. 27, 1778, AGI, Audiencia de Guadalajara,
270.
19. These provisions are all found in grants made to the towns of San Miguel de
Carnué and San Antonio de Padua in Tijeras Canyon, just east of Albuquerque. See
Robert Archibald, "Cañon de Carnué: Settlement of a Grant," *New Mexico Historical
Review* 51 (October, 1976), p. 323.
20. The legal issues will be treated in the discussion of Spanish colonial water law in a
later portion of this study.

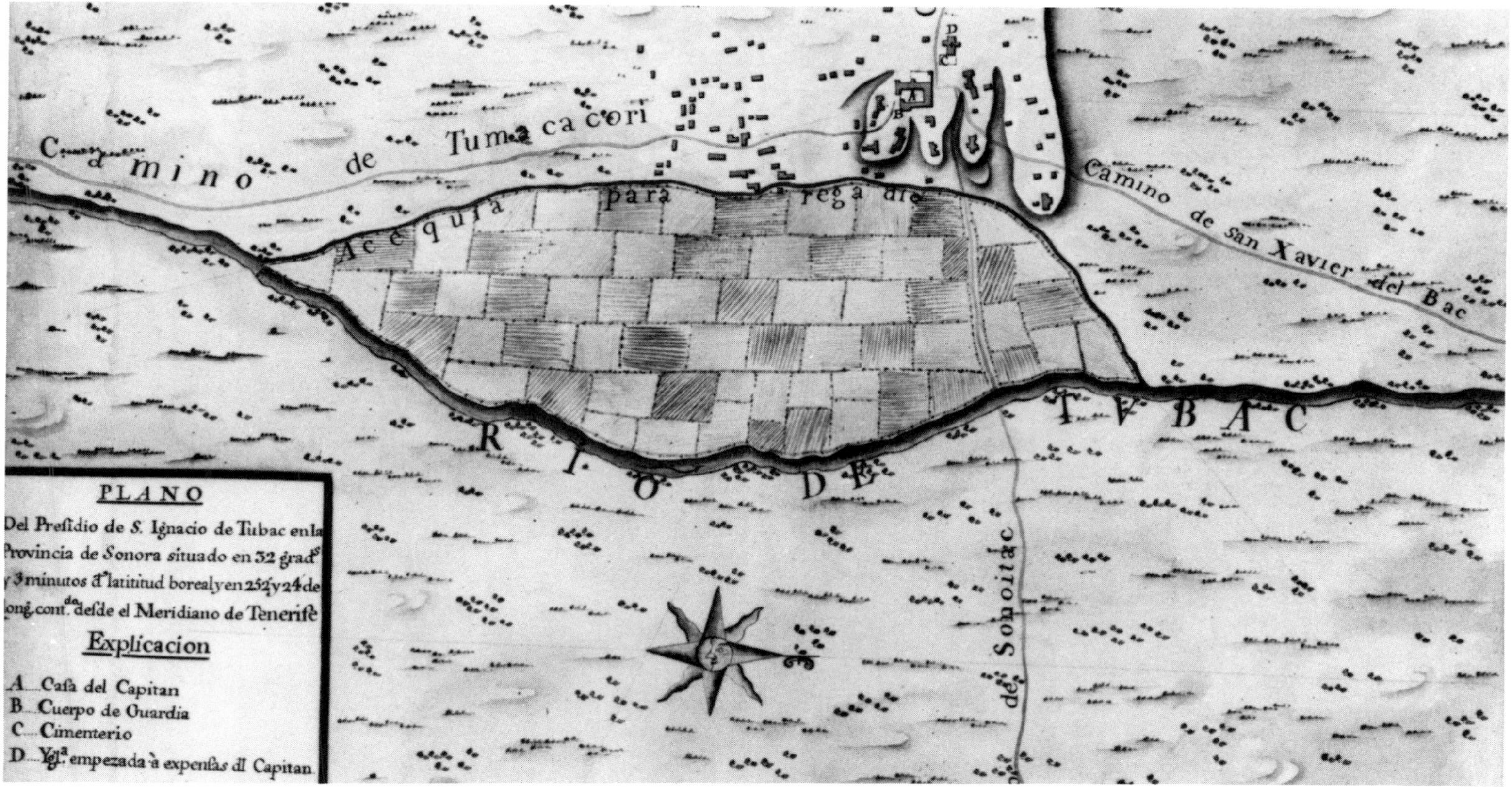
Camino de Tumacacori
Acequia para regadio
Camino de San Xavier del Bac
RIO DE TUBAC
de Sonoitac
PLANO
Del Presidio de S. Ignacio de Tubac en la Provincia de Sonora situado en 32 grad.s y 3 minutos d' latitud boreal y en 252 y 24 de long. cont.da desde el Meridiano de Tenerife
Explicacion
A...Casa del Capitan
B...Cuerpo de Guardia
C...Cimenterio
D...Ygl.a empezada à expensas dl Capitan

Figure 2.1 *Acequia at the Tubac Presidio.* By permission of the British Library, courtesy Arizona State Museum

Ynstruccion aprovada por S.M. que se formó para el establecimiento de la Nueva Villa del *Pitic* en la Provincia de Sonora mandada adaptar à las demas Nuevas Poblaciones proyectadas y que se establecieren en el distrito de esta Comandancia General.

1°. . . . . . . Aunque por la Ley 6.ª tit. 8. Lib. 4. se prohive à los Virreyes, Audiencias y Governadores conceder Titulos de Ciudades ò Villas ò eximir de sus Caveceras principales à los Pueblos de Españoles ò Indios es limitada esta providencia à los que ya estuvieren fundados, pues en quanto à las Nuevas Poblaciones y fundaciones previene se guarde lo dispuesto refiriendose à las otras Leyes que tratan del asunto, y como la 2.ª tit. 7. del mismo libro dispone que elegida la tierra, Provincia y lugar en que se huviere de hacer nueva Poblacion, y averiguada la comodidad y aprovechamientos que puede aver declare el S.r Governador en cuyo distrito estuviere ò confinare, si hade ser Ciudad, Villa, ò Lugar, y que conforme à lo que declarare se forme el Concejo Republica y oficiales de ella, en uso de esta facultad, teniendo presente las proporciones del Sitio elegido, y las ventajas q.e prometen sus Terrenos fertilizando con el beneficio del Riego por medio de la gran Azequia construida à este fin, puede V.S. declarar Villa à la Nueva Poblacion señalandole el Nombre que deva traer, y tenerla p.r su diminucion, y conocimiento.

2°. . . . . . . Con arreglo à lo dispuesto en la Ley 6.ª tit. 5. del mismo Lib. 4. p.a las Villas de Españoles, que se fundaren por capitulacion ò asiento y por la 10.ª para las que a falta de Asentistas se exigieren por particulares Pobladores q.e se fundaren y concedieren en forma se podia conceder à la de que se trata quatro leguas de termino en

town of Hermosillo states that the formula and instructions for the division of water and land shall have applicability not only in Hermosillo but in all of the Provincias Internas, a vast northern political division encompassing almost all of the modern states which share the United States–Mexican border.

Myra Jenkins, for many years the archivist for the state of New Mexico, has questioned the authenticity of the Plan de Pitic.[21] The most fundamental problem, although not the only, is that the villa of Pitic was not founded in 1789, but six years earlier. The presidio which evolved into the town dates from 1742 and the original pueblo from 1700, but authorization for the establishment of a formal villa came on July 6, 1783.[22] Dr. Jenkins builds her case largely on the absence of corroborative evidence, specifically that Hubert H. Bancroft makes no mention of it in his multivolume history of California during the colonial period;[23] that Luis Navarro García's biography, *José de Gálvez y la Comandancia General de las Provincias Internas*, does not mention it;[24] and that copies of the document could not be found in the Sonoran holdings of the Bancroft Library, the Provincias Internas section of the Archivo General de la Nación in Mexico City, or in the official Spanish Archives of New Mexico. She concludes that "there is no evidence that such a plan, if promulgated, was intended to be applied anywhere except in Pitic, Sonora."[25]

Dr. Jenkins' conclusions, although based largely on negative evidence, would be strongly suggestive if her contentions were all correct. Some of the contentions are inaccurate, however, and others are misleading. Hubert H. Bancroft does mention the Plan de Pitic in his *History of California*;[26] there is a copy in the Archivo General de la Nación, although it is in the Tierras section, not the Provincias Internas section;[27] there is a copy in the Spanish Archives of New Mexico,

21. Myra Jenkins, "Spanish Administration of Indian Affairs during the Sixteenth Century," (Unpublished manuscript), pp. 53–62.

22. Juan Antonio Ruibal Corella, *Memoria: Festejos conmemorativos del sesquicentenario de Hermosillo como ciudad* (Mexico: Editorial Libros de México, 1979), pp. 120–121.

23. Hubert H. Bancroft, *History of California* 7 vols. (San Francisco: A. L. Bancroft and Company, Publishers, 1884–1890).

24. Luis Navarro García, *José de Gálvez y la Comandancia General de las Provincias Internas* (Seville: Escuela de Estudios Hispano-Americanos, 1964).

25. "Spanish Administration," p. 63.

26. Bancroft, *History of California*, I, 610–612.

27. Año de 1794. Californias. El Gobernador Interino de Californias, AGN, Tierras, Vol. 2773, Exp. 22. Professor Richard Greenleaf led me to this copy.

although it is not identified as the Plan de Pitic;[28] and there is still another copy in the Nettie Lee Benson Archives of the University of Texas.[29] We are still left with the problem of the six-year discrepancy in the date, however.

Richard E. Greenleaf has studied this problem and suggests that the plans for the establishment of the Villa de Pitic were forwarded to Spain by Governor and Intendant Pedro Corbalán in 1783 at the time of the founding. Royal approval was delayed because of the provisions which made the instructions applicable to the entire Provincias Internas. This special situation made careful study, and possibly even revisions of the original plan, likely. There might have been additional delay after the plan was finally approved in Spain and sent to Chihuahua City. Additional modifications could have been made at that point. Without question. Spanish colonial bureaucracy was notoriously dilatory. As Greenleaf concludes, "such a delay was in no way unusual, nor would it have been unusual for the Chihuahua authorities, looking to future application of the Pitic regulations, to assign a date when those regulations were refined and elaborated."[30]

Although six years is a long time, Greenleaf's explanation of the discrepancy in dates has much to recommend it. There is another possible explanation, however, and one that does preclude his hypothesis of bureaucratic procrastination. It does address itself to any lingering doubts about the six-year interregnum. The original document has never been uncovered and possibly has been lost. The 1789 date appears to be the date of a copy from which subsequent copies were made. Although the original copy should have included the original date, in practice this procedure was not always followed. The copy in the Spanish Archives of New Mexico, for example, does not carry even the 1789 date. It is dated 1800.

After the last sentence of the Plan, both the document in the Archivo General de la Nación and the document in the University of Texas Archives read, "This is a copy, Chihuahua 14th of November of 1789, Juan Gasiot y Miralles." It is significant that the words "This is a

28. This copy was found by Professor William Taylor during his preparation of a historical report for the United States District Court in Albuquerque in the water case of *The State of New Mexico vs. R. Lee Aamodt et al.* See his "Colonial Land and Water Rights of New Mexico Indian Pueblos." (Unpublished Report, 1979?), p. 40.

29. Año de 1796. Californias . . . Erección de la Villa de Branciforte, University of Texas, Nettie Lee Benson Latin American Collection, W. B. Stephens Collection 9. Hereafter cited as UT WBS 9.

30. Richard E. Greenleaf, "Land and Water in Mexico and New Mexico, 1700–1821," *New Mexico Historical Review* 47 (April, 1972), p. 102. James Vlasich errs when he suggests that the Commandant General's office drew up the document in 1789. Vlasich, "Pueblo Indian Agriculture," p. 81.

copy" precede the date. If the date preceded the indication that the document was a copy, one could conclude that the date was part of the original document. But, because the reverse is true, it is clear that November 14, 1789, was the date of the copy, and Juan Gasiot y Miralles was the copyist. Many other documents in Mexico City's Archivo General de la Nación carry his signature as copyist.[31] The original Plan de Pitic was undoubtedly dated closer to the actual foundation of the Villa de Pitic in 1783. There remains no question concerning the authenticity of the document.[32]

Article 6 of the Plan directs itself to the question of water and ethnicity. When a new town is laid out, the water is to be shared by Indians and non-Indians: "its pastures, woodlands, waters, hunting grounds, fishing areas, quarries, fruit trees and other things it produces shall be for the common benefit of Spaniards and Indians."[33] The following article expanded the principle, indicating that Spaniards and Indians were also to share the water on all royal lands surrounding the village. Ethnicity was clearly not to be an issue in the division of water.

The size of land grants for individual houses and garden plots was left flexible because families of different sizes had different requirements. Common pasture land was to be selected from those sites that held out small promise for the growing of wheat, fruit, and vegetables. Agricultural land was divided into suertes, 400 *varas* by 200 varas.[34] Each family was granted two, one of which was to carry water rights with it. Whenever possible, these grants were to be contiguous with one another for the convenience of the owner. All land was granted in perpetuity, with rights of inheritance passing to the heirs. Eight suertes, with water rights, were reserved for the town itself. The income from these properties (*propios*) was to be used to defray municipal expenses.

31. See, for example, Domingo Díaz to Jacobo Ugarte y Loyola, May 1, 1788, AGN, Provincias Internas, Vol. 112, Exp. 1; Jacobo Ugarte y Loyola to Domingo Díaz, Apr. 29, 1788, AGN, Provincias Internas, Vol. 112, Exp. 1; Juan de Ugalde to Jacobo Ugarte y Loyola, Apr. 13, 1788, AGN, Provincias Internas, Vol. 112, Exp. 1; Juan de Ugalde to Jacobo Ugarte y Loyola, Nov. 1, 1788, AGN, Provincias Internas, Vol. 112, Exp. 1.

32. The application of the Plan de Pitic beyond Hermosillo is established, in part, by the fact that Diego de Borica enclosed a copy of it when he instructed Engineer Extraordinary Alberto de Córdoba to plan out the new villa de Branciforte in California, Año de 1796, Californias, UT WBS 9. This fact is confirmed in Daniel Garr, "Villa de Branciforte: Innovation and Adaptation on the Frontier," *The Americas* 35 (July, 1978), 102.

33. Plan de Pitic, Article 6.

34. A vara is a linear measure of approximately 33 inches or .8359 meters.

Article 19 heralds irrigation as the prime means of making the land fertile and the most important factor contributing to the future development of the new town. Because of water's undeniable importance, a special commissioner was to divide it in such a way that all the land subject to irrigation (that portion previously designated as subject to irrigation) would receive its benefits, especially during the spring and summer, the seasons most crucial to a successful harvest. When irrigable plots were apportioned, each inhabitant was to have access to the *acequia madre* (the main irrigation ditch) through individual outlets and ditches cut to the respective pieces of land. Each landowner was to be informed of his outlet on his ditch so that he would not abuse the water of his neighbors. Furthermore, nobody was to use more water than absolutely necessary. This was deemed especially important to protect the interests of those landowners downstream on the acequia madre. Because a broken diversion outlet upstream could deny downstream users any water at all, these outlets, if possible, were to be constructed of stone and lime at the cost of each user.

Although Article 19 enjoined the farmers in the new community to be considerate of others in their water use, the founders of Pitic knew that a simple word of caution might be insufficient. Some farmers inevitably would try to use more than their fair share. Therefore, this article anticipated such an occurrence by specifying in great detail the actual mechanism for water distribution.

> So that these [settlers] will enjoy with equity and justice the benefits of the water, in proportion to the needs of their respective plantings, the *ayuntamiento* [town council] will name annually an *alcalde* or *mandador* for each outlet, whose function it will be to divide the water to the fields in proportion to the needs of each. A list will be drawn up indicating the hours of the day or night a farmer must irrigate his fields.[35]

In order to implement the irrigation times assigned, the alcalde or mandador would hire a special assistant (a *peón* or *jornalero*) to check each outlet at the specified time. If he found that a farmer was not irrigating when he was supposed to, the assistant would open the outlet and irrigate the fields for him, and the alcalde would subsequently charge the farmer a fair price for the service.

The Plan de Pitic was to be the model for water distribution in all of the towns subsequently founded in the Provincias Internas. As was the case in the 1573 ordinances of King Philip II, some variation

35. Plan de Pitic, Article 19.

continued as local circumstances mitigated against a single plan for every settlement. In general, however, the principles contained in this document formed the basis for water practice in northern New Spain. In effect, the Plan de Pitic represents a codification of water practice prior to and at the time of its promulgation.[36]

With amazing regularity, the construction of an irrigation system for the new communities of the north began even before the houses, public buildings, and churches were finished. Prior to the completion of the ditches, water had to be conveyed by *aguadores*, who carried heavy buckets hanging from yokes across their shoulders.[37] The human toll was substantial. In addition, it was crucial to have the ditches in place before the first sowing. The initial project in Santa Fe, New Mexico, has been described by Marc Simmons:

> The first citizens of Santa Fe, probably with the aid of Mexican Indian servants and conscripted Pueblo laborers, dug two ace-quias madres (main ditches) to water fields on either side of the small river that passed through their villa. From the canal on the north, known after the Reconquest as the Acequia de la Muralla, a lateral ditch was brought to the vicinity of the plaza and the Governor's Palace, although at times, it seems, a smaller acequia leading from a marsh or cienaga near the parish church served this area.[38]

This same process occurred nearly everywhere in the north. Francisco Cuervo y Valdez, for example, in reporting on the foundation of Albuquerque in 1706, stated in April of that year that the irrigation ditch had already been completed. His report to the King indicated that the church had been completed, some of the houses were finished, and others were under construction, but "the acequias were ditched and running (*sacadas y corrientes*)."[39] The pattern was the same in California. Reporting on the progress of the newly established pueblo of Los Angeles in October 1781, Felipe de Nerre wrote to the

36. This argument was first advanced in Greenleaf, "Land and Water," p. 103. It was tested and found to be correct in the case of colonial New Mexico. See Michael C. Meyer and Susan M. Deeds, "Land, Water and Equity in Spanish Colonial and Mexican Law: Historical Evidence for the Court in the Case of the State of New Mexico vs. R. Lee Aamodt," (Unpublished manuscript, August, 1979), pp. 60–68.

37. Esther MacMillan, "The Cabildo and the People, 1731–1784," in *San Antonio in the Eighteenth Century* (San Antonio: San Antonio Bicentennial Heritage Committee, 1976), p. 87.

38. Marc Simmons, "Spanish Irrigation Practices in New Mexico," *New Mexico Historical Review* 47 (April, 1972), 138–139.

39. Paleographed with facsimile reproduction in Lansing B. Bloom, "Albuquerque and Galisteo: Certificate of Their Founding, 1706," *New Mexico Historical Review* 10 (January, 1935), pp. 48–49.

viceroy that construction of the houses and corrals was underway, the main irrigation ditch having already been completed.[40] Similarly, when Alberto de Córdoba reported to Governor Diego de Borica on the founding of the Villa de Branciforte in 1797, he indicated that some of the houses had already been built and the well dug for irrigation had been completed.[41] Even in the missions, the construction of dams and an irrigation system took precedence over the building and adornment of the mission church.[42] The missionaries of the El Paso region reported to their superiors that one of their first accomplishments was to teach the local Indian community how to build "a beautiful irrigation ditch."[43]

Because construction of the water system antedated the building of houses, public edifices, and churches, and because it required the mobilization of a large work force for the digging, dredging, transportation of materials, and feeding humans and animals, it was often one of the first endeavors which brought Indians and Spaniards together in a labor-management relationship. When the irrigation ditches of San Antonio were built, the local missionaries, fearing Indian restiveness, asked for military support, "enough soldiers to cause respect."[44] In the face of threats and coercion, Indian resentment is not difficult to understand. But forced labor was only one source of the friction. Although Spanish settlers and missionaries repeatedly assured the Indian work force that a new or better irrigation network would serve the interests of all, a Spanish acequia upstream from the Indian village caused an obvious diversion of the Indian water source. Conflict was not long in surfacing.

Building a mission, a presidio, or a town close to a river or a stream and digging simple irrigation canals from a single water source by no means assured a plentiful harvest. Water was only one of a number of requisites to be considered. The capricious nature of the desert climate taught harsh lessons to the early Spanish colonists; the best irrigation system could not forestall an unexpected frost in the

---

40. Felipe de Nerre to Viceroy Marques de Croix, Oct. 29, 1781. Quoted in *The City of Los Angeles vs. The City of San Fernando*. Court of Appeal, Second Appellate District, State of California, Second Civil No. 33708, p. A81.

41. Garr, "Villa de Branciforte," p. 104.

42. Thoribio de Urrutia to Sr. Auditor Gral de Guerra, Dec. 17, 1741, AGN, Provincias Internas, Vol. 32, Exp. 5; Diego Yragorri to José Luciano, May 26, 1748, AGN, Misiones, Leg. 11.

43. Fernando Ocaranza, *Establecimientos Franciscanos en el Misterioso Reino de Nuevo México* (Mexico: n.p., 1939), p. 68.

44. Edwin P. Arneson, "Early Irrigation in Texas," *Southwestern Historical Quarterly* 25 (October, 1921), 127.

late spring or a hailstorm in the summer. In some areas, the high caliche content of the soil thwarted the best irrigation system, as water, even when bountiful, could not be absorbed.[45] Even if climate and soil were good, human nature could not be predicted; although against the law, unauthorized use of the acequia madre occurred repeatedly and denied an adequate water supply to those entitled to use it. Water theft was especially serious during the early history of San Fernando de Béxar in Texas.[46] Even when unauthorized pilfering did not occur, a single stream often proved inadequate to supply the ditches, and it was necessary to construct diversion dams, reservoirs, and more elaborate irrigation networks to take advantage of all the water sources within a confined area to match supply and demand. The Jesuit padre José Pascual, assigned to the Tarahumara region of western Chihuahua in the middle of the seventeenth century, commented on this dilemma as follows:

> Although this mission was founded on the banks of the Río Conchos, it is not rich because there is not enough water to irrigate its many fields. Thus, those who live here suffer from want. For six years in succession the corn crop has been lost. . . . The padre, seeing these difficulties year after year, decided that natives of both this village and its visita of Santa Cruz should develop an adequate irrigation system. This mission would then cease to be so sterile and would begin to produce, for the lands of these two villages are extensive and fertile.[47]

Initial reconnaissance of a proposed site for settlement could be misleading. A river running to its banks during a wet year might carry not a drop during the next two or three. A number of towns and missions, including Saltillo, were relocated when an ostensibly adequate water supply turned out to be a chimera.[48] The town of Branciforte, one of the few civilian settlements in California, was abandoned altogether in the early nineteenth century, and among the

---

45. Noticia que el Coronel Dn Dom⁰ Cabello, Govʳ y Comᵗᵉ de las Armas de Dha Prov . . . Dec. 31, 1785, Bexar Archives, Reel 17. Hereafter cited as BA with appropriate information. The original documents in the Bexar Archives are housed in the University of Texas Archives, Austin, Texas.

46. Franᶜᵒ Delgado, Alcalde Segundo, San Fernando, Apr. 29, 1752, BA, Reel 9.

47. "An Account of the Missions, Taken from the Report of Padre José Pascual for the year 1651," in Thomas E. Sheridan and Thomas H. Naylor (eds.) *Rarámuri: A Tarahumara Colonial Chronicle, 1607–1791* (Flagstaff, Arizona: Northland Press, 1979), p. 29.

48. Joseph Antonio Rodríguez to Sr. Thenᵗᵉ Joseph Juachin Ecai y Muzquiz, Dec. 3, 1721, AGN, Provincias Internas, Vol. 32, Exp. 5; Vito Alessio Robles, *Francisco de Urdiñola y el norte de Nueva España* (Mexico: Imprenta Mundial, 1931).

reasons for the decision was the determination that the San Lorenzo River carried insufficient water for both the town and the neighboring mission of Santa Cruz.[49] The same lack of water prompted the Jesuits to abandon the Baja California mission of Nuestra Señora de Guadalupe.[50] In other cases, water scarcity limited the growth of towns and missions. In 1772 the governor of Baja California reported to the viceroy in Mexico City that the mission of Loreto had reached its maximum size because available water would not allow further expansion.[51]

When aridity threatened the survival of a new town, the options were limited. One could implore the local curate to ask for divine intervention, or neighboring Indians could be secretly encouraged to appeal to their god of rain. The town could be abandoned, of course, and many were. A final option was to request government help. In 1731 the citizens of Santa Eulalia, Chihuahua, having suffered several consecutive dry years, asked for government funds for the construction of a stone and lime dam near the town. The citizens would provide the labor if the government would pay the costs of materials. Their request for the assistance was denied, and they were given suggestions on how they might raise the money by taxing themselves.[52]

Other water problems plagued new communities as well. When the mission of San Diego de Alcalá was founded in 1769, marking the first permanent settlement in upper California, the colonists planted the first harvest in a broad river plain. Heavy rains caused the river to rise, and the entire crop was lost. The second year they sowed fields farther away from the river, but because of the lack of surveying equipment, the irrigation system was poorly engineered, and only a few fanegas of wheat survived.[53]

49. José Joaquín Yrrillaga to Viceroy Yturrigaray, July 18, 1806, AGN, Jesuitas, Leg. 1–14, and Borbon to Fiscal del Re Hacienda, Oct. 9, 1803, AGN, Jesuitas, Leg. 1–14.

50. Francis J. Weber, "Jesuit Missions in Baja California," *The Americas* 23 (April, 1967), 411.

51. Governor Phelipe Barri to Viceroy Antonio María de Bucareli, Jan. 4, 1772, AGN, Californias, Vol. 13.

52. Autos Quese formaron para Construir un tanque para recoger las aguas que entiempo dellubias derramaren los serros de Santa Eulalia, Año de 1731, Archivo Hidalgo de Parral, Reel 1731B. Hereafter cited as AHP with appropriate information.

53. Informe de los Aumentos que han tiendo en todo el Año, Feb. 5, 1775, AGI, Audiencia de Guadalajara, 1775; Noticias de la Antigua y Nueva California, DHM, VII, 13. San Diego overcame these intital difficulties within a few years and prospered. A large dam, 12 feet high and 245 feet long, was built on the San Diego River, and the irrigation system was redesigned. Between 1783 and 1832, the mission ranked fourth in agricultural production of all twenty-one missions in Upper California. See Zephyrin Engelhardt, O.F.M., *The Missions and Missionaries of California*, 4 vols. (Palo Alto, California: N-P Publishers, 1902–1915), p. 3.

Occasionally the design and execution of an irrigation network for a new community was handled with consummate skill. The canals of San Antonio, Texas, were well planned, lined with stone, and lasted for many years.[54] Some of the ditches on the lands of the Sánchez Navarro family in Coahuila also were lined with masonry to minimize seepage and prevent erosion.[55] In a few instances technology helped overcome the laws of gravity, as Spaniards introduced the *noria*, a waterlifting device to raise the precious liquid from a well or sunken seep and deposit it in an irrigation canal. But the overwhelming evidence suggests that these kinds of acequias were exceptions. The irrigation systems of most northern communities were scarcely models of hydraulic engineering. Skilled *acequeros* (ditch specialists) were scarce, surveying techniques crude, and communities had to rely on the talent that was available. In many cases the local missionary, the best-educated man in the community, served as amateur engineer, but mistakes were frequent and costly. Dug by hand with the most primitive tools, the ditches ranged in depth from two to eight or nine feet and in width from a foot to seven feet. They were seldom straight. It was easier to go around a hill than cut a ridge through it, or to go around a large tree rather than chop it down and dig up the roots. On occasion, the ditches were so poorly designed that they served no function at all. When the Seri Indians were relocated in Hermosillo, Sonora, in the 1770s, the intendant, Pedro Corbalán, ordered that a new acequia be built for their lands.[56] The digging was completed in several months, but because of an incorrect calculation of the slope, gravity refused to allow the water to work its way through the new ditch. Most of the ditch had to be deepened by three feet, and, when the diggers encountered huge rocks, the work was suspended.[57] Many months passed before it was ultimately finished. Twenty years later, the same problem befell the newly constructed acequia of Chihuahua City. The system had to be destroyed and built again.[58]

Stone diversions and floodgates, often located far upstream to take advantage of the most propitious gravitational flow, were the

54. Mardith K. Schuetz, "Excavation of a Section of the Acequia Madre in Bexar County, Texas," Texas Historical Survey Committee, *Archeological Report Number 19* (July, 1970); Arneson, "Early Irrigation in Texas," pp. 123–125.
55. Harris, *A Mexican Family Empire*, p. 47.
56. Providencia de Pedro Corbalán, May 4, 1772, AGN, Provincias Internas, Vol. 232, Exp. 1, and Pedro Corbalán to Viceroy Antonio María de Bucareli, June 15, 1773, AGN, Provincias Internas, Vol. 91, Exp. 1.
57. Francisco Messica to Pedro Corbalán, Oct. 12, 1772, AGN, Provincias Internas, Vol. 232, Exp. 1.
58. Anselmo Rodríguez to Viceroy, May 8, 1779, AGN, Alhóndigas, Vol. 11, Exp. 3.

most common method of channeling water from the stream to the principal and secondary channels. When properly installed, they served their intended function. But on many occasions they broke, and water was needlessly diverted into fallow or well-watered fields to the obvious disadvantage of those downstream who needed the water for irrigation. Poor design also made the ditches themselves vulnerable to the vagaries of nature. Throughout the region, they broke during heavy rainfalls or during the spring thaw and had to be repaired, thus diverting human energy from other pressing aspects of the agricultural cycle.[59] This particular problem was especially severe in El Paso, which drew irrigation water from the Río Grande, the largest of the northern rivers. Bishop Pedro Tamarón y Romeral visited the area in 1760 and explained the unique method the citizens of El Paso used to cope with excess water in the irrigation canals.

> That settlement suffers a great deal of trouble caused by the river. Every year the freshet carries away the conduit they make to drain off its waters. . . . The method of restoring the conduit every year is to make some large round baskets of rather thick rods. When the freshets are over, they put them in the current, filling them with stones, and they act as dams and force the water to seek the mouth of the ditch.[60]

In some cases irrigation systems were designed properly to bring water into the fields but were too ambitious in scope to help the struggling farmer. Excessively long ditches, even though the gradation was designed perfectly, invariably lost huge amounts of the precious liquid to evaporation and seepage. One eighteenth-century mission in Coahuila found itself sixty-five miles away from the principal water source. The acequia brought in water without difficulty, but for every 800,000 gallons that entered the ditch at its source, 700,000 gallons were lost to evaporation and seepage before the fields received any moisture at all.[61] When water is at a premium, it is obvious that the loss of seven-eighths cannot be tolerated without serious repercussions.

The problem of constructing effective irrigation systems was of sufficient concern to authorities in northern New Spain to prompt them to seek professional help. In the 1760s, the Royal Corps of

59. Juan Nentvig, S.J., *Rudo Ensayo: A Description of Sonora and Arizona in 1764* (Tucson: University of Arizona Press, 1980), p. 88.

60. Adams (ed.), *Bishop Tamarón's Visitation,* pp. 35–36.

61. "Misiones del Colegio de Pachuca en 1793," Nov. 16, 1793, in *Estudios de historia del noreste* (Monterrey: Editorial Alfonso Reyes, 1972), p. 159.

Engineers arrived and began to make its presence felt in the north. In charge of town planning and major construction projects, including dams, roads, and bridges, the corps was responsible for improving the design of some irrigation networks. In 1774 a special section of the engineers was established exclusively for hydraulic projects, but the corps was spread thin in the north, and many communities continued to suffer from irrigation systems inadequate to the task.[62]

The quality of water, the nature of the surrounding land, and other climatic factors caused colonists and missionaries many difficulties. Generally, water quality in the north was excellent, but on occasion high mineral content made it unfit for either drinking or irrigation. When Jesuit fathers Victoriano Arnes and Juan José Díaz founded the Baja California mission of Calamajue in 1766, the crops were all destroyed the first year because of the high salt content in the irrigation water.[63] The same problem plagued the Baja California mission of San José del Cabo.[64] In Chihuahua, at the presidio of Janos, it was the soil that was bad. The river carried sufficient water, but, when it was conducted to the fields, it was absorbed by the sand before it could irrigate the crops.[65] In the Guazapares region of Chihuahua the water resource seemed adequate for irrigation, but the constant winds thwarted the most persistent irrigation efforts. Steady winds increased the rate of evaporation and dried out the fields before the crops could be harvested.[66]

Huge masonry aqueducts were generally unnecessary in the new communities of the north. They were very prominent in central and southern Mexico and dominated the landscape in the towns of Querétaro, Oaxaca, Morelia, Atlacomulco, Zempoala, and Guadalajara.[67] Northern towns generally were located not in deep valleys but on broad river plains where simple ditches and gravity obviated the

62. For a discussion of the engineers, and especially their concern with water projects, see Janet R. Fireman, *The Spanish Royal Corps of Engineers in the Western Borderlands: Instrument of Bourbon Reform, 1764–1815* (Glendale: Arthur H. Clark Company, 1977), pp. 28, 42, 129, 160–161.

63. Engelhardt, *Missions and Missionaries*, I, 260–261.

64. Fr. Vicente de Mora to Antonio Bucareli y Ursua, Feb. 20, 1777, AGN, Californias, Vol. 36, Exp. 5.

65. Juan Bautista Peru to Comandante Gral., Dec. 28, 1778, AGI, Audiencia de Guadalajara, 270.

66. Guazapares, Descripción Geográphica que. . .asse el Padre Fray Buenaventura Fernández de Lizi, Sep. 27, 1777, cited in *Relaciones del siglo XVIII relativas a Chihuahua* (Mexico: Biblioteca de Historiadores Mexicanos, 1950), I, 17.

67. Adolfo Orive Alba, *La política de irrigación en México* (Mexico: Fondo de Cultura Económica, 1960), pp. 33–34; Marcos Arana Cervantes, *Agua para todos* (Guadalajara: Gobierno del Estado de Jalisco, 1980), pp. 21–30.

Figure 2.3   Aqueduct in San Antonio, Texas, constructed in the 1730s to carry water from the Acequia Espada over the Río Pideras. Courtesy San Antonio Conservation Society

need for tall, arched aqueducts. One exception was Chihuahua City, which authorized the construction of an aqueduct in 1751. The cabildo paid for it by levying a special tax on the rich silver mines in the area.[68] San Antonio also built a small aqueduct, part of which still stands today (fig. 2.3).

68. Francisco R. Almada, *Resumen de historia del estado de Chihuahua* (Mexico: Libros Mexicanos, 1955), p. 110.

The many problems faced by newly established communities in the Hispanic Southwest differed tremendously from area to area but not from time to time. The decade or even century of settlement did not exert any major influence on the water problems encountered. Settlers who moved from one area of the northern desert to another could help the founders of a new town anticipate recurrent ecological problems, but for the most part the physical environment had to be experienced in each locale and special solutions had to be devised for the countless idiosyncracies of nature. The only predictable problem, but one without a predictable solution, was that water scarcity would occur and would bring with it social polarization and confrontation. The variety of water conflicts was limited only by human ingenuity, but the conflicts themselves, as well as their solutions, fashioned some of the most important configurations of southwestern society.

CHAPTER 3

Water and Social Conflict

Social discord is born of many causes, some more morally reprehensible than others. Without question motivations no more laudable than greed and envy prompt some to appropriate the property of others. Almost invariably they are encouraged, directly or indirectly, by ineffective or corrupt officials whose lack of dedication to their public charge holds out high promise for impunity. The search for power, as a means to an end or an end in itself, also yields its share of group hostility. In conflicts of these kinds the pathologically weak are victimized by the strong, and they have little recourse. Some of the water disputes in northern New Spain can be attributed fairly to the moral reprobates of society. Spanish colonists knew from experience that water was a source of power and did not hesitate to use it in the quest for both material goods and influence. But not all water quarrels were rooted in the debased and selfish actions of the power seekers. The majority of conflicts pitting individual against individual and group against group were the product of an imperfect world in which scarcity came to dominate human action. In many years and in specific areas there simply was not enough usable water to meet the needs of all. In the disputes which ensued, the weak were also victimized by the strong, but at least they did have recourse to the administrative and judicial mechanism of the state. Some fared better than others.

Land disputes in the Hispanic Southwest were almost always based on contentions over water. No area in northern New Spain was densely populated. Land was readily available and in large quantities. Land with a reliable and permanent water source, however, was scarce.

As Spanish settlers moved into areas occupied by Indians, disputes
arose, and they are often treated as land confrontations. As one begins
to examine the documentation, it becomes obvious that in most cases it
was not the land that was an issue, but rather the water that went with
it.[1] Certainly there were some controversies over grazing land and
boundaries, but in most cases land was not contested unless it was
attached to a water source.[2]

It is not surprising that Spanish settlement of the arid far north
was accompanied by heated contests over water. Spaniards vied for
existing water supplies not only with the Indian populations but with
other Spaniards. Spanish landowners with adjacent boundaries
fought one another constantly in the effort to increase their water
supplies.[3] In addition Spanish clergymen and military men both believed that they were serving the Crown, but, when water was at issue,
each group argued that its mission was supreme and, as a result, that
its claims to water should be considered paramount.[4] Each group
rationalized that its own presence was needed to assure the happiness
and tranquility of the surrounding Indian population, but the documentation suggests forcefully that in most cases Indian water interests
were served by neither.

It is a common presumption that the majority of water disputes
between Indians and non-Indians were registered between large and
powerful Spanish hacendados and the neighboring Indian population. Controversies of this kind did indeed occur and often had dire
results for the Indians. When hacendado Felipe Montano cut off the
Indian water supply in the pueblo of Santa Cruz in southern

1. Archival examples abound. For a sampling of New Mexico "land cases" that are in
actuality water cases, see Joseph Visente Ortiz to Alcalde de Laguna, Sep. 26, 1816,
Spanish Archives of New Mexico, I, 668, hereafter cited as SANM with appropriate
information. Petition of Juan Antonio Lobato, Oct. 30, 1823, SANM, I, 1292; Pedro
Martin and Fr. José Benito Pereyra to Senor Gov^or D^n Alberto Maynez, SANM, II,
2596; Bartolome Baca to Alcalde Constitucional de Alameda, Apr. 27, 1824, University of New Mexico, Seligman Collection. Hereafter cited as UNM SC with appropriate information.

2. Even the complicated and litigious Atrisco land grant case in New Mexico has a
strong water dimension. For the importance of acequias in this litigation see Richard
E. Greenleaf, "Atrisco and las Ciruelas, 1722–1769," *New Mexico Historical Review* 42
(Jan., 1967), 5–25. The eighteenth-century water disputes in Coahuila among the
Vásquez Barrego, Ignacio Elizondo, and Sánchez Navarro families were also based
on water. See Harris, *A Mexican Family Empire*, pp. 19–20, 24–26.

3. Struggles between Spaniards over water followed on the heels of the foundation of
many northern settlements. This process is described for Coahuila in Harris, *A
Mexican Family Empire*, p. 5.

4. See, for example, Pedro Antonio Albares de Azebedo to Governor, June 2, 1740,
and June 4, 1740, AGN, Californias, Vol. 80, Exp. 28, and Capellan Antonio Tempis
to Pedro Antonio de Alvarez, June 15, 1740, AGN, Californias, Vol. 80, Exp. 28.

Chihuahua, the local inhabitants were forced to flee into the mountains "and search for food like deer."[5] Some died because their water source had been denied. Other cases with similar results can be found in the surviving documentation, but most of the water controversies in the Mexican north pitted Indians not against hacendados, but against Spanish towns, presidios, missions, small Spanish landholders, and other Indians. The results, if often less dramatic, were no less dire.

In no way did water conflict in the Mexican north result from population increase. The decline of the native population in those decades following the original Spanish contact more than offset the number of Spanish and mestizo arrivals. Water controversy more properly was a product of demographic and economic change. Even though the total population of the Hispanic Southwest was less in the seventeenth century than it had been in the sixteenth, it was a much more concentrated population. Almost as a matter of faith, Spaniards considered seminomadic or widely scattered Indians as uncivilized. Not only were they beyond the effective reach of the missionaries and civil authorities, but, persisting in a non-European lifestyle, they were *gente bárbara*. Even when the grand design called for the Indians to serve as the agricultural labor force, they first had to be concentrated in villages or missions. Unlike the Anglo-American ideal of isolating the single-family farm, the Spaniards preferred the close human interaction that could be offered by the community. The Spanish penchant for town life and the concerted policy of bringing the Indian population together in missions strained water sources almost everywhere. The total amount of water available in the north easily could have supported a population one hundred times greater (even with limited technology), but it was not always available where it was needed and even less when it was needed.

More important than the demographic pressure resulting from the concentration of the population were changes in economic orientation. Private land and water ownership probably did not exist anywhere in the pre-Columbian Southwest; if it did, it was an extremely rare exception.[6] With the Spanish settlement of the north and with the

5. Don Juan Tepeyuan, Casique del Pueblo de Santa Crus to Gran Señor y tlatoani Mayor de Nuestras Tierras . . . July 12, 1649, AHP, Reel 1653 B.

6. Private ownership of land, if it did exist in the Indian Southwest, would have been found most logically in those areas inhabited by sedentary agriculturalists. But Ralph M. Linton hedges on the issues in the Pueblo region of New Mexico. "The Río Grande Pueblos have had individual ownership of farmlands for many generations . . . this may be due to Spanish influence. . . ." See Linton's "Land Tenure in Aboriginal America," in Oliver La Farge (ed.)., *The Changing Indian* (Norman: University of Oklahoma Press, 1942), p. 52.

introduction of capitalism, private ownership of land and private use of water became the norm. A well-watered piece of land could produce a profitable cash crop. Agricultural surpluses could be used to sustain the extension of the mission frontier. They could be used to foster the goals of the Spanish monarchy in its rivalry with other European interlopers. These notions were foreign to native American mentality and were bound to occasion conflict as a resource formerly controlled by the Indians themselves now had to be obtained from others.

Irrigation came to dominate agricultural practice to a much larger extent than ever before. But it was not the only new drain on the water reserve. Domesticated animals introduced by the Spaniards greatly increased water demand. Animal water consumption greatly surpasses that of humans, and the animal population, multiplying rapidly in the new environment, soon outnumbered the human population by many times. An eighteenth-century census for Nuevo Santander, for example, listed six settlements along the lower Río Grande with a total population (Indian and non-Indian) of 2,273. The number of livestock for the same six settlements exceeded 209,000.[7] Over-grazing prompted soil erosion and reduced the normally scarce water supply. It was a classic example of ecolturation. The cattle introduced by the Spaniards consumed the grasses more readily than they could regrow. The desert topsoil was slow to regenerate because the natural groundcover played a crucial role in its formation. In this process of desertification, aridity increased and with it the demand for additional water. There is strong documentary evidence that this particular ecolturative problem prompted sporadic water shortages in the Pueblo region of New Mexico and indirect evidence that it plagued Arizona as well.[8] Other new economic activities were water-consumptive also. A medium-sized mining enterprise demanded more water than a half a dozen towns or missions. Although the mines were only occasionally located immediately adjacent to a town, they nevertheless drew on the same limited water sources. It did not matter to town dwellers if their water was diverted one mile or seventy-five miles upstream. The introduction of new technology strained water reserves as well. Water was not used as a source of energy prior to the arrival of the Spaniards, but gristmills, powered by water, were used throughout New Spain by the eighteenth century.

7. Edwin J. Foscue, "Agricultural History of the Lower Río Grande Valley Region," *Agricultural History* 8 (1936), 128.
8. Sandos, *The Pueblo Indians*, p. 52.

Water conflict occurred occasionally in wet and normal years, but, not surprisingly, it manifested itself most dramatically in years of drought. Preliminary studies indicate that New Spain registered eighty-eight droughts between 1521 and 1821, some lasting for only a matter of months and others several years.[9] Scarcely a decade passed without one. In addition, very localized droughts in restricted areas of the north must be added to the list of eighty-eight more general ones. On a few occasions water scarcity stimulated cooperation among potential competitors. The more general pattern, however, was for scarcity to engender conflict which almost invariably prejudiced the interests of the weak: poor Spaniards, poor mestizos, and most obviously, poor Indians.

When a new Spanish town, presidio, or mission was founded, existing Indian communities were generally guaranteed a share or percentage of the water supply. On many occasions, however, that percentage was subsequently reduced through both legal and illegal means. Spanish encroachments on Indian land almost always implied appropriation of the local water supply. The process occurred in different areas of the borderlands at different times and in varying degrees of intensity, but the process itself appeared to be inevitable.[10] In her discussion of Spanish incursions in the Pueblo area of the Upper Río Grande valley of New Mexico, Myra Ellen Jenkins explains the phenomenon well:

> The Pueblo Indians, already living in settled villages, became wards of the Crown, entitled to the full protection of the innumerable royal cedulas and viceregal and *audiencia* ordinances passed for the benefit of the Indians. The intent of Spanish law and administration was both to protect the Indians in their personal and communal land-water rights, and to convert them to the Christian religion so that they would be loyal vassals of the Crown. . . . Indian conversion, coupled with humane and equitable treatment of royal wards, however, was but one principle of Spanish colonial administration. Of comparable importance was the economic exploitation of the New World for the benefit of an expanding empire. Often these principles were incompatible.[11]

9. Enrique Florescano, "Una historia olvidada: La sequía en México," *Nexos* 32 (Aug. 1980), 9–18.

10. For the water dispute between the heirs of Francisco Urdiñola, founder of Saltillo, and the local Indian population, see Alessio Robles, *Francisco de Urdiñola*, pp. 103–106.

11. Myra Ellen Jenkins, "Spanish Land Grants in the Tewa Area," *New Mexico Historical Review* 47 (Apr., 1972), p. 113.

There is some evidence to suggest that in New Mexico the process began in the early seventeenth century, prior to the famous Pueblo Rebellion of 1680, and indeed was one of the factors which combined with other religious and cultural conflicts to produce that major insurrection.[12] Shortly after the Spaniards were forced to abandon New Mexico and take refuge in El Paso, an Indian captive reported to them that Popé, the leader of the rebellion, had instructed all of the pueblos "to enlarge their cultivated fields."[13] The implication of land and water pressure is certainly there, but the documentation is stronger for the late seventeenth and early eighteenth century, following the reconquest of the Pueblo region. Governors Diego de Vargas, Pedro Rodríguez Cubero, Francisco Cuervo y Valdez, and Gaspar Domingo de Mendoza made many land grants to individual Spaniards in the heart of the Pueblo region[14] and in 1695 permitted the establishment of a new Spanish town, Santa Cruz de la Cañada. The founding document for the new town is clear in stating that the boundaries of the new settlement were not to extend into the lands of the Pueblos. The Spanish grant was made "as far as the Pueblos of Nambe, Pojoaque, Jacona, San Ildefonso, Santa Clara, and San Juan de los Caballeros."[15] During the formal act of possession which took place a few days after the grant was made, Indian rights were even more clearly protected, as Governor Vargas specified: "I again made them [the Spaniards] their grant . . . revalidating their lands which belong to them and the boundaries set forth, and which limit the said pueblos mentioned in the said declaration . . . *without prejudice to the boundaries of land which belong to each one* [emphasis mine]."[16] In spite of the unmistakable protections, land and water disputes were not long in surfacing as Spanish population in the Pueblo region increased

12. The period is discussed thoroughly in France V. Scholes, *Church and State in New Mexico, 1610–1650* (Albuquerque: University of New Mexico Press, 1937), and in France V. Scholes, *Troublous Times in New Mexico, 1654–1670* (Albuquerque: University of New Mexico Press, 1942).

13. Myra Ellen Jenkins, "Taos Pueblos and its Neighbors, 1540–1847," *New Mexico Historical Review* 41 (Apr., 1966), p. 89.

14. Jenkins, "Spanish Land Grants," pp. 118–132.

15. The grant was signed by Governor and Captain General Don Diego de Vargas Lujan Ponze de Leon, Santa Fe, Apr. 19, 1695, SANM, I, 882, contained in Microfilm of New Mexico Land Grants, Miscellaneous Archives, Reel 9.

16. ". . . y de nuevo les hize merzed . . . rebalidandoles sus tierras q les pertenezen y terminos deslindados y que caen a los Pueblos dhos en dho bando de Merzed . . . sin perjuizio de terminos de sus tierras q les perteneze a cada uno. . . ." Posesion y Juramento de dha Villa, Governor Vargas Zapata Lujan Ponze de Leon, Villa de Santa Cruz, Apr. 22, 1695, SANM, I, 882.

tremendously during the next century.[17] Contentions over land and water dominated Spanish-Indian relations in the Tewa pueblos of Nambe, Tesuque, San Ildefonso, and Pojoaque.[18]

One of the best-documented water disputes between Indians and non-Indians in northern New Spain was the case of Taos and San Fernando de Taos against the Spanish settlers of Arroyo Seco, New Mexico. The case emerged at the end of the colonial period, but the actual decision was rendered in 1823, shortly after Mexico won its independence from Spain.

The Taos area of northern New Mexico had grown slowly during the colonial period. At the time of the Pueblo Rebellion of 1680, there were fewer than seventy-five Spaniards in the Taos Valley. The non-Indian settlement increased rapidly following the reconquest. In the eighteenth century, large Spanish land grants, especially the Cristóbal de la Serna Grant and the Antoine Leroux Grant, attracted many settlers to the north. By 1800, the Spanish population numbered about 1,330. As happened elsewhere in northern New Spain, growth occasioned conflict between Indians and Spaniards. In 1815 a major land dispute occurred when the Taos Indians charged that a group of Spaniards had settled on their grant. The *alcalde* (justice of the peace), Pedro Martín, had what he thought was an easy solution. The Spaniards should pay the Indians fifty cows and horses for the land they had appropriated. The Indians angrily rejected the scheme and demanded that the alcalde take the case to Governor Alberto Maynez in Santa Fe.[19] The alcalde did forward the case to the governor and advised that a bad decision could cause serious problems between Spaniards and Indians. The governor ultimately upheld the Indian rights to the land in question.

The land dispute of 1815, and its resolution by the governor, was the long-range cause of the water dispute a few years later. Some of the Spanish settlers who were forced to leave the Taos Pueblo founded the

17. Judicial proceedings over land and water, pitting Spaniards against the Indians of Pojoaque, Nambe, San Ildefonso, Tesuque, and Santa Clara, are outlined in Jenkins, "Spanish Land Grants," pp. 113–134. Additional information can be gleaned from Auto de Alfonso Real de Aguilar, Santa Fe, June 14, 1715, SANM, I, 7, and Juan Perez Hurtado to Ignacio Roybal, Santa Fe, Sep. 18, 1704, SANM, I, 1339.

18. Some of these disputes, based upon the Twitchell documentary guide but not on the actual documents themselves, are discussed in Vlasich, "Pueblo Indian Agriculture," pp. 84–95.

19. "Espucimos elque los vecinos entregaron cinquenta animales, entre vacuno y cabayos . . . pero los indios lleno de petulancia renunciaron toda combencion y esponen que S.S. subtanze el litiz. . . ." Pedro Martin, Alcalde Interino, and Fr. José Benito Pereyra to Señor Gov[or] D[n] Alberto Maynez, May 13, 1815, SANM, II, 2596.

village of Arroyo Seco, probably in 1815.[20] Arroyo Seco was located on a grant originally assigned to Diego Lucero and reassigned after the Pueblo Rebellion to Antonio Martínez. Under both Spanish landlords, the Taos Indians claimed that they had been allowed to use part of the land for agriculture and to draw water from the Río Lucero (named after the first grantee).[21] Shortly after the new village was founded, a few of the Spanish settlers, including Joaquín Sánchez and José Sánchez—who may or may not have held legal titles—sold portions of their land to the Taos Indians.[22] The Indian claims to the water of the Río Lucero thus had two bases: they had used the water for many years (and thus could claim prior usage), and they had more recently purchased land fronting on the Río Lucero and in that purchase gained additional water rights. The Indian claims seemed well founded, but did the Spanish settlers of Arroyo Seco have water rights as well?

At the request of the Governor of New Mexico, the case was heard by the cabildo of Taos in March of 1823. The Arroyo Seco settlers argued that as descendants of the original grantees, they had founded their village in 1815 and since that time had irrigated their fields from both the Arroyo Seco and the Río Lucero. The Indians countered that they had used the water of Río Lucero even before the arrival of the Spaniards and in 1818 had purchased additional land with water rights on the Río Lucero. The Taos cabildo, with Alcalde Juan Antonio Lobato presiding, ruled that the Indians had total right (*derecho total*) to the water on both grounds. But their total right did not mean that they were entitled to the total water of the Río Lucero. The Spanish settlers of Arroyo Seco needed water, too. Their other water source, the Arroyo Seco, as might be surmised from the name itself, did not supply them with an adequate water source. Therefore, the

20. The early history of Arroyo Seco and the water dispute with the Taos Pueblo is discussed in Myra E. Jenkins, "The Río Hondo Settlement," (unpublished manuscript, 1974) and Jenkins, "Taos Pueblo," pp. 85–114. Further information can be gleaned from Harold H. Dunham, "Spanish and Mexican Land Policies in the Taos Pueblo Region," in *Pueblo Indians I* (New York: Garland Publishers, Inc., 1974), pp. 151–331.

21. There is no reason to doubt prior usage of the water from the Río Lucero by the Taos Indians. When Fray Anastasio Domínguez visited the area in 1776, he reported that the lands were fertile ". . . and those on the north are watered by the Lucero River." See Eleanor B. Adams and Fray Angélico Chávez (eds.), *The Missions of New Mexico, 1776* (Albuquerque: University of New Mexico Press, 1975), p. 112.

22. In litigation which followed, it was argued that Joaquín Sánchez, one of the Arroyo Seco settlers, hoodwinked the Taos Indians by selling them land that was not his to sell but rather belonged to the legitimate heirs of Antonio Martín. Juan Eusevio García de la Mora to Governor Antonio Narvona, Santa Fe, Apr. 25, 1826, SANM, I, 389.

alcalde, speaking for the entire cabildo, awarded the Spaniards of
Arroyo Seco one *surco*[23] of water from the Río Lucero when the
stream was abundant and a proportionately lesser amount when water
was scarce.[24] The settlement was an equitable one and forestalled new
hostility between Pueblo Indians and newly arrived Spaniards.

Unfortunately, the reduction of Indian water supplies often precipitated violent confrontation. At approximately the same time as the
Pueblo Rebellion in New Mexico, hostility surfaced some five hundred
miles to the southwest in the Tarahumara country of Chihuahua.
Spanish encroachments on Tarahumara water supplies began at least
as early as the 1670s,[25] but major difficulties were still two decades
away. A series of silver strikes were made in the 1680s at Coyachic, San
Bernabé, and Cusihuiriachic. The population explosion which followed brought new pressure on Indian labor, land, and water and
ultimately resulted in a series of rebellions in the 1690s.[26]

To the west in Tucson, the reduction of Indian water supplies
occurred later, but occurred, nevertheless. Throughout the late colonial period, there were four competing demands on the limited Tucson water supply: the Pima village of Tucson (on the west bank of the
Santa Cruz River); the Royal Presidio of San Agustín de Tucson (on
the east bank of the Santa Cruz); the communal mission lands of San
Xavier del Bac; and the individual Indian plots of San Xavier.
Whether living on mission lands or in their own pueblo, the Indians
ranked low on the water priority scale.

Shortly after Father Eusebio Kino founded the Jesuit mission of
San Xavier del Bac in 1700, new agricultural fields were opened there.
For irrigation purposes water was drawn from the Río Santa Cruz and
from a few small valley springs. This use caused no hardship during
the years of normal precipitation, but during dry years irrigation at
the mission prejudiced the Pima village of Tucson, north and downstream of the mission. Periodically, until the expulsion of the Jesuits in
1767, quarrels over water were recorded.[27] Seventeen-sixty-one was an
especially bad year. Padre Manuel de Aguirre at the Mission of San
Xavier del Bac reported to civil authorities that there was plenty of

23. A *surco* entitled the grantee or grantees to 3,081 gallons per hour, 73,944 gallons per day, or over half a million (517,608) gallons per week. For additional hydraulic measures see pp. 90–91.
24. "Seles esceda un surco de agua del Río de Lucero quando este en abundancia y quando este escaso seles dara a proporcion." Decision of Juan Ant° Lobato, Oct. 30, 1823, SANM, I, 1292.
25. Pedro Cano to Joseph García, Nov. 10, 1672, AHP, Reel 1671A.
26. Sheridan and Naylor (eds.), *Rarámuri*, pp. 39–70.
27. Dobyns, *Spanish Colonial Tucson*, p. 62.

land for everyone, but not enough water to sustain the existing Spanish and Indian population.[28] A similar report reached Viceroy
Bucareli in 1772,[29] but the situation went from bad to worse a few
years later.

Shortly after the Franciscans replaced the Jesuits in the Pimería
Alta, the Spanish crown made the decision to move the presidio of
Tubac north to Tucson. By the late 1770s many civilians had attached
themselves to the military fort, and the local commander, Don Pedro
de Allande y Saavedra, began making land grants to them. This
added to the water shortages of the Pima pueblo of Tucson.[30] An
accord was ultimately reached awarding three-quarters of the Santa
Cruz water to the Indians and one-quarter to the presidio.[31] But the
agreement was not kept, and the Pima continued to be denied an
adequate water supply. By the 1790s the situation was sufficiently
serious that it was reported to the King by Franciscan Friar Diego
Bringas:

> . . . I must inform Your Lordship that since the presidio is so near
> the pueblo the farming practiced by the inhabitants and the
> soldiers causes a scarcity of water for the Indians. . . . For this
> reason, I humbly beg Your Lordship to order that the damage be
> repaired and that the Indians be permitted the water they need.[32]

The Commandant General's office in Chihuahua City was not at
all impressed with Bringas' accusation against the Tucson presidio. It
simply reminded Bringas that an agreement had already been
reached on the division of water.[33] Friar Bringas was furious at the
lack of concern. Rather than simply referring to an old accord that was

28. Manuel de Aguirre to Governor Juan de Pineda, 1761, AGN, Provincias Internas,
Vol. 17, Exp. 15.
29. Governor Mateo Sastre to Viceroy Bucareli, Oct. 19, 1772, AGI, Audiencia de
Guadalajara, 513.
30. Dobyns, *Spanish Colonial Tucson*, p. 67.
31. I have been unable to locate a copy of the agreement, but reference to it is made in
at least two subsequent documents, one dated 1796 and one dated 1828. Galindo
Navarro to Señor Comandante General, Chihuahua, Dec. 9, 1796, cited in Daniel S.
Matson and Bernard L. Fontana (eds.), *Friar Bringas Reports to the King: Methods of
Indoctrination on the Frontier of New Spain, 1796–1797* (Tucson: University of Arizona
Press, 1977), pp. 67–75, and Manuel Escalante y Arvizu to Governador José María
Gaxiola, Dec. 9, 1828, Archivo Histórico del Estado de Sonora, Film 12. Hereafter
cited as AHES with appropriate information. The Arizona Historical Society holds a
microfilm copy of this film. The particular document cited here was kindly brought to
my attention by Kieran McCarty.
32. Galindo Navarro to Señor Comandante, Dec. 9, 1796, cited in Matson and
Fontana (eds.), *Friar Bringas*, p. 66.
33. Matson and Fontana (eds.), *Friar Bringas*, p. 73.

not being honored, he argued, "it would have been more fitting to have decreed . . . that they should put the aforementioned provisions into effect. . . . Everyone knows that there are laws, but many do not respect them. It is not enough to tell them that the laws exist. They must be compelled to obey them."[34]

Friar Bringas' recommendations fell on deaf ears. Action was taken shortly after Mexican independence, but it was scarcely what the clergyman had in mind. Manuel Escalante y Arvizu, the jefe político, wrote to Governor José María Gaxiola recommending a new formula for water distribution. The Indians, instead of being guaranteed three-fourths, should have their percentage reduced to one-half.

> The little [Pima] town of Tucson is older than the presidio. For this reason it enjoys a water grant from a beautiful spring that gently irrigates the immense agricultural fields. The inhabitants of the presidio, because of a formal agreement, are limited to one-fourth of the water for agricultural fields that belong to the presidio.
>
> I have stated to Your Excellency in all truth the reasons for the complaints and the ultimate decision of the citizens of Tucson (to abandon the presidio). Now it would be profitable for me to indicate the measures that should be undertaken to alleviate the problems.
>
> In Tucson, more than in any other place, it is necessary to have a very active military commander, one who sleeps with his arms rather than his wife. The little [Pima] village of Tucson . . . has very few Indians who enjoy, through legal right, three-quarters of the water. It would be best to look for legal means to award the [Spanish] citizens of Tucson half of the water.[35]

The Governor accepted the recommendation, and, when Tucson passed from Mexican to United States sovereignty with the Gadsden Purchase, the presidio, then called the colonia militar, had legal right to half of the water.[36] Why did the Indians of the Tucson area not rebel? Undoubtedly, the presence of the presidio first, and then the colonia militar, discouraged rebellion.

Similar scenarios were repeated all over northern New Spain and,

---

34. Ibid., p. 80. Manuel de Aguirre to Governor Juan de Pineda, 1761, AGN, Provincias Internas, Vol. 17, Exp. 15.

35. Manuel Escalante y Arvizu to Governor José María Gaxiola, Dec. 9, 1828, AHES, Film 12.

36. Petition of Ignacio Saenz, Dolores Gallardo, Jesús Castro, and José Zapata to Governor José Aguilar, May 6, 1852, AHES, Film 48.

after independence, in northern Mexico.[37] In the struggle for survival, Indians found themselves contending for water, and not very successfully, with Spanish towns, Spanish presidios, and individual Spanish settlers.[38] Even when Indians received water in amounts adequate to their needs, there were subtle reminders of Spanish priorities. At El Paso del Norte, the acequia designed to irrigate Indian fields was bled off the acequia madre, placing Indian water use at the mercy of Spanish landowners (fig. 3.1). In the Hermosillo region in the 1770s the local Indians received one day of water per week to irrigate their fields and orchards. Their designated day was Sunday.[39] Maybe the Spaniards needed one day of rest; the Indians obviously did not.

When the Indians found themselves on the short side of water allocations, they often asked for judicial relief, but their record in courts, with a few major exceptions such as the Taos settlement, left much to be desired. Armed with what they believed to be legal documentation to support their case, they were often turned away by officials who informed them that their papers were not valid,[40] or, that if they were valid, their water right came not from the main river of their land, but from an arroyo that might carry water only a few weeks during the year.[41] Mexican independence brought no relief to the Indian population. Although they were considered citizens for the first time, the same pressures for land and water continued. In most cases the Indians were at a decided disadvantage when litigation occurred. They were required to submit their titles to the proper authorities, and sometimes the titles were never returned.[42] In the

37. In his study of water practices in the Pueblo region of New Mexico, James Vlasich has reached conclusions similar to those expressed in this work concerning the relative unimportance of Mexican independence in water disputes and resolutions. He concludes, "It can be generally stated that Mexican law concerning the Pueblo Indians was not much different than that of their Spanish predecessors . . . concerning water rights, Mexican law continued to implement the policies that originated under the Spaniards. . . ." "Pueblo Indian Agriculture," pp. 117 and 118.

38. The struggle for water between the missions and the presidio of the San Antonio, Texas, area is synopsized in Joseph Antonio Rodríguez to Sr. Then.te Joseph Juachin Ecai y Muzquiz, Dec. 3, 1721, AGN, Provincias Internas, Vol. 32, Exp. 6.

39. Juan Antonio Meave to S.or Intendente d.n Pedro Corbalan, AGN, Provincias Internas, Vol. 91, Exp. 1.

40. It is not uncommon to find in the litigation phrases such as "es un ynstrumento simple alqe no sele puede dar ninguna fee ni credito para proseguir estas diligencias." Testimonios de los Autos Formados Sobre el Repartimiento de Tierras en la Colonia del Nuevo Santander Perteneciente a las Misiones de Californias, Año de 1770, AGI, Audiencia de México, 1369.

41. Sobre posesion a los indios . . . en Las Bocas, gestion del P. Francisco Velasco, 1700, AHP, Reel 1700a.

42. Juan Ant.o Chaves to Sr. Srio de Estado y del Despacho de Justicia, Sep. 30, 1829, and Mar. 15, 1830, AGN, Justicia, Vol. 48, Exp. 19.

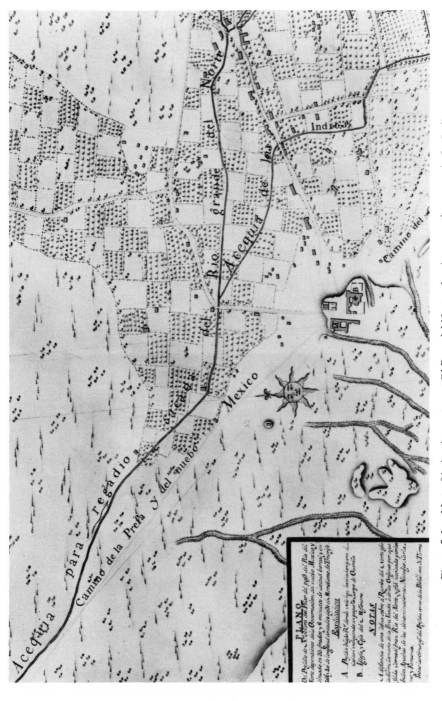

Figure 3.1   Map of irrigation system at El Paso del Norte, showing secondary acequia for Indian
use. By permission of the British Library, courtesy Arizona State Museum

colonial period at least they had a *protector de indios* to represent them. After independence, they were on their own.

It is not unlikely that droughts increased an entire spectrum of social tensions in the Southwest even before the arrival of the Spaniards. The new water pressures which followed Spanish settlement simply exacerbated the problem. Examples from the seventeenth, eighteenth, and nineteenth centuries abound in the surviving documentation.

In 1645 Nicolás de Zepeda described the Tarahumara region of Nueva Vizcaya as experiencing a severe drought ("five years of barrenness in which it has not rained") during which Indian hostility increased dramatically: "so many deaths, so many robberies, so many dangers and so many enemies. . . . "[43] In the next century Viceroy Antonio María de Bucareli attributed Indian hostility in Chihuahua to "the drought, the poor state of the horse herds, and the fact that the rains have not arrived."[44]

Dendrochronology establishes that 1805 was the driest year in the history of colonial Texas. For the same year the archival documentation is replete with examples of greatly heightened tensions between Indians and non-Indians, and even between various groups of Indians. The Tahuayace rebelled;[45] Indians attacked a number of ranches, killing the inhabitants;[46] the Coco Indians attacked José Estrada and stole his cattle;[47] the Taboaya Indians engaged in constant raiding, pillage, and murder;[48] warfare broke out between the Tahuacanes and the Tanacagues;[49] and the Lipan Apaches caused repeated depredations.[50] Relations between Indians and non-Indians in colonial Texas were not good in wet years either. None of these activities can be attributed only to a severe drought, but the lack of water seems to be significant in the mix of factors which precipitated inter- and intraracial hostility beyond that which was normal.

Throughout northern New Spain the missionaries learned that

43. Nicolás de Zepeda to Francisco Calderón, Apr. 28, 1645, DHM, Serie 4, Tomo III.
44. Viceroy Antonio María de Bucareli to Conde de O'Reilly, Nov. 28, 1772, AGI, Audiencia de México, 1242.
45. Antonio Cordero to Governor Juan Bautista Elquesaval, Apr. 20, 1805, BA, Reel 33.
46. Nemesio Salcedo to Governor Elquesaval, Apr. 23, 1805, BA, Reel 33.
47. Dionisio Valle to Juan Bapᵃ de Elquesavⁱ, May 6, 1805, BA, Reel 33.
48. Nemesio Salcedo to Governor Elquesaval, May 7, 1805, BA, Reel 33.
49. Dionisio Valle to Juan Bapᵃ de Elquesavⁱ, May 3, 1805, BA, Reel 33.
50. Francisco Viana to Juan Bautᵃ de Elquesabal, June 18, 1805, BA, Reel 33; Francisco Viana to Gov. D. Antonio Cordero, Oct. 4, 1805, BA, Reel 33, and Compania Presidial de Bexar, Nov., 1805, BA, Reel 33.

water and the conflicts it produced had a major impact on the religious effort. Aridity sometimes helped and sometimes hindered the missionary process. When crops shrivelled because of the lack of rain or sufficient irrigation water, Indians who had previously resisted the proselytizing effort could be more easily persuaded to join a mission settlement administered by the local regular order. This phenomenon occurred in Tucson in 1768 when the summer rains arrived very late.[51] It occurred again in 1796, when drought forced 134 Papagos to join the Tucson mission of San Xavier del Bac.[52] But the attraction of mission life was often transitory. Centuries of Indian adaptation to life in the desert mitigated against the sedentary life of the mission. Where water is scarce, mobility makes it possible to take advantage of plant and animal resources in the effort to supplement a meager agricultural yield.[53] Indians who left the mission without permission were counted on the rolls of the apostates.

Many missionaries saw the aridity of the northern desert as a factor limiting their success. On occasion they were dissuaded from carrying the word of God to isolated Indian villages in a parched desert. Friars in seventeenth-century Coahuila reported to superiors that their venture into isolated Indian rancherías was not worthwhile. There was not enough drinking water to go around.[54] The Jesuits in Arizona reported exactly the same situation in discussion of the missionary effort among the Papagos. "These Papagos ... cannot be served in their own lands, because of the total absence of irrigated cropland and even of drinking water."[55] The situation was not always better in some of the missions themselves. The Papagos at Father Kino's Mission of Remedios resisted Christianization because the missionaries "pastured so many cattle that the watering places were drying up."[56] On the Texas mission of Espíritu Santo, Indians were

51. Francisco Garcés to D. Juan de Pineda, July 29, 1768, DHM, Serie 4, Tomo II. In this dispatch Garcés reported that "Algunos [Indios] del Monte me had dado esperanzas que se agraran [a la mision] y yo he prometido que si enfermo me llaman a confesion voy y que ire a ver sus ranchos que dichen estar faltos de agua."

52. John L. Kessell, *Friars, Soldiers, and Reformers: Hispanic Reformers and the Sonora Mission Frontier, 1767–1856* (Tucson: University of Arizona Press, 1976), p. 197.

53. This point is developed in Sheridan and Naylor (eds.), *Rarámuri,* p. 72.

54. "... y por vivir en partes tan incomodas que no se puede ir en donde ellos viven por la escasez del agua. Lo que ellos beben es de magueyes pequeñas si no es en tiempo de aguas que cae algun aguacero y aun entonces es bien poca la agua." Nicholás de Arnaya to Francisco Baez, Feb. 9, 1601, DHM, Serie 4, Tomo III.

55. Manuel Aguirre to Señor Teniente Coronel D. Juan de Pineda, Mar. 20, 1764, DHM, I, 126.

56. Quoted in Fontana, *Of Earth and Little Rain,* p. 45.

expelled from mission lands because of the lack of accessible water to be used for irrigation.[57]

Water could cause major controversy for the men of God, and there are examples of Indian uprisings against missionaries who diverted waters designated for Indian plots to the mission lands.[58] The charges that the missionaries sacrificed Indian water interests to their own are as recurrent in the documentation as they are difficult to evaluate. Civilian officials and military commanders often found themselves in conflict with the clergy, and the accusations of water diversions come from these same civilian and military leaders. On occasion, they appear to be vindictive, exaggerated, and contrived, but at other times they have the ring of truth. There seems to be no doubt, for example, that in the 1740s Father Salvador de Amaya, head of the mission of Santa María de los Dolores in the Nuevo Reyno de León, believed that mission lands should carry priority over Indian plots.[59] He acted accordingly.

Ultimate responsibility for creating water hardships among the Indians may not rest entirely with the clergy, because clergymen often found themselves competing for the same water with nearby presidios or towns.[60] During dry years, soldiers simply helped themselves to mission water as they did in Santiago, Baja California, in 1740 and in Tucson, Arizona, in 1796.[61] The clergy, in turn, passed the shortages on, but in the process mission lands seem to have taken precedence over individual Indian plots.[62]

The rules and precepts which theoretically governed the northern missions were laudable in their expressed concern with the protection of Indian rights.[63] Civil law also concerned itself with Indian rights in

57. Del Weniger, "Wilderness, Farm, and Ranch," in *San Antonio in the Eighteenth Century,* p. 109.

58. Dn Joseph de Berrosteran to Dn Pedro de Ravago y Teran, Apr. 17, 1748, AGI, Audiencia de Guadalajara, 513; Joseph Antonio Rodríguez to Sr. Then[te] Joseph Juachin Ecai y Muzquiz, Dec. 3, 1721, AGN, Provincias Internas, Vol. 32, Exp. 6.

59. Dn Fran[co] Antonio de Echavarri to Auditor Gral de Guerra, Mar. 6, 1741, AGN, Provincias Internas, Vol. 32, Exp. 9.

60. As one example, the Pima mission of Tumacácori had to share its water from Río Santa Cruz with the downstream presidio of Tubac. A weekly water rotation was instituted by Captain Juan Bautista de Anza. See Manuel Barragua, Francisco Castro, and Antonio Romero to Captain Pedro de Allande y Saavedra, Nov. 24, 1777, cited in Kieran McCarthy, *Desert Documentary* (Tucson: Arizona Historical Society, 1976), pp. 31–34. Hereafter cited as DD with appropriate information.

61. Autos seguidos en razon del aguaje y sitio registrado en nombre . . . 1740, AGN, Californias, Vol. 80, Exp. 28; Kessell, *Friars, Soldiers, and Reformers,* pp. 197–198.

62. Berrasteran to Ravago y Teran, Apr. 17, 1748, AGI, Audiencia de Guadalajara, 513.

63. Charles W. Polzer, *Rules and Precepts of the Jesuit Missions of Northwestern New Spain* (Tucson: University of Arizona Press, 1976), passim.

the missions. As early as 1604, the Marqués de Montesclaros issued an ordinance guaranteeing an irrigated plot for each Indian who joined a mission.[64] But the rules, precepts, and laws were not always followed. There is no doubt that Indians were sometimes shortchanged in matters of land and water by the missionaries themselves. When José de Gálvez made his famous visita to New Spain, he was informed of charges (some valid, some exaggerated, and some inaccurate) that prompted him to issue detailed instructions for the governing of the missions in Baja California, one of the driest areas of the northwest desert. With the expulsion of the Jesuits from New Spain in 1767 and the assumption of the missions by the Franciscans the following year, there was great hope that a less-than-thriving Baja California could be revitalized. Plans were being made for the settlement of upper California, and the missions of the lower peninsula could perhaps carry out a supporting role. If they were to do so, however, they had to be placed in order themselves. The possibilities were good. When Gálvez toured the Baja California missions, he was appalled by their condition but found the soil and temperature adequate for a greatly increased agricultural yield.[65] A more equitable distribution of the scarce water reserves was fundamental to the process. In his report on the reorganization of the southern missions he ordered that once the mission lands had been marked out, all Indian heads of families should be granted irrigation land measuring fifty square varas. These plots were to be held privately, not communally, were to be legitimized through legal title, and were to be passed on from father to son. Realizing that water shortages, especially in the Mission of Santiago in the extreme southeast corner of the peninsula, might preclude implementation of the instructions, Gálvez further ordered that as many individual irrigated plots as possible be distributed, the older heads of families receiving them first. To accommodate those who were left without water when the distributions occurred, the missionaries were to encourage the digging of wells and the building of storage ponds.[66]

The Franciscans and Dominicans followed Gálvez' instructions, and within a few years the missions in Baja California were flourishing. Private Indian lands and the communal lands were productive. In

64. Cited in Genaro V. Vásquez, *Doctrinas y realidades en la legislación para los Indios* (Mexico: Departamento de Asuntos Indígenas, 1940), p. 249.
65. Joseph de Galves to King, Sep. 18, 1768, AGI, Audiencia de Guadalajara, 415; Relacion del reconocimiento de la Bahia de Sn Bernabe en el Cabo de Sⁿ Lucas, Sep. 1, 1765, AGI, Audiencia de Guadalajara, 416.
66. Instruccion para el Govierno Civil y Economico de las Misiones del Sur [de California], Oct. 3, 1768, AGI, Audiencia de Guadalajara, 1768.

1775, for example, San Francisco reported "the sowings are about the same as in 1774 and with good results; two additional fanegas of land and fifty new garden plots have been brought under cultivation. They are irrigated by a new ditch and supplied with water from the dam that was repaired with stone and lime, leaving a pond of about a hundred varas."[67] The reports from Nuestra Señora de Guadalupe and San José Comondú were similar. Guadalupe increased cropland by two fanegas by building a new irrigation ditch, while Comondú planted new vineyards with water from newly built canals.[68] A similar process was also initiated in Sonora and Arizona shortly after the expulsion of the Jesuits. Although the results were not as spectacular, the shift from communal to individual cropland (*milpas*) was evident.[69]

José de Gálvez was not alone in his concern that mission Indians were being shortchanged in the allocation of water. Fray Antonio de los Reyes, later to become the first Bishop of Sonora, Sinaloa, and the Californias, reported to Viceroy Bucareli in 1772 that because of neglect and greed the mission Indians were worse off than those living in their own villages. He believed that it was against their very nature to be forced to work on the communal lands of the missions. They would do much better if they were allowed to work their own individual plots. But to do so, they had to be guaranteed water. Each family should therefore be given two plots of land: one, of two hundred yards square, would be unirrigated (*de temporal*), and the other, of the same size, would carry water rights with it.[70]

Water conflict molded many institutions of government, as it was necessary for Spanish towns to appoint special water judges with a wide variety of functions. As early as 1563 a royal cédula ordered local officials to appoint water judges whenever necessary.[71] The practice continued throughout the colonial period and during the first half of the nineteenth century, although the titles of these officials varied; some were called *comisionados,* others *alcaldes de agua,* others *jueces de*

---

67. Notas Relativas al Estado Actual de las Misiones Antiguas de la Peninsula de Californias, Feb. 25, 1776, AGI, Audiencia de Guadalajara, 515.

68. Ibid.

69. Cynthia Radding de Murrieta, "The Function of the Market in Changing Economic Structures in the Mission Communities of Pimería Alta, 1768–1821," *The Americas* 34 (Oct., 1977), 155–159.

70. Albert Stagg, *The First Bishop of Sonora and Arizona: Antonio de los Reyes, O.F.M.* (Tucson: University of Arizona Press, 1980), p. 42.

71. Diego de Encinas, *Cedulario Indiano,* 4 vols. (Madrid: Ediciones Cultura Hispánica, 1945–1946), I, 69. The cédula is entitled "Que manda el Presidente y Oydores nombren juez que reparta las aguas, cada vez que fuere necesario."

agua, and still others *mandadores.*[72] Indian towns were supposed to have water judges, too, called either *topiles* or *alguaciles,* but in practice only the large Indian communities appointed special officials to take charge of water distribution.[73] In smaller Indian towns the Indian governors exercised the functions of the water judge.[74]

In the case of the Spanish towns, on occasion the water judges were appointed from the ranks of the cabildo itself (an *alcalde ordinario* could at the same time serve as an *alcalde de agua*), but in other instances different officials held these positions. When water shortage was acute, a town might have more than a single water judge. In the case of the Presidio of Altar three or four water judges were appointed to apportion water among the ninety-two families in residence there in 1779.[75] No matter what the specific title or the number, the functions of the office were the same. When called upon by circumstance, the water judges were responsible for initiating and implementing strict rotations for water usage. They generally worked with a *mayordomo* or ditch boss who was charged with implementing the decisions. When water shortages threatened the vitality of a community, the mayor-domos were ordered to "divide up the available water by turns, giving first one user, and then another, a fixed period of time so that every-one will have the chance to irrigate his fields."[76] Because physical conditions often made it necessary to set up the rotations on a twenty-four hour basis, and because few farmers preferred to irrigate their fields at night, irrigation times were drawn by lot.[77] If one individual irrigated out of turn, the violation would be reported to the water judge, who would make a determination, render a decision, and order its implementation.

Because water rights under Spanish law could be passed on from

72. Nombram to y Orden de Juezes para el Repartimiento de lagua, Santa Fe, July 16, 1720, SANM, II, 317a. Plan de Pitic, Art. 20, AGN, Tierras, Vol. 2773.

73. By the middle of the eighteenth century, every Indian town was to have "un topil o alguacil del Pueblo hade tener encargo de que no falte agua. . . ." Consulta que hace a S.M. Dn Fernando Sanchez Salvador, Alcalde de la Sᵗᵃ Hermandad. . . . Provincias de Sinaloa, Sonora y Costas del Mar del Sur, May 19, 1751, AGI, Audiencia de Guadalajara, 137.

74. Notificaz.ᵒⁿ a Anttonio Zarzillo, Gobernador de los Indios, Feb. 1, 1755, A. L. Pinart Collection, Bancroft Library, PE-51. Hereafter cited as ALPC with appropriate information.

75. Caballero de Croix to Exmo Señor Don Joseph Galvez, Dec. 23, 1780, AGI, Audiencia de Guadalajara, 272.

76. Juan Estevan Rebolledo, Dec. 15, 1731, AGN, Provincias Internas, Vol. 163, Exp. 3.

77. Pedro de Rivera to Viceroy, Dec. 1, 1731, AGN, Provincias Internas, Vol. 163, Exp. 3: ". . . quando fueren escasas las aguas debran repartirse de suerte, que por tandas gozen de su beneficio."

parents to children, the special judges were consulted when wills were
called into question.[78] They also adjudicated a seemingly endless
number of disputes among the living, punishing those guilty of water
theft and those whose unattended cattle damaged irrigation ditches.
When a pressing water issue faced the community, they were empowered to convene a general meeting of the entire citizenry to
discuss how the problem might best be resolved.[79] In short, they
comprised an integral part of a judicial system which adapted general
Spanish jurisprudence to the exigencies of a society in which water
was scarce. Their role was judged to be of sufficient importance that in
1704 a royal decree made them all subject to *residencia*, or judicial
review, when their term of office expired.[80]

If the special water judges had primary responsibility for the just
distribution of irrigation and industrial water, the cabildo or ayuntamiento was charged with the chores of providing clean drinking water
for the community. Towns located along a reliable river most often
took their water directly from the stream. But when the flow diminished, either because of climatic changes or upstream diversions, the
water stagnated and could cause health problems of major proportion.
In instances such as this, it fell to the town council to devise a solution.
Confronted with just this situation, the Chihuahua cabildo decided to
build an entirely new potable water system in 1797.[81]

The cabildos or ayuntamientos shared responsibility with the alcalde de agua in funding the construction and administering the
principal irrigation ditch (*acequia madre*) which ran through or ran
close to most towns. If the acequia was not carrying a sufficient water
supply throughout the year, the cabildo could authorize the construction of a dam or reservoir to steady the supply. In Monterrey, Nuevo
León, the local ayuntamiento not only ordered that a new dam be built
in 1795, but also secured funding and provided prison labor ("*presos
. . . en la carcel por pequeños delitos*") for the construction.[82] In Hermosillo, Sonora, the government contracted with a private citizen for

78. See, for example, Ygnacia Castro to Governor, Sep. 19, 1771, BA, Reel 11, and
Marcos de Castro to Governor, Sep. 19, 1771, BA, Reel 11.

79. Autto de Obedim[to], 1754, ALPC PE-51.

80. Real Cédula, May 10, 1704, cited in Antonio Muro Orejón, *Cedulario Americano de
siglo XVIII: Colección de disposiciones legales indígenas desde 1680 a 1800 contenidas en los
cedularios del Archivo General de Indias* (Seville: Escuela de Estudios Americanos de
Sevilla, 1969), pp. 123–124.

81. Anselmo Rodríguez to Viceroy, May 8, 1797, AGN, Alhóndigas, Vol. 11, Exp. 3.

82. Governor of Nuevo León to Viceroy, June 14, 1795, AGN, Provincias Internas, Vol.
34, Exp. 6.

the work and provided him with Indian labor to do the job.[83] The Commandant General of the Provincias Internas, Teodoro de Croix, diverted funds from the presidio to pay for the supplies. In Chihuahua the 1,900 pesos needed for constructing a new municipal acequia came from the city's *propio* funds, an account replenished annually as the city rented out community land and sold community water.[84] Funding for a proposed dam in El Paso in the middle of the eighteenth century was raised by a special tax. All Spaniards and Indians were assessed four reales for every hundred grapevines they had under cultivation.[85]

By the eighteenth and early nineteenth centuries numerous small frontier villages occupied the deserts of the Greater Southwest. Tiny communities of a dozen or two dozen families, they scarcely needed the formal bureaucratic structure of the larger towns. But most of them had at least one informal agency to supervise governmental affairs. Not surprisingly, it was the ditch or acequia association. The irrigators met annually to elect their mayordomo and to set a salary for his efforts during the coming year. As the only genuine official of the tiny villages, the mayordomo had prestige and competence extending beyond regulation of the local water supply. Even if he limited his activities to the acequia itself, however, he most assuredly earned his salary.[86]

The controversies surrounding the acequia madre in northern New Spain are endless and their variety limited only by human imagination. By no means are all of them related to the apportionment of water. In a formally established town the acequia madre was generally built by the citizens and was considered common property. It was used not only for irrigation but also for the domestic water need of the town, for the watering of animals, for washing clothes, and for sewage and garbage disposal. It is obvious that these diverse uses are not entirely compatible with one another and, in spite of royal ordinances proscribing pollution of the water source,[87] those who lived down-

83. Juan Honorato de Rivera received the contract in May, 1772. Thirty Opata Indians were assigned to him. Pedro Corbalan to Fr. Mariano Buena y alcalde, May 5, 1772, AGN, Provincias Internas, Vol. 232, Exp. 1.

84. Anselmo Rodríguez to Viceroy, May 8, 1797, AGN, Alhóndigas, Vol. 11, Exp. 3.

85. Manuel Antonio San Juan to Governor Velez Cachupin, July 17, 1754, ALPC PE-51; Junta de los Vezinos e Indios deste Pueblo, Feb. 9, 1755, ALPC PE-51.

86. See Simmons, "Spanish Irrigation Practices in New Mexico," pp. 140–141, and Roxanne Dunbar Ortiz, *Roots of Resistance: Land Tenure in New Mexico, 1680–1980* (Los Angeles: Chicano Studies Research Center Publications, 1980), p. 56.

87. Articles 122 and 123 of King Philip II's ordinances on the laying out of new towns

stream were often victimized by the carelessness of their upstream neighbors. Human excreta, kitchen and bathing wastes, and small dead animals dirtied the communal ditch. Chihuahua City found itself with an especially unhealthy situation caused by an incipient form of industrial pollution. Lead tailings from upstream mines polluted the municipal system and caused disease.[88] In the San Antonio missions, an area of extensive sheep grazing, the fleeces were washed in the acequia after the annual shearing.[89]

Obviously there were no careful standards for drinking water in the Hispanic Southwest. But one did not need to count coliform bacteria or to evaluate concentrations of turbidity to be repulsed by the sight of fecal matter or scum floating on the domestic water supply. Because filtering methods were primitive at best, and chemical coagulation centuries in the future, the only answer was to prohibit the contamination at its source. The cabildos issued ordinances repeatedly to govern the use of acequia water. In Santa Fe, New Mexico, people bathed and engaged in "other filthy practices," ruining the drinking water of those downstream. Those who were caught were fined four reales.[90] The village of San Fernando in Texas had a similar problem but a more imaginative penalty. In 1775 Amador Delgado, the local alcalde, had to outlaw the washing of clothes in the acequia because those living further down were denied clean drinking water. His order stated: "Clothes will not be washed in the acequia of the city. Penalty for the woman or other person who violates the ordinance will be the confiscation of any clothes washed in the said acequia."[91] An even worse problem was that of stray animals polluting the acequia. The

---

specified that polluting activities were to be located downstream of the town. See Zelia Nuttall, "Royal Ordinances Concerning the Laying Out of New Towns," *Hispanic American Historical Review* 4 (Nov., 1921), 747. A detailed mining code adopted in 1783 reiterated that the mines could not pollute domestic water supplies, but they often did. See Ordenanzas del Tribunal General de la Minería de Nueva España, Mar. 22, 1783, in Eusebio Ventura Beleña, *Recopilación de todos los autos acordados de real audiencia y sala de crimen de esta Nueva España.* 2 vols. (Mexico: Universidad Nacional Autónoma de México, 1981), II, 262–263.

88. Anselmo Rodríguez to Viceroy, May 8, 1797, AGN, Alhóndigas, Vol. II, Exp. 3.

89. Mardith K. Schuetz, "The Indians of the San Antonio Missions, 1718–1821," (Ph.D. dissertation, University of Texas, 1980), p. 272.

90. Lynn I. Perrigo (ed.), "Review Statutes of 1826," *New Mexico Historical Review* 27 (Jan., 1952), p. 71.

91. Dn Amador Delgado, Alcalde de la Villa de Sn Fernando Provincia de los Tejas, Jan. 15, 1775, BA, Reel 11.

ayuntamiento of San Antonio de Béxar was forced to levy a fine of one peso against anyone who allowed his pigs to run loose.[92]

Some northern towns, most notably those of California, developed simple pollution control systems. A laundry tank (*lavandería*), two or three feet wide and a couple of feet deep, could be found near the central plaza. Built with mortar and sometimes lined with tiles, the lavandería discharged the dirty water, not into the main acequia, but into the fields. Unlike the synthetic detergents in use today, the lye soap then in use did not damage the crops. The system helped assure a more healthful domestic water supply.[93] But Spanish Californians' early concern with environmental issues did not solve the water problems of a growing population. After Mexican independence the cabildo of Los Angeles issued repeated ordinances against laundering in the city irrigation ditch, against using it for garbage disposal, against leading waste pipes into it, and against building cesspools in the immediate vicinity.[94]

The annual spring cleaning and repair of the acequia madre (not inappropriately called *la fatiga*) was a major community activity supervised carefully by the local cabildo. Debris and silt had to be removed, and, if erosion damage was apparent, the banks had to be reinforced. On many occasions the entire ditch had to be widened or deepened. If the acequia was the common property of the town, all persons who had used it during the previous year were required to participate in this activity under the threat of fine.[95] The number of hours to be devoted to the cleaning and repair was pro-rated to the number of hours each irrigator was entitled to water. After independence, the same practice prevailed. When the province of New Mexico articulated its legal statutes in 1826, a fine of four reales was authorized for any individual who did not participate in the annual cleaning, "two for his disobedience and two for the work he should have lent."[96]

During both the colonial and early national periods, the wealthiest men in the community hired others to do their cleaning for them, but

92. Jose Anto Saucedo to Sr. Alcade 1º D. Gaspar Hores, Feb. 5, 1824, BA, Reel 76.

93. For information on the lavanderías, see John Q. Ressler, "Indian and Spanish Water Control on New Spain's Northwest Frontier," *Journal of the West*, 7 (Jan., 1968), 15–16.

94. See John Caughey's direct testimony for the court in *Los Angeles vs. San Fernando*, p. A134.

95. Petition of Pedro Fuentes, Jph Antonio Bustillos y Saballas, et al., Mar. 30, 1784, BA, Reel 15; Bandos de Policia y Hordenes de buen govierno, Jan. 10, 1802, BA, Reel 30.

96. Perrigo, "Revised Statutes of 1826," p. 70.

they had to provide horses and wagons and other equipment. Payment in kind was more common than payment in cash.[97] Female heads of household were assessed a tax in lieu of the actual physical labor.[98] Presidio commanders hired peones to clean and repair the ditches of the forts.[99] But there is some good evidence to suggest that in most cases the majority of the population participated directly. In Béxar, for example, the cleaning and repair of the community acequias, upstream and downstream, so depopulated the town that the residents requested troops be sent in to guard the women and children while the men were away.[100] This annual activity was considered so basic to the life of the community that when water requests were made, petitioners sometimes promised to do more than their fair share of the cleaning, hoping that this factor would have a positive impact on the granting agency.[101] Similarly, when water disputes occurred in the late colonial period and early national period, the record of the cleaning participation of the contending parties was taken under advisement in the adjudication.[102]

Not all acequias were community owned. Some were the property of individuals, others were owned jointly by a corporation of rural users, and still others were shared by a town or mission and a group of farmers who resided near that town.[103] Cleaning and repair of these ditches was the responsibility of those who had used them. Ditches of twenty or thirty miles in length were not uncommon. In Coahuila the

97. In eighteenth-century New Mexico, payment often consisted of stock animals or bulls. Two examples of this payment procedure for acequia work can be found in Autos de la Visita General de este Reino de la Nueva Mexico fechos por el Señor Sarx^to Maior D^n Joachin Codallos y Rabal Govr y Cap^n Gral . . . Aug. 16 to Oct. 20, 1745, SANM II, 470.

98. María Carmen Calvillo to Jefe Político, Oct. 29, 1823, Béxar County Archives, Mission Records G. Hereafter cited as BCA MR with appropriate information.

99. Pedro de la Fuente to Viceroy, Aug. 1, 1776, AGI, Audiencia de Guadalajara, 511.

100. Ayuntamiento to José Antonio Saucedo, Jan. 20, 1826, BA, Reel 26, and Mateo de Almada to Ayuntamiento, Jan. 25, 1826, BA, Reel 26.

101. One petitioner in Texas, hoping for favorable action on a request for a large amount of water, promised to match the number of acequia cleaners provided by all the other users combined: ". . . si los demas parcioneros pucieren diz mozos, otros tantos pondree yo. . . ." Juan Manuel Zambrano to Governor Cordero, Jan. 1807, BA, Reel 35. The same kind of argument was advanced by Carlos Rodríguez in his water dispute with Joseph Saenz near Santa Rosa, Chihuahua. Carlos Rodríguez to Alcalde Mayor, Oct. 25, 1767, AHP, Reel 1767. See also María del Carmen Calvillo to Jefe Político, Oct. 29, 1823, BCA, MR 6.

102. Testimonio, Bernalillo, Nuevo México, July 18, 1829, UNM SC; Santa Ana—Angostura, and Ysabel Jorge, Phelipe Gallegos, and Antonio de Garule vs. Xristopal García, Jan. 7 to Feb. 9, 1733, SANM, I, 379.

103. The best discussion of the various patterns of acequia ownership is found in Wells A. Hutchins, "The Community Acequia: Its Origins and Development," *Southwestern Historical Quarterly* 31 (Jan., 1928), 261–284.

mission of San Bernardo de Río Grande had ditches totalling forty-four miles, and the neighboring mission of San Juan Bautista almost thirty-one miles. Cleaning and repair was an immense task which occupied the mission Indians for the entire months of February and March. On occasion, the friars had to hire non-mission Indians to help with the work.[104]

Spanish law made special effort to guard the interests of those landowners whose property did not have a direct outlet to the water source. Through practice, custom, and law (*jus aquoeductus*), an individual was allowed to construct an acequia on another man's land if there was no other way to conduct the water to his own.[105] A landowner could drive his cattle through his neighbor's property to water them (*jus aquoe hausius*) if there were no watering holes on his own land.[106] Even the foundations of houses and churches could be altered so that water could pass through them.[107] It was also possible for an individual to be given permission by the courts to construct a dam on another man's property to feed an acequia which ultimately watered his own land.[108] In all such eventualities, however, the owner had to be compensated for any damage to the property on which waterworks were constructed.[109]

By the eighteenth century, irrigation ditches crisscrossed most of the best land in the Hispanic Southwest. Because the water sources were sometimes distant, and because the shapes of farming plots were often irregular, on occasion the acequias had to be built across one another. This phenomenon caused innumerable difficulties among neighbors. One ditch owner could easily break down the canal of another while crossing it with his own. But more importantly when ditches crossed, unanticipated water diversion, or even water theft, could ensue. The situation in New Mexico was sufficiently serious to

104. Estado Actual de las Misiones de la Provincia de Coahuila y Río Grande de la Misma Jurisdicción, Año de 1786, cited in *Estudios de historia del noreste* (Monterrey: Editorial Alfonso Reyes, 1972), p. 138.

105. Ayuntamiento de Abiquiu to Jefe Político Santiago Abreu, July 4, 1832, Mexican Archives of New Mexico, Reel 15. Hereafter cited as MANM with appropriate information.

106. Joaquín Escriche, *Diccionario razonado de legislación civil, penal, comercial y forense* (Madrid: Calleja e Hijos, 1842), p. 650.

107. Manuel Martínez to Jefe Político, July 3, 1832, MANM, Reel 15.

108. See Malcolm Ebright, "Manuel Martínez's Ditch Dispute: A Study in Mexican Period Custom and Justice." *New Mexico Historical Review* 54 (Jan., 1979), pp. 21–34.

109. Autos de la Visita General de este Reino de la Nueva Mexico fechos por el Señor Sarx[to] Maior D[n] Joachin Codallos y Rabal Govr y Cap[n] Gral de dho Reino . . . Aug. 16 to Oct. 20, 1745, SANM, II, 470.

prompt one alcalde mayor, Ignacio Sánchez Vergara, to issue a strong proclamation in 1813.

> Those who must irrigate by bringing water from up above another ditch, should construct a flume (*canoa*) wherever the water crosses, so that owners of the other ditches will not be harmed and to avoid theft of water from one irrigation ditch to another. In such an event, other parties would be denied the benefit of their own work and would lack water they need, so that their crops would be held back and damaged. And he who does not build a flume when he should, must pay consequences, suffering four days of imprisonment in the public jail.[110]

Acequia disputes arose proportionately with the complexities of ownership, title, location, and use. Illustrative of the kinds of issues that could arise, and for which there was no easy answer, was a controversy that occurred in the San Fernando area of Texas in the late colonial period. A group of sixteen farmers constructed an irrigation ditch more than five miles in length from a water source to their cropland. Most of this main ditch was not on their property. At the point where it reached their own land, smaller ditches (*sangrias* or *contra-acequias*) were bled off the acequia madre to water the individual fields. As the builders and users of the five-mile acequia, the sixteen farmers gladly assumed responsibility for its maintenance, from the outlet to its end, even though it ran across the property of others. They even built bridges across it so as not to interfere with the activity of itinerant merchants and travelers.

During the course of years, however, Spanish population along the five-mile stretch began to grow and, with growth, problems ensued. Not only did persons living along the route begin helping themselves to the water, but they threw garbage into the ditch, broke down the banks, and even ruined several of the bridges with heavy carts. The sixteen farmers protested to the governor that they should no longer have full responsibility for the cleaning and maintenance of the ditch. Since their upstream neighbors were both using and abusing it, they should pay for their carelessness by contributing to the work that had to be done each year. The governor agreed and in 1806 ordered

---

110. Marc Simmons (ed.), "An Alcalde's Proclamation: A Rare New Mexico Document," *El Palacio* 75 (Summer, 1968), 5–9. On occasion, small aqueducts were used in the Southwest to carry one water source across another, but the canoa or flume was most common. See T. Lindsay Baker, Steven R. Rae, et al., *Water for the Southwest: Historic Survey and Guide to Historic Sites* (New York: ASCE Publications, 1973), pp. 11–12.

everyone whose property fronted on the ditch to clean and maintain that section.[111]

The compromise solution lasted for fifteen years, but in 1821 the upstream residents convinced the cabildo of San Fernando de Béxar that they should be relieved of their responsibility. It was not a community acequia and therefore the sixteen owners should clean and maintain it. The owners protested that a fair agreement had been reached and it should be honored. The cabildo responded that since the farmers could produce no formal documentation showing the order of an earlier governor, they would be obliged to maintain their own acequia.[112] The sixteen owners then decided to appeal their case directly to the current governor, Antonio Martínez.[113] He was not convinced that the absence of a formal order by a previous governor should be a factor of great significance in the dispute. He told the cabildo that since the acequia benefited the entire population, it was only fair that the responsibilities be shared by all.[114] Even though the acequia was not owned by the community, cleaning and maintenance was so basic to the prosperity of the region that all persons had to participate.

Water conflict was as constant in the Hispanic Southwest as was water scarcity. The bickering, although unremitting, was far from petty because the stakes were so high. Without access to water, personal ambitions remained unfulfilled, security was a farfetched dream, and the hope for a better life nothing more than a chimera. Water was transcendent in its impact on the formation of social values, on the multifaceted activities of economic development, and on the major struggles for power among competing interest groups.

111. Los Ciudadanos Labradores de la Labor de Abajo . . . to Governor Antonio Martínez, Feb. 14, 1822, BA, Reel 70.
112. Sala Capular de San Fern[do] de Bexar, Feb. 14, 1822, BA, Reel 70.
113. Los Dueños de la Labor de Abajo to Governor Martínez, Feb. 22, 1822, BA, Reel 70.
114. Antonio Martínez, no date, BA, Reel 70.

CHAPTER 4

The Social, Economic, and Military Impact of Water

In the infinitely complex but subtle processes of socialization, his-panicization, and cultural syncretism which followed the original settlers, soldiers, and missionaries to the Mexican north, water exerted a constant presence. Within a century of the original Spanish coloniza-tion, maps of the region commemorated the importance of water with their place names. On many occasions, the Spaniards simply adopted Indian reverence for this precious liquid in their own names for towns, presidios, and missions. The Yaqui town of Bahcum (meaning "where the water comes out") became Bacum, the Pima Pitiquim ("where the rivers come together") became Pitic, the Towa word *payokona* ("place of water") became Pecos, the Tewa words *posoong wa ghay* ("drink water place") became Pojoaque, and the Papago designation *ali shonak* ("place of the small spring") became Arizonac and later Arizona. The word *bac*, or water in a number of other Uto-Aztecan languages, came to dot the maps of Arizona and Sonora in names such as Tubac, Bacanuche, Bacatete, and Bacuachi. On other occasions, Spanish was mixed with the local language to honor the importance of water to the desert. The celebrated mission of San Xavier del Bac near Tucson is perhaps the best example. Spanish stood alone in other places. New Mexico had its Ojo Caliente, Agua Salada, Arroyo Hondo, and Ar-royo Seco; Nuevo León its Agua Blanca and Ojito de Agua; Chihuahua its Agua Verde and Ciénaga de Olivos; Sonora its Cienaguita and Agua Prieta; Arizona its Pozo Verde and Agua Cal-iente; and California Rancho Rodeo de las Aguas, La Zanja, Laguna Seca, and Agua Mansa.

When Spanish culture and religious concepts were conveyed to local Indian groups, they often maintained the essence of meaning but were dressed in new linguistic coats reflecting holdovers from the native value systems. Spanish Jesuits in Sonora in the seventeenth century were able to indoctrinate the Yaqui with the meaning of *compadrazco*, but the word adopted for godfather (the person who will care for children in time of need) in the Yaqui language became *bato-achai*, or "water father." Similarly, godmother became "water mother."[1] It did not matter much to the missionaries that the Yaqui Indians converted godfather to water father, but many clerics in the Pueblo region of New Mexico expressed dismay when the Indian religious leaders organized dances to the old rain gods in front of the new Catholic chapels. Such occurrences offered graphic proof that although the outer forms of Roman Catholicism had been adopted, there were serious problems in conveying its substance.

Cultural syncretism became engrained in the folklore as well. Indian and Spanish custom meshed in the inexact "science" of weather forecasting. Rain was predicted if the cattle became frisky, if snails climbed out of their holes, if one donkey answered the bray of another, or if a ring surrounded the moon.[2] Folk tales and songs incorporated water symbolism in abundance.

It would scarcely be an exaggeration to suggest that the daily concern over water became an obsession on the northern edges of New Spain. It created a subculture which in turn produced individuals whose very thought processes differed from their counterparts in central and southern Mexico. If Spaniards farther to the south were concerned with water, and many were, they might ask for a grant of water to go along with some land they already had. It would never have occurred to them, however, to ask for a grant of water with some land to go with it. Yet this juxtaposition of requests occurred in the north.[3] When land grants were made, they often incorporated the same priority. In 1823 José Antonio Saucedo, jefe político of the Province of Texas, granted José Manuel Granado "two days of water

1. Edward H. Spicer, *The Yaquis: A Cultural History* (Tucson: University of Arizona Press, 1980), pp. 22–23. The same kinship designations, "water father" and "water mother," were used by the neighboring Mayo Indians. See Crumrine, *The Mayo Indians*, p. 69.
2. Arthur L. Campa, *Hispanic Culture in the Southwest* (Norman: University of Oklahoma Press, 1979), p. 201.
3. See, for example, Espediente de concesion de cinco suertes de labor ... en el Pueblo de Todos Santos a Favor de Hilario Carrillo hecha por José de Galvez, Aug. 2, 1768, AHBCS, Leg. 2, Doc. 1.

with the land that belongs to it"[4] and granted María del Carmen Calvillo "one dula of water with its corresponding land."[5]

A landowner in the north might build permanent structures on a neighbor's property without occasioning a dispute, but if he began to tamper with his neighbor's water, they would both soon wind up in court.[6] Residents of central and southern New Spain trying to validate a cloudy land title with the argument of effective occupation generally offered that they had built a house or a corral on the property, or had cultivated the land. In the north effective occupation was argued on the grounds that a well had been dug or an irrigation canal initiated.[7]

When the Papagos at Father Kino's Mission of Remedios realized that the horses and cattle were drying up nearby watering holes, they decided that they would rather do without the animals. Water obviously held a higher priority in the Papago scheme than did reliable sources of transportation and food.[8]

Military men in southern and central Mexico might be sent out to look for pasture land and water for the horses. In the north, they were dispatched more often to search for water and pasture land.[9] When northern haciendas were put up for sale, the description of available water preceded and took precedence over the description of the land and other property.[10] When taxes were assessed in the north, they were based not on the land and its corresponding water but on "the water and its corresponding land."[11] All over New Spain, rivers and lakes were named and the designations duly placed on early maps, but in the arid north even tiny ponds, dry arroyos, muddy watering holes, and minuscule springs were given formal names.[12] As Josiah Gregg

4. José Antonio Saucedo to José Manuel Granado, Feb. 5, 1824, BCA, MR 5.

5. José Antonio Saucedo to María del Carmen Calvillo, Feb. 5, 1824, BCA, MR 6.

6. Caytano Trevino to Governor Bruno Barreras, June 9, 1818, AGN, Tierras, Vol. 1419, Exp. 3.

7. Pedro Foxas and Manuel Justel to Sor Subdelgado, Aug. 1809. AGN, Tierras, Vol. 1424, Exp. 11.

8. Fontana, *Of Earth and Little Rain*, p. 45.

9. Pedro Antonio Albares to Governor, May 30, 1740, AGN, Californias, Vol. 80, Exp. 28. See also Malcolm Ebright, "The San Joaquín Grant: Who Owned the Common Lands? A Historical-Legal Struggle," *New Mexico Historical Review* 57 (Jan., 1982), 18.

10. Aviso al Público, Monclova, Coahuila, June 4, 1834, BA, Reel 6.

11. Yndice de ventas de casas en la extinguida mision de San Franco. de la Espada Hechos por D. Gaspar Flores, Año de 1823, BCA MR 63.

12. For examples see Relacion de la expedicion que de ordn del Sr. Capitan y Justica Mar . . . Don Pedro de la Fuente hizieron los soldados. . . , Sep., 1765, AGI, Audiencia de Guadalajara, 511, and Testimonio de las dilixencias y derrotero practicado en virtud de Superior Horn . . . por el Gral. Don Pedro de Rabago y Theran . . . Año de 1748, AGN, Historia, Vol. 52.

noted in his diary during a trip to New Mexico in the 1830s, "The scarcity of water in these desert regions, gives to every little spring an importance which, of course, in more favored countries it would not enjoy."[13] The body of evidence is persuasive that, on the scale of relative values, water often was held in higher esteem than the northern land it might make productive.

If water contributed to a change in the value structure of northerners, it had an even more direct impact on the three main economic pursuits in which the citizens of the north would become involved: agriculture, mining, and commerce. Intensive irrigation was necessary in the north for all save subsistence farming. Town life, much more pronounced after the Spanish conquest, was supported by surrounding farms, generally drawing their water from the same sources as the communities they served. Mission settlements, administered by the regular orders, also used intensive irrigation in the quest to produce a food surplus adequate to withstand any natural disaster and to support new missions as the frontier was extended steadily to the north. Water demands increased not only because of settlement patterns, but also because the Spaniards introduced a variety of new food crops from Europe and from central Mexico: wheat, barley, oats, citrus fruits, apples, apricots, pears, grapes, chickpeas, carrots, radishes, and onions. Unlike the drought-resistant native crops such as maize, squash, and beans, none of these new food crops could survive for long on desert rainfall alone.

New crops and intensive irrigation farming hastened the process of ecolturation. Wheat and fruit trees became the home for new insects, but, more importantly, every area that was artificially moistened left a corresponding area drier downstream. Natural desert life withered and died, changing an entire spectrum of plant and animal associations and displacing both from their former habitat. Wind erosion ensued, and blowing sand and silt blanketed previously fertile desert oases with a sterile top cover. A damaging chain reaction slowly set in as even with crop rotation repetitive clearing and plowing tired the upstream soil, reduced agricultural yields, and made it necessary to bring additional areas under irrigated cultivation. Clearing and burning of natural desert cover altered the landscape, while new water diversions, of course, hastened the browning of more downstream desert belts.

Demographic change took an ecolturative toll as well. European diseases might well have reached the far north even before the first

13. Gregg, *Commerce of the Prairies*, p. 33.

Spaniard set foot on the desert soil. Without question smallpox and measles epidemics devastated the northern Pima population in the sixteenth century. Thousands died, and many of the survivors migrated to new areas. Although not remembered for extensive irrigation networks, Pima flood farmers had built small diversion dams and check dams which tended to slow excessive runoff and percolate into underground aquifers. The tremendous demographic changes of the sixteenth century found these crude water-control structures abandoned and then collapsing from natural deterioration. Erosion and flooding ensued.[14]

The hydraulic changes introduced by the Spaniards yielded positive results, too. By the middle of the seventeenth century, Indian communities with access to water for irrigation purposes also began producing agricultural surplus for sale. The Tarahumara country of western Chihuahua affords one example. Commenting in 1651 on the social and economic conditions of the Tarahumara living along the Río Papigochic, Father José Pascual noted, "Their lands are good because of irrigation, as can be confirmed by the many people who come to them to buy provisions."[15] Similarly, the Jesuits introduced improved irrigation techniques among the Yaqui in the middle of the seventeenth century. The increased agricultural yield permitted food exports from the Yaqui valley; these were very important in the subsequent colonization of Baja California and the Pimería Alta.[16]

Patterns of land ownership were different in the Hispanic Southwest from what they were in the better-watered south. In the first place the shape of farming grants was more likely to be rectangular than square. The fields were often long, adjacent to the water source, and with very short frontage on the stream or acequia. The lots were generally more than three times longer than they were wide.[17] This practice assured that the largest possible number of farming plots had direct access to the water source. Land grants for grazing in the north were more generous than they were in the south and, as a result, the size of an average hacienda, that hybrid institution that was part feudal and part capitalist, was considerably larger. The semi-arid

14. One need not accept the chronology or extent of the Pima population decline postulated by Henry F. Dobyns to accept that he is essentially correct in his description of the process synopsized in this paragraph. See *From Fire to Flood*, pp. 45–56.

15. "An Account of the Missions . . . for the year 1651," in Sheridan and Naylor (eds.), *Rarámuri*, p. 28.

16. Spicer, *The Yaquis*, p. 30.

17. Alvar W. Carlson, "Long Lots in the Río Arriba," *Annals of the Association of American Geographers* 65 (Mar., 1975), 50. Long lots were also used in the San Antonio area. See MacMillan, "The Cabildo and the People," pp. 86–87.

grasslands of Texas and New Mexico provided adequate pasture for horses, cattle, and sheep but, because the groundcover was not dense, large areas were needed for grazing. In Arizona and Sonora natural pasture was more sparse and domesticated livestock more exotic to the landscape. Because more grazing acreage was required per animal, the capacity of the land to sustain wild game was lowered. Pasturage adequate to support a herd of cattle or sheep in the Southwest desert was often found in areas without nearby streams or watering holes. The animals could survive for several days, perhaps even a week, without water, but then they would have to be rounded up and led to water, or water would have to be taken to them. In New Mexico in the early nineteenth century, shepherds would fill large *guages* (gourds) with water, load them up on burros, and take them out into the fields to sustain the sheep.[18]

The *fundo legal*, or land designation for Indian towns, was also larger than its counterpart in the south. In central and southern Mexico the fundo legal came to be standardized at about 600 square varas or 250 acres. It comprised the townsite and the cropland assigned to the town, but grazing land and woodland were granted in addition to the fundo legal. In the north, Indian towns were more likely to receive a square league (a league is a linear measure of 5,000 varas or approximately 2.6 miles) or 4,338 acres as their fundo legal, but grazing land and woodland were included within the grant. The northern land grant was over seventeen times larger than its southern counterpart, and, even conceding that much of the difference was consumed by the grazing land and woodland, the proportion set aside for crops, and carrying rights to water for irrigation, was undoubtedly larger.[19]

In excessively arid parts of the north, such as Baja California and parts of Sonora, Arizona, and Chihuahua, individual requests for land were often not honored unless the petitioner could demonstrate that he had uncovered a water source adequate to sustain himself on the land.[20] As a result, individuals buttressed their requests for dry land with the caveat that, if it were approved, they would assume the expense of dam construction to convert a worthless plot into a piece of

18. Gregg, *Commerce of the Prairies,* p. 62.

19. A 1687 royal cédula authorized additional size for the fundo legal if the extra acreage was necessary to sustain the Indian community. Real Cédula sobre el fundo legal de los llamados Indios, June 4, 1687, contained in Juan N. Rodríguez de San Manuel, *Pandectas hispano-mexicanas* 3 vols. (Mexico: Universidad Nacional Autónoma de México, 1980), II, 305.

20. Javier Aguilar to Governor José Pérez Fernández, Oct. 27, 1805, AHBCS, Leg. 1, Doc. 453.

productive land that would be of economic and social benefit to the larger community.[21] The same practice occurred farther to the south, but less frequently.

The construction of a large storage dam or a sophisticated irrigation system for any piece of land required a large capital outlay, even in the time of a cheap and ready labor supply. Most of the dams that were built in northern New Spain were small diversion dams or crude earthen blockages of a water source, designed to provide a drinking hole for animals.[22] A few logs thrown across an acequia would cause water to rise sufficiently to permit secondary canals to be fed.[23] Only in the most general sense can these be considered dams, yet they adequately served the purpose of dams.

The building of large masonry storage dams simply was not financially feasible, except in large community grants or in the most prosperous individual grants. The same financial restraints limited the irrigation system. The majority of individual small landowners could not afford more than a simple and relatively short drainage ditch. The Jesuits, the best economic managers among the regular orders, embarked upon large-scale agriculture in Mexico in the eighteenth century and had the necessary financing to improve their holdings through ambitious water projects. The improvements brought about through the construction of dams and extensive irrigation networks not only paid handsome dividends in terms of agricultural yield, but also increased the value of their property enormously.[24]

Land prices fluctuated tremendously with the availability or absence of water. A prolonged drought could dry up springs and wells, prompting the owners to seek new land.[25] Land prices rose with the increased demand. In Arizona at the end of the colonial period, land with running water was appraised at twice the amount of a similar strip of land without a reliable water source.[26] In Texas at the end of

21. Acordado de Diligencias . . . a la mrd q[e] solicita el Reg[or] dn Fran[co] Man[l] de la Puente, Dec. 2, 1753, AGN, Mercedes, Vol. 70, Fol. 154.

22. See, for example, Autos seguidos en razon del aguaje y sitio registrado en nombre del Real Dro . . . 1740, AGN, Californias, Vol. 80, Exp. 28.

23. Alvin R. Sunseri, "Agricultural Techniques in New Mexico at the Time of the Anglo-American Conquest," *New Mexico Historical Review* 47 (Oct., 1973), p. 332.

24. Hermes Tovar Pinzón, "Elementos constitutivos de la empresa agraria Jesuita en la segunda mitad del siglo XVIII en México," in Enrique Florescano (ed.), *Haciendas, latifundios y plantaciones en América Latina* (Mexico: Siglo Veintiuno Editores, 1975), pp. 132–166.

25. Francisco Man[l] Gomez Campillo to Sor Subdelgado, Mar. (?), 1808, AGN, Tierras, Vol. 1424, Exp. 10.

26. Richard R. Willey, "La Canoa: A Spanish Land Grant Lost and Found," *The Smoke Signal* 38 (Fall, 1979), 154.

the colonial period, a piece of land with a small well on it commanded a price three times higher than the same piece of land without it, while land with surface water running through it cost six times more than comparable dry land.[27] Grazing land in the north was relatively cheap, but good cropland with a reliable water source was extremely expensive. In eighteenth-century Chihuahua a prospective buyer could acquire a *sitio* of grazing land (4,388 acres) for less than 300 pesos, but a *caballería* of cropland (105 acres), with an irrigation system already installed, could cost 2,600 pesos.[28] The increased cost to the owner of land with water did not end with its purchase. Throughout the colonial period land and taxes were indirectly tied to water availability, but in 1806 they were tied directly. A royal cédula of that year ordered that land with running water could be evaluated at no less than sixty pesos, land with a good well or spring at no less than thirty, and land lacking water at no less than ten.[29] Land sales in the north indicate that for the most part the decree was enforced.[30] The same general pattern continued after independence. Immediately following Mexico's separation from Spain, taxes on land in Texas were based in part on the number of days that the land enjoyed the right of irrigation.[31] In 1825, for example, water taxes yielded a revenue of 309 pesos for the Ayuntamiento of Béxar.[32] At about the same time, water sales from one recently secularized mission brought in 110 pesos annually for the treasury of the Provincial Deputation of Texas.[33]

Just as today, the agricultural use of water often came into direct conflict with its industrial use. If an individual wanted to divert irrigation water for a mining operation, for a mill, or for some other kind of industrial use, special permission had to be obtained. In late 1806 and

27. Unidentified dispatch, Aug. 27, 1805, BA, Reel 33.

28. H. Bradley Benedict, "The Sale of the Hacienda of Tabaloapa: A Case-Study of Jesuit Property Redistribution in Mexico, 1771–1781," *The Americas*, 32 (Oct., 1975), p. 177.

29. Remate de Tierras a favor de D. Francisco Gutiérrez, Vecino de la Villa de Horcasitas, 1819, AGN, Tierras, Vol. 1421, Exp. 12.

30. Remate de Tierras a favor de Francisco de Escalante, Feb. 15, 1815, AGN, Tierras, Vol. 1421, Exp. 8; Joseph Peres to Sor Gov.ᵒʳ Ynte Ynt.ᵒ, July 26, 1815, AGN, Tierras, Vol. 1421, Exp. 8; Remate de Tierras a favor de Francisco García, Abaluo de un Sitio, n.d., AGN, Tierras, Vol. 1421, Exp. 9; and Remate de Tierras a favor de D. José Antonio de Bustamante, 1816, AGN, Tierras, Vol. 1421, Exp. 10.

31. ". . . cinco pesos anuales q por termino de quatro años les impuso la ex-Diputacion Provincial sobre cada dia de agua. . . ." Rafael Gonzales to Sr. Gefe del Departamento de Texas, Oct. 7, 1825, BA, Reel 84.

32. Cuenta de Cargo y Data que manifesta el Ylustre Ayuntamiento de esta Ciudad. . . . Dec. 31, 1825, BA, Reel 87.

33. Provᵃ de Tejas, Año de 1824, BCA, MR 91.

early 1807, for example, the subdeacon of the mission of La Purísima Concepción in Texas, Juan Manuel Zambrano, wanted to build a flour mill at the mission. He reported to Governor Antonio Cordero that, in order to do so, he would have to use water from the acequia madre. In his request he added that there was plenty of water for everyone, and that nobody who was using the water would be denied his customary share.[34] Governor Cordero was aware that missionary use of water had prompted Indian uprisings in that area in the past and appointed Vicente Amador as a special protector of the Indians in this case.[35] Amador visited the mission, accompanied by Captain Francisco Amagual, head of the Presidio of Bahía del Espíritu Santo. The two men interviewed a number of Indians, including the Indian governor, and determined that, in spite of the claims in Zambrano's petition, water was scarce and the Indians were strongly opposed to the new flour mill if it meant a reduction in agricultural water supply. In addition, there was a good chance that in the near future a group of new Indians, Mazorrales, would join the mission, thus adding to the pressure on water.[36] The report on the petition was so negative that Zambrano knew that he stood only a small chance of receiving a positive response. The day after the report was filed, he wrote to the governor himself, stating that he actually agreed with the objections raised by the Indians. He withdrew his request and advised Cordero to simply dispatch the file to the archives.[37] In this case, agricultural use of water by the Indians won out over increased industrial use by the missions.

In many other cases, however, the Indians were not as well organized nor as well represented. In addition, the milling capacity in the north was small almost everywhere. On many occasions water diversion was approved for industrial needs, even at the expense of agricultural necessity. Much depended on the political influence of the petitioner. There seems little doubt, for example, that the leverage enjoyed by José Eugenio de la Garza Falcón at the highest level of provincial government was significant in his obtaining not one, but two water grants for mills in Coahuila in 1734.[38]

34. Juan Manuel Zambrano to Governor, undated (Jan., 1807?), BA, Reel 35.
35. Marginal annotation of Governor Cordero, Ibid.
36. Fran[co] Amangual and Bisente Amador to Governor Cordero, Mar. 3, [?] 1807, BA, Reel 35.
37. ". . . puede archibar estas diligencias. . . ." Zambrano to Cordero, Mar. 4, 1807, BA, Reel 35. The governor's annotation was "send it to the archive [archivese]."
38. Confirma la Composicion de las Tierras que se espresan hecha por el Señor Juez Privativo de Ventas y Composiciones, Sep. 18, 1734, AGN, Mercedes, Vol. 73, Folio 99.

Mining operations, no matter where they were located, required substantial amounts of water. The patio process of amalgamation, much more common during the colonial period than smelting, needed water for almost every step. To carry out the procedure, refineries had to be located close to a water source.[39] The floor of the pits in which the ore was ground consisted of clay that had to be kept constantly wet. It was covered with very hard rock that was repeatedly washed. Where water was abundant, it was used to power the grinding stones which ground the ore into a powder. In the arid areas of the north, such as in the silver mines surrounding Alamos, Sonora, mules and oxen more commonly provided the power for turning the drag stones. But even in the north, water in large quantities was needed to turn the powder into slime to prepare it for the addition of the mercury. After several days, when the mercury amalgamated with the silver, the mud was thrown into vats. More water was added so that the heavy amalgam could sink to the bottom and be secured. Water was then summoned again as the mud and tailings had to be washed away to begin the process anew.[40]

When water became scarce, mining production declined. A 1782 dispatch from Baja California attributed the decline of mining activity to two main factors: a shortage of quicksilver and the lack of water.[41] The following year, water shortages in Sonora forced many mine owners to cease their operations entirely, or at best to cut back their production.[42] And in 1790, Sonora mine owners had to shut down entirely because of a severe drought.[43] In eighteenth-century Sonora and Chihuahua, potentially rich mines were not developed fully because of the absence of an adequate water supply.[44]

39. D. A. Brading, *Miners and Merchants in Bourbon Mexico, 1763–1810* (Cambridge: Cambridge University Press, 1971), p. 138.

40. The differences in the patio processes in wet and dry areas consisted of little more than the power source. Aside from the grinding, the water requirements were roughly the same. See Robert W. Randall, *Real del Monte: A British Mining Venture in Mexico* (Austin: University of Texas Press, 1972), pp. 20–23, and Albert Stagg, *The Almadas of Alamos, 1782–1867* (Tucson: University of Arizona Press, 1973), pp. 13–15.

41. Sargento Fran^{co} de Aguan to Ant^o de Osio, May 18, 1782, AHBCS, Leg. 2, Doc. 49.

42. Pedro Corbalán to Viceroy Antonio María Bucareli y Ursua, May 14, 1773, AGN, Provincias Internas, Vol. 91, Exp. 1.

43. Henrique de Grimerest to Viceroy Revilla Gidego, Nov. 12, 1790, AGI, Indiferente General, Leg. 1560.

44. Autos quese formaron para construir un tanque para Recoger las aguas que entiempo dellubias derramaren los Serros de Santa Eulalia, Año de 1731, AHP, Reel 1731b. This document discusses the negative impact of the lack of water in the Chihuahua mining zone of Santa Eulalia. Additional information is contained in Alvaro López Miramontes, *Las minas de Nueva España en 1753* (Mexico: Instituto de Antropología e Historia, 1975), p. 87, and Joseph Och, S.J., *Missionary in Sonora* (San Francisco: California Historical Society, 1965), p. 143.

The case of Cieneguilla, Sonora, is illustrative. Gold in promising amounts was discovered there in 1771, but two years later the decision was made not to develop a settlement to exploit the mines because the nearest water source for the placers was over five miles away. When mines were not developed, the Spanish crown lost the revenues of the mining tax and needed explanation. They were forthcoming in this case.

> The place where the ore must be washed is over two leagues away and it is simply impossible to construct a ditch from there [to the mines]. . . . The notable lack of water where the placers are is tremendous. I conducted a test at the mines, digging down to a depth of 16 varas [44 feet] and the earth there was just as dry as that on the surface. There was no reason to continue.[45]

Miners in the mountains of northern New Mexico found a unique solution to water scarcity in the 1820s. They restricted their activities to the winter months when there was snow cover on the ground. The process they employed was described by Josiah Gregg.

> Water in winter is obtained by melting a quantity of snow thrown into a sink, with heated stones. Those employed as washers are very frequently the wives and children of the miners. A round wooden bowl called batea, about eighteen inches in diameter, is the washing vessel, which they fill with the earth, and then im-merse it in the pool, and stir it with their hands; by which opera-tion the loose dirt floats off, and the gold settles in the bottom. . . . Some attempts have been made to wash with machinery but as yet without success; partly owing to the scarcity of water. . . . [46]

Mines in Sonora did not have the advantage of winter snow to melt. The system devised there to cope with the lack of water was less than satisfactory, as evidenced by a late-eighteenth-century report:

> Lack of water . . . is our main problem. Where there is no water we have to throw the dirt and sand into the air. The wind carries the loose material away, including the finer gold, and only the heavier particles fall back to the ground. A great deal is lost in this way. Since most of the placers are six to ten miles away from available water here at the settlement, it is not only difficult to carry the water but we have nothing to carry it in. In most cases we have to

45. Melchor Peramas to Viceroy, Jan. 27, 1773, AGI, Audiencia de Guadalajara, 513. A year after the problem was first described, water had not yet been discovered and the mining operation had almost come to a halt. Expediente formado con motivo del Ynforme que hizo el Governador Dn Francisco Crespo del estado Real de la Cieneguilla, 1774, AGN, Provincias Internas, Vol. 247, Exp. 16.
46. Gregg, *Commerce of the Prairies*, p. 54.

resort to throwing the dirt in the air, hoping that most of the gold will fall back into our wooden trays [bateas]. If we had water we could double the gold we take.[47]

If the absence of water retarded economic development in the mines, its presence where it was not wanted did the same. Mine shafts dug two or three hundred feet deep often struck the water table, even in the arid north. The resulting seepage and flooding caused the closing of many mines. Available technology permitted only two rather ineffective methods of draining. An adit or *contramina* (horizontal drainage ditch) could be cut from the surface to the level in which the water was encountered, but this was a slow and expensive process and one which had to be engineered with great skill if it was to succeed. The deeper the mine, the more difficult the chore. In addition, if the mine shaft proceeded subsequently to a depth below the adit, it would, of course, be useless.

A second, more common method of drainage was that of the *malacate*, or windlass hoist (fig. 4.1). A heavy rope was wound around a vertical drum on a spindle. The drum was turned by horses, mules, or oxen. Bags filled with water were secured to the rope and lifted to the surface to be emptied and returned. Large mining operations needed fifteen or twenty malacates, while a smaller enterprise might have only one. As long as the seepage problem was minor, the system worked. If the mines hit a large underground spring, it was a losing battle, as the mine would flood more quickly than the water could be removed.[48] Even when the malacate system of drainage proved successful, production was very slow and the cost of producing an ounce of ore doubled.[49] The Spanish crown recognized the problem and, in an effort to stimulate mining production, exempted all equipment needed for drainage from the *alcabala* or sales tax.[50]

European technology was considerably ahead of drainage methods used in the New World, and this undeniable fact prompted José Antonio de Alzate, Mexico's most famous eighteenth-century scientist, to pen an article in 1768 calling for the adoption of the steam-driven pump to drain the country's mines.[51] The call did not go unheeded.

47. Pedro Tueros to Pedro Corbalan, July 23, 1772, DD, p. 21.
48. Contramina and malacate technology are discussed in Randall, *Real del Monte,* pp. 18–19, 27, and Brading, *Miners and Merchants,* pp. 134–136.
49. Och, *Missionary in Sonora,* p. 149.
50. Decreto del govierno y acuerdo de la junta superior de hacienda, para no cobrar alcabala a varios artículos en favor de la minería, Sep. 2, 1685, Rodríguez de San Miguel, *Pandectas,* II, 232.
51. José Antonio de Alzate y Ramírez, *Obras: I Periódicos* (Mexico: Universidad Nacional Autónoma de México, 1980), pp. 31–35.

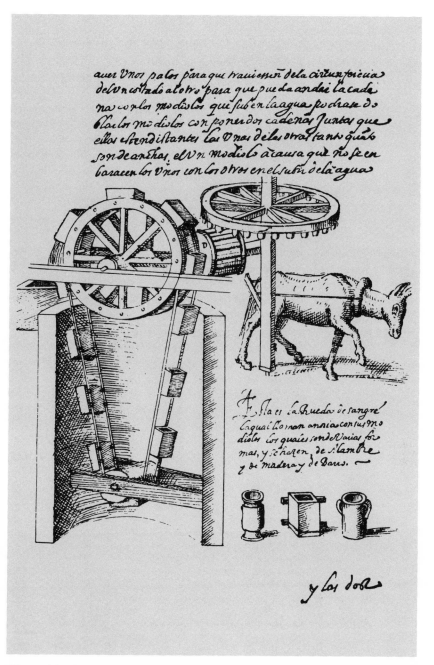

Figure 4.1   Water lift, easily converted to a malacate, *designed by Cristóbal Iranzo in 1570.* From Ramón Sánchez Flores, *Historia de la tecnología y la invención en México* (Fomento Cultural Banamex A.C., 1980); courtesy of the author.

Steam-driven pumps were introduced in Mexico during the late colonial period and had reached even Chihuahua by 1820.[52] However, there were too few to make a notable difference in the north.

When Mexico gained independence, many rich mines were shut down. La Quintera, the richest mine in Sonora, was closed by flooding in 1806 and not reopened until 1835, when it fell into the hands of the Almada family of Alamos.[53] The same problem befell other Sonora mines. Juan Bautista Echaves had to abandon the mine of San Francisco Javier; Juan Bautista Munguía gave up La Clarina when it flooded in 1781 and drainage attempts were unsuccessful; Nuestra Señora de Jalpa was abandoned for the same reason during the same year; a similar fate awaited Prudencio de Covarrubias, who gave up trying to drain Las Animas.[54] The rich Sonora mines of San Antonio de la Huerta were closed because they became waterlogged,[55] and miners in Cananea had to work very close to the surface because of the shallow water table.[56] In neighboring Chihuahua and New Mexico the same story was repeated. Flooding caused Francisco González Ramírez to give up working his Santa Eulalia mine.[57] In the Chihuahua mining district of Real de Guanavesi, summer rains caused the underground water level to rise sufficiently to flood many of the mines.[58] When Francisco Manuel de Elguea began copper mining at Santa Rita del Cobre in the southwest corner of New Mexico in about 1804, he found that it did not pay to try to cope with inundation. Whenever his miners hit water, he would simply abandon the shaft and begin a new one.[59] The northern mines did not live up to their anticipated potential. Viceroy Marqués de Croix commissioned Joaquín Velásquez de León to report on the situation. He related that in the mines of Baja California the principal problem encountered was flooding.[60]

52. Almada, *Resumen de historia*, p. 169.
53. Stagg, *The Almadas of Alamos*, pp. 64–67.
54. Mario Hernández Sánchez-Barba, *La última expansión española en América* (Madrid: Instituto de Estudios Políticos, 1957), pp. 65–67.
55. Governor Joseph Tienda de Cuervo to Marqués de Cruillas, Feb. 15, 1761, AGN, Provincias Internas, Vol. 86, Exp. 2.
56. Governor Joseph Tienda de Cuervo to Marqués de Cruillas, Mar. 16, 1762, AGN, Provincias Internas, Vol. 86, Exp. 2.
57. López Miramonte, *Las minas de Nueva España*, p. 88.
58. Relacion que se dirige del Sor Dⁿ Joaquin de Amerguetta sobre los puntos que enella se espresan, Jan.–Apr., 1794, AHP, Reel 1794.
59. Billy D. Walker, "Copper Genesis: The Early Years of Santa Rita del Cobre," *New Mexico Historical Review* 54 (Jan., 1959), p. 12.
60. Roberto Moreno, *Joaquín Velásquez de León y sus trabajos científicos sobre el valle de México, 1773–1775* (Mexico: Universidad Nacional Autónoma de México, 1981).

The ecolturative process accompanied mining activities as well. Not only did intensive mining deplete nonrenewable natural resources, but the exploitation of mineral reserves prompted a deforestation of surrounding mountains to provide the timber and firewood necessary for the mining enterprise. The most perceptible and immediate impact on the desert was the scarring of the earth's surface, but the beauty of the desert landscape is only skin deep. Not only beauty but the ecosystem fell victim to thoughtless exploitation of the forests. The felling of trees left mountainsides unnaturally vulnerable to erosion and flooding during summer months. The results were not all negative, as some rich mountain topsoil was deposited in the valleys below. The more common result, however, was an increase in the sedimentation of desert streams and a smothering of rich alluvial soils. Even in the best of circumstances the destructive force which accompanied the floods far outweighed any possible good. The long-range impact was severe as well. Deforestation encouraged a much more rapid evaporation at the higher altitudes, and in the process lessened the usual annual water supply on the desert floor.

The exchange of goods and services in northern New Spain was carefully controlled by crown policy, just as it was everywhere in the Spanish American empire. Although many of the regulations were cumbersome, they were no more influential at the local level than the wild fluctuations in the water supply. When water was scarce and agricultural productivity declined, prices rose and local commerce suffered catastrophic decline. It was not unusual for the prices of corn and other staples to double during a dry year,[61] and many goods could not be obtained at all. Because the rivers were not navigable, almost all trade moved on land. Shippers often refused to move their mule trains or oxcarts out on the roads when watering places dried up; if any shipping was done during dry times, the freightage charges, passed on to the consumers, were excessive.[62] Government intervention was not uncommon. A 1749 drought and resultant food shortages prompted a decree ordering all haciendas to plant additional corn on any available land.[63] However, emergency measures such as this did little to alleviate human suffering.

---

61. Razon de los tiempos que han esperimentado en el semestre primero del presente Año, Aug. 3, 1790, AGI, Indiferente General, Leg. 1560.

62. Informe que el Visitador General de la Sinaloa y Sonora hase en cumplim[to] de su obligasion. . . . Aug. 12, 1756, AGN, Provincias Internas, Vol. 29, Exp. 6; Manuel Concha to Sor D[n] Joaquin de Amerguetta, May 24, 1798, AHP, Reel 1798.

63. Bando del Superior Gobierno de 29 de Noviembre de 1749, in Beleña, *Recopilación sumaria*, I, 67, tercero foliage.

In the spring of 1773 Intendant Pedro Corbalan explained the
impact of a recent Sonora drought to Viceroy Bucareli.

> Because of the scanty rains last year you cannot find pasture or
> water along the roads and if you are lucky enough to find any
> food, it is at very high prices. A *fanega* [2.58 bushels] of corn is
> selling at between ten and twelve pesos. A *carga* [5.15 bushels] of
> wheat at twenty-five pesos, and one has to pay as much as two
> pesos for an *arroba* [25 pounds] of meat. Other foodstuffs have
> risen proportionately.[64]

The 1770s were generally dry years throughout the Mexican
north. They exerted a heavy toll on the sheep industry of Coahuila,
where thousands of head died.[65] But the 1790 drought in Sonora was
even worse. The pasture land dried up, and entire herds of horses and
cattle perished. Cows were too weak to give milk. The crop seeds in
areas of dry land farming refused to germinate, and there was insufficient water to keep grains and vegetables alive even in the irrigated
plots. Food was in such short supply that people were reduced to
eating roots and grass. Illness of epidemic proportion set in. Mines,
haciendas, and *obrajes* (workshops) shut down, unemployment reached
gargantuan proportions, and commerce came to a halt. Many small
towns were abandoned as people fled to avoid starvation.[66]

During normal years, water affected the economic life of the
northern colonies in more subtle ways. It was itself an important
exchange commodity, to be bought and sold, sometimes in liquid
amounts and sometimes by time allotments. Liquid amounts were
determined by the size of the opening (the *abertura* or *toma*) through
which water was channeled from the main source into the individual
ditch. The largest unit of measurement was the *buey*. Originally esti-
mated as the amount of water that could pass through an ox's legs in
one minute, the buey came to be standardized as an opening of one
square vara, which released 2,597 gallons per minute. The buey was
subdivided into surcos (sometimes rendered as *sulcos*), which released
slightly over fifty-one gallons per minute, or the amount needed to fill
an average trench dug by a simple plow. The surco, in turn, was

64. Pedro Corbalan to Viceroy Antonio María Bucareli y Ursua, May 14, 1773, AGN,
Provincias Internas, Vol. 91, Exp. 1. Although Spanish law provided that muleteers
and cart owners had to be given water while on route, the law, of course, could not
guarantee that water would be available. For the pertinent legislation see Providencia
de Beleña, July 12, 1785, Rodríguez de San Miguel, *Pandectas*, II, p. 304.

65. Harris, *A Mexican Family Empire,* p. 40.

66. Henrique de Grimerest to Viceroy Revilla Gigedo, Nov. 12, 1790, AGI, Indiferente General, Leg. 1560.

further divided into *naranjas* (17.13 gallons), *reales* or *limones* (2.14 gallons), and *pajas* (1.18 gallons).[67]

The purchase and sale of water by liquid measures was less common in the Mexican north than by time allotments, which were generally by the day, but sometimes by the hour or even by the minute.[68] Unless specified deliberately, all times were calculated on a weekly basis. The purchase of one day of water theoretically carried the right to use as much water as needed for fifty-two days during the year, but, since the water was used primarily during the growing season, the yearly allotment for which one paid was little more than an abstraction. The crucial element in the agreement was that no more than a fixed number of days or hours could be drawn from the source in any one week.[69] With permission of the owner, and in agreement with other users, a daily allotment could be divided up over several days. Depending upon temperature, humidity, and wind, it was often preferable to irrigate for twelve hours twice a week than for twenty-four hours once a week.[70]

Just as with any other commodity, the price of water was dictated by what the market would bear. In most cases the flow rate of the stream and the number of potential users determined the price.[71] When purchased by the poor for irrigation purposes, payment was often deferred until the harvest, and, at least on some occasions, repayment consisted of a percentage of the crops.[72] An important potential source of income to those who held legal right, it often saved businessmen whose other economic ventures had gone sour.[73] Local

67. Manuel Carrera Stampa, "The Evolution of Weights and Measures in New Spain," *Hispanic American Historical Review* 29 (February, 1949), p. 14, and Galván Rivera, *Ordenanzas de tierras y aguas*, pp. 151–156.

68. Marcos de Castro to Governor, Sep. 19, 1771, BA, Reel 11; Copias de los Originales Firmados por el Teniente d. Juan Ygnacio Arranmide, Feb. 7, 1805, BA, Reel 26.

69. In the San Antonio area in the middle of the eighteenth century, daily allotments were made on the basis of a twenty-day period, rather than a week, but the aberration is stipulated in the grants themselves. See Dobkins, *The Spanish Element in Texas Water Law*, p. 120.

70. Both methods, time and amount, were used in Spanish and Mexican Texas, but an additional, less precise measure is also found in the Texas documentation. Water was bought and sold by *dulas*, an amount necessary to water one's irrigable land. If an individual purchased only half a dula, he could irrigate only half of his irrigable land.

71. A sampling of water prices in Coahuila in the 1820s and 1830s can be found in Harris, *A Mexican Family Empire*, p. 161.

72. En el Real y Minas de Sn Jose de Parral, Nov. 25, 1783, AHP, Reel 1783b.

73. For two examples, see Demanda de Geronimo Barrera Contra Juan Josef Montes de Oca, [1779] BA, Reel 13, and Fran^co del Prado y Arze to Juan Baut^ta Elquesabal, Apr. 8, 1805, BA, Reel 33.

units of government found water sales to be a lucrative source of income for municipal treasuries.[74]

It is one of those ironies of nature that a region most remarkable for its aridity should also be characterized by extreme periodic flooding, the quintessential expression of Tlaloc's revenge. Two related desert conditions help explain this phenomenon: the pattern of annual rainfall and the characteristics of desert soil. The rainfall is not evenly distributed throughout the year, most of it coming in the three summer months. Late afternoon summer storms can be violent. On occasion one-sixth or one-seventh of an entire year's precipitation will fall within a four- or five-hour period. The best natural drainage systems cannot carry off such excess water, and the situation is especially precarious in many areas of the desert because of the land formations, desert cover, and quality of the soil. Steep slopes and a relatively barren surface encourage rapid runoff. In addition, high alkali content in the soil yields a caliche formation only a few inches below the surface. So hard that a pick and shovel can barely penetrate it, the caliche refuses to absorb more than minuscule amounts of water, and in the process contributes to excessive runoff and flash floods. A placid stream or an arroyo which has carried no water for years can suddenly crest at 100,000 or 200,000 cubic feet per second.

Ecolturation also took its toll. Human tampering with the natural flow of a stream or the surrounding groundcover exacerbated the flooding problem. A poorly designed diversion from a major water source, such as the Río Grande, could cause flooding not preordained by nature alone. The town and presidio at El Paso del Norte were subjected to repeated flooding by uncontrolled Río Grande water in the irrigation network itself.[75] Deforestation, a by-product of all settlement patterns, reduced the natural absorptive qualities of the soil and increased flood potential. The introduction of domesticated animals contributed to these water tragedies. The daily watering of a herd of cattle or sheep wore down streambanks precariously close to newly established town sites. Poorly engineered upstream dams, while impounding water for beneficial use during times of scarcity, were time bombs simply awaiting impressive cloudbursts.

It is not surprising that the Spanish towns, missions, and presidios were built in river valleys. It would have been impossible for life to exist, much less flourish, if locations far from a water source had been

74. At the time of independence the Provincial Deputation of Texas was selling water at the annual rate of 2 pesos, 4 reales for a half dula or 5 pesos for a full dula. See Prov^a de Tejas, Año de 1824, BCA, MR 91.

75. Decreto del Sr. Gov^or dn Thomas Veliz Cachupin, 1754, ALPC PE-51.

chosen. But those first Spanish settlers had no way of knowing that, centuries in the future, climatologists and soil physicists would be engaged in the business of defining dangerous floodplains (some quite innocent looking), and local zoning boards would refuse to grant construction permits in areas susceptible to flooding once every hundred years. The temptation to construct homes, public buildings, and churches very close to the streambed or arroyo was strong. In the first place, water in relatively large amounts was needed to build adobe bricks for construction.[76] The bricks, of course, could be transported anywhere, but the lure of close proximity to the water source was great. If the homes and buildings were located close to the banks, large trees shaded them from the blistering summer sun. Water for domestic purposes had to be channeled or carried in pots, skins, gourds, or jars for only short distances.[77] However, the price paid for this innocent indiscretion was high.

The summer rains, even falling in normal amounts, caused rivers to swell and retarded travel, transportation, and communications.[78] But when the rain fell in torrents, the resultant flooding caused devastation to life and property. Quite naturally the first things to go were the waterworks themselves: ditches, headgates, flumes, reservoirs, and watering holes for animals.[79] Once the banks of the river overran or the ditches collapsed, there was little that could be done. It was virtually impossible to rebuild the water system before the streams ran dry. The best that could be hoped for was that only one harvest would be lost. In 1767 summer flooding was so severe in the Yaqui and Mayo river valleys of Sonora that the crops could not be planted.[80] In 1773 and again in 1791 flooding in the same area washed away crops already in the fields. The havoc wreaked by the 1773 flood was so great that local officials forgave the Indians the payment of their tribute for a time.[81]

76. Lorenzo Cancio to Juan de Pineda, June 25, 1767, DHM, 4, II, 262.

77. See, for example, Domingo Elizondo to Marqués de Croix, Dec. 20, 1770, AGN, Provinicias Internas, Vol. 226.

78. Cabello to Phe° de Nebe, July 20, 1784, BA, Reel 16.

79. Dn Joseph de Berroteran to Pedro de Ravago y Teran, AGI, Audiencia de Guadalajara, 513; Jose Man¹ Granados to Gov°ʳ Dn Ant° Cordero, June 7, 1808, BA, Reel 38; Juan Manuel Zambrano to D. Antonio María Martínez, Oct. 29, 1818, BA, Reel 82; Manuel Martínez to Jefe Político, July 3, 1832, MANM, Reel 15.

80. Lorenzo Cancio to Juan de Pineda, Oct. 3, 1767, DHM, 41, II.

81. Extracto de las Noticias de Temporales y cosechas que se han esperimentado . . . de las provincias de Sonora y Sinaloa . . . al segundo semestre del año pasado de 1791, AGI, Indiferente General, Leg. 1560; Real Orden del Consejo, Aug. 19, 1773, AGI, Audiencia de Guadalajara, 242.

On a number of occasions floods destroyed entire settlements built precariously on low ground. The same large trees coveted so much for their shade could be uprooted and crash down on the roofs of those houses they had protected from the summer sun. The foundations of buildings collapsed under the brunt of rushing water. The 1773 Sonora flood carried away the church at the Visita of Charay.[82] The year before, the same fate befell the church at Culiacán. The Culiacán inundation also left many people homeless; some abandoned the town, while others rebuilt on higher ground.[83] Fifteen years after the founding of Monterrey, heavy rains caused the Río Santa Catalina to go on a rampage. This 1611 flood carried away houses and destroyed crops. The city itself had to be rebuilt farther away from the river.[84] A 1751 flood devastated Reynosa in the lower Río Grande Valley.[85] An 1802 flood destroyed 150 adobe structures in Monclova, Coahuila, as well as many others in the surrounding area.[86]

Spanish settlements in Texas experienced some of the most severe floods of the entire colonial period. The city of Béxar was all but destroyed on July 5, 1819, when the rivers spilled over their banks with tremendous force. Those homes that did nót collapse were left in shambles.[87] Military installations were by no means immune. In the late summer of 1818 seventy-one houses were destroyed at the Texas presidio of Bahía. This same flood left severe breaches in the presidio wall, making the installation vulnerable to enemy attack.[88]

Floods had a devastating effect on the economic life of a community. Normal economic activities ground to a halt during the long and tedious process of reconstruction. Stores and factories could be closed for months. Food shortages caused suffering, and mail, medicine, and supplies were difficult to obtain.[89] The pollution or destruction of city

82. Pedro Corbalan to Viceroy, Feb. 19, 1773, AGN, Provincias Internas, Vol. 98, Exp. 1.
83. Governador Mateo Sastre to Viceroy Antonio Bucareli, Oct. 14, 1772, AGI, Audiencia de Guadalajara, 513.
84. José Fuentes Mares, *Monterrey: Una ciudad creadora y sus capitanes* (Mexico: Editorial Jus. 1976), p. 15.
85. Foscue, "Agricultural History of the Lower Río Grande Valley Region," p. 126.
86. Harris, *A Mexican Family Empire*, pp. 40–41.
87. Antonio Martínez to Joaquín de Arredondo, July 9, 1819, BA, Reel 63; Relacion delas casas pertenecientes ala Rl Hacienda . . . que han padecido ruina en la Ynundación dela Ciudad de Béxar en la Mañana 5 de Corrte, BA, July 8, 1819, Reel 63.
88. Juan Manuel Zambrano to Antonio Martínez, Aug. 20, 1818, BA, Reel 61.
89. Cabello to Pheᵉ de Nebe, July 20, 1789, BA, Reel 16; Ramón de Castro to Gov. Manuel Muñoz, Aug., 1791, BA, Reel 21; Antonio Cordero to Manuel de Salcedo, Mar. 3, 1809, BA, Reel 40.

waterworks prompted disease, as did water holes, which quickly pu-
trefied following major flooding.

People came together in interesting ways in the aftermath of a
serious flood. The natural disaster brought out the best in some but
the worst in others. Flood relief was well organized during the colonial
period and combined both government and private initiative. After
the San Antonio flood in the summer of 1819 the governor of the
province immediately made 2,000 pesos available to flood victims.[90]
Charitable donations followed from individuals living hundreds of
miles away.[91] Some of the donors undoubtedly hoped that their gener-
osity would later be rewarded with official favors, but others seem to
have desired only to help. Some local inhabitants were less altruistic.
Not only did looting follow the San Antonio flood, but profiteering
occurred as well. When neighboring communities donated 84 fanegas
of corn to alleviate hunger, a local muleteer charged the citizens a
whopping 129 pesos in freightage costs to bring the corn into the
city.[92] Even worse, local officials skimmed off the top of the official
flood relief allocation. Of the 2,000 pesos made available by the
governor, only 1,118 pesos, distributed to seventy-five individuals,
could be accounted for.[93] The private donations seem to have been
better managed. Citizens from Coahuila sent 675 pesos, 495 of which
went to 93 individuals (mainly women) in amounts ranging from 4 to
12 pesos each. In addition, 150 pesos was set aside for three neighboring missions which also suffered flood damage. The remaining 20
pesos was used to provide food for soldiers from the presidio who
helped with a variety of flood relief projects.[94]

Not even national security and defense were immune from water
influence. Because the isolated settlements and missions of the northern frontier were easy prey to both Indians and potential foreign
rivals, the Crown decided that small forts or presidios were needed to
protect the colonies and missions. The original presidios were not
carefully planned out, however. Not only were they placed in poor
defensive locations, but the garrisons often found themselves in competition with the missions and colonists for the scarce water supply. In
1766 the Marqués de Rubí set out on an extensive inspection of the

90. Conde de Venadito to Antonio Martínez, July 28, 1819, BA, Reel 63.
91. Conde de Venadito to Antonio Martínez, Apr. 12, 1820, BA, Reel 63.
92. Relacion que manifesta los vecinos que de esta Capital han sido socorridos . . . .
May 14, 1820, BA, Reel 64.
93. Arredondo to Martínez, Feb. 20, 1820, BA, Reel 63; Conde de Venadito to
Martinez, Dec. 22, 1819, BA, Reel 63.
94. Relacion que manifesta. . . . BA, Reel 64.

presidios. His tour took about two years, during which time he covered 7,500 miles of the borderlands. His recommendations, made in 1768, called for the abandonment of some of the presidios and the establishment of others. In total, there would be fifteen, extending from Altar in Sonora to Bahía del Espíritu Santo in Texas. They would be located at intervals of about forty leagues (104 miles). Of greatest importance, he reported, they must be placed in areas "that will assure the two indispensable requisites: water and grazing land for the horses, without taking into consideration the possibilities these lands might hold out for future settlement."[95] The recommendations were carried out by Don Hugo O'Conor between 1773 and 1775. When the presidio of Tubac, Arizona, was moved north to Tucson, O'Conor noted that the new site "fulfills the requirement of water, pasture and wood and effectively closes the Apache frontier."[96]

When war broke out in the north, and it often did, water availability dictated much of the military strategy. Military scouts searching for hostile Indians first checked the known watering holes.[97] Military campaigns were planned to coincide with those months when water was anticipated to be most plentiful. On a military map from a report on Sonoran campaigns against the Indians in 1768, the most prominent feature of the legend is the affirmation that the arroyo does not carry water except during the rainy season (fig. 4.2). Not only did the troops and mounts need drinking water, but a cavalry march across a parched desert plain threw up huge clouds of dust visible for miles. Surprise attack was thus rendered impossible.[98] Water shortages limited the military activities of both Indians and Spaniards, but it seems to have had an especially negative impact on the Spanish troops, who sometimes refused to carry out expeditions in the desert if an adequate water supply was not assured. Viceroy Bucareli on one occasion explained the lack of military success in Chihuahua on the following grounds: "after [Hugo O'Conor] took command of the Chihuahua frontier, we didn't have much success there, unfortunately. The lack of

95. ". . .pa asegurar los dos indespensables Requisitos de Agua y Pastos pa la cavallada y sin respecto alguno alas Proporciones pa poblacion qe Fomentara en los terrenos." El Marques de Ruvi, *Dictamen Sobre los Presidos d. N. España, Año de 1768,* AGI, Audiencia de México, 2477. See also Max L. Moorhead, *The Presidio: Bastion of the Spanish Borderlands* (Norman: University of Oklahoma Press, 1975), passim.

96. Hugo O'Conor, San Xavier del Bac, Aug. 20, 1775, DD, 25–26.

97. *Diario que formo oi 24 de Febrero de 1768 años . . . de orden del Senor Gov°ʳ Dn Juan de Pineda. . . .* AGN, Historia, Vol. 24, Exp. 9.

98. Navarro García, *José de Gálvez,* p. 68.

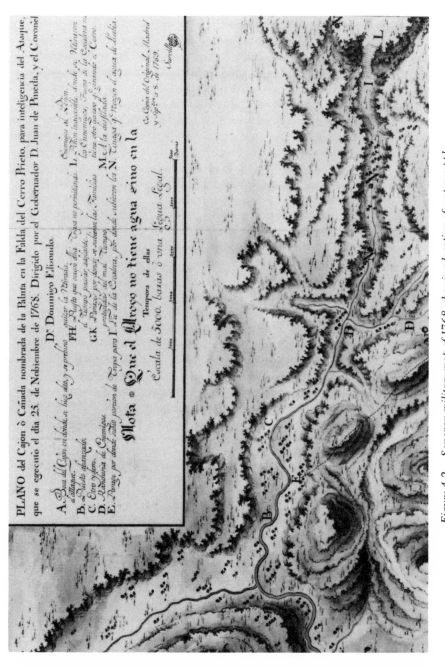

*Figure 4.2   Sonoran military map of 1768, showing location of water supply.
By permission of the British Library, courtesy Arizona State Museum*

rain at the beginning of the summer has hindered the military operations of the troops."[99] Juan de Pineda, the governor of Sonora, was
more specific. His soldiers were unable to respond to Indian attacks
because all of the horses were weak from lack of water.[100] Felipe de
Goychea, governor of Baja California, had a similar story to tell. So
many of his army mounts were dying for lack of water that his cavalry
was quickly turning into infantry.[101] Not infrequently, military expeditions were dispatched to engage hostile Indians but returned before
carrying out their objectives because of the lack of water.[102] When
water shortages occurred on a military campaign, the expedition
would simply stop and scouts (generally Indian auxiliaries) would be
sent out in all directions to search for water.[103] By the time it was
uncovered, the Indians who were being pursued were long gone.

Shortly after the reconquest of New Mexico by Diego de Vargas,
Governor Félix Martínez decided that the time was ripe to bring the
Hopi pueblos under Spanish control. For a number of years they had
resisted the efforts of Franciscan friars to convert them, and the
governor opted to lead his troops personally. The march west from
Santa Fe was uneventful, but, by the time Hopi country was reached,
the Spaniards and their animals were suffering from lack of water.
Initial contact with the Hopi proved disappointing, and Governor
Martínez concluded that they would have to be defeated by force of
arms. However, his own troops and mounts were weakened, and he
ordered his men to create several artificial ponds by damming a
diminutive stream. As he later reported to his superiors, the desert
terrain of the Hopi country thwarted his best efforts:

> I, the same Governor, ordered them to ascertain if there was any
> water in the two pools and dams that were constructed yesterday,
> and whether there was enough to supply me and the said army

99. Viceroy Antonio María de Bucareli to Conde de O'Reilly, Sep. 26, 1772, AGI,
Audiencia de México, 1242.

100. Juan de Pineda to Viceroy Marqués de Cruillas, May 21, 1765, AGN, Provincias
Internas, Vol. 86, Exp. 1.

101. José Manuel Ruiz to Felipe de Goycochea, Feb. 5, 1813, AHBCS, Leg. 1, Doc.
575.

102. "Que de los tres destacamentos q salieron arecorrer las immediciones del Cerro
Prieto y parages donde pudieron retirarse los Yndios, pr falta de aguas en el Volvio a
los siete dias el de D. Domingo Elisondo sin otra ventaja qè matar dos Yndias apresiar
a dos ninos, cojer 21 cavallos y descubrir dos aguages nuevos, que faciliaran en
mucholos reconocmmientos subcesivos," Noticias Recividas de Sonora, June 17, 1768,
AGI, Audiencia de Guadalajara, 416.

103. Diario de la Campana Executada de Orden del Exmo Señor Conde de Revillagigedo Expedida el 1º de Diciembre de 1748 por Dⁿ Josef Berroteran, AGI,
Audiencia de Guadalajara, 513.

during all the time that I might stay. It was done, and it was found that there was none, the sand having absorbed it all.[104]

Defeated by the environment, as many other Spanish commanders before and after him, Governor Martínez acquiesced and ordered the retreat to Santa Fe.

Throughout the Southwest the Indians seemed better equipped to function militarily when water was scarce. In 1786, when Bernardo de Gálvez advised Commandant General Jacobo Ugarte y Loyola on how to engage the Indians of the north, he indicated that they were more effective in battle than the Spaniards because, among other things, they were willing to suffer thirst.[105] Perhaps gradual biological adaptation made it possible for them to survive on lesser amounts, but, more importantly, they were wise in the ways of the desert. Indian warfare was finely tuned to the vagaries of an arid land. Seldom would they travel in the heat of a summer day, and, when they did, special precautions would be taken. In the Hopi country of northern Arizona, for example, women would accompany military expeditions simply for the purpose of carrying water in large gourds. Half of these would be buried in the sand for use on the return. The Pueblo of Acoma in western New Mexico was built on top of a mesa rising 350 feet above the surrounding plain. There was no water source on top; water had to be carried up in earthen jars by the women from a spring below. A military vulnerability? Not really. Water was stored in large stone cavities carved out of the rock mesa, and the virtually impregnable pueblo could withstand a long siege.

The Indian populations were very aware of Spanish liabilities during the dry season, as evidenced by a military report dispatched in the early summer of 1768: "Nobody better than you knows the circumstances of this dry and hot season and that the enemies [the Indians] use it as an excuse to make war on us and to destroy our troops and horses . . . before the benefit of the rains."[106]

The military tactics of both Spaniards and Indians often included the destruction of enemy water supply systems and dams.[107] In an

---

104. "A Campaign Against the Moqui Pueblos under Governor Phelix Martínez in 1716," *New Mexico Historical Review* 6 (Apr., 1931), 211.

105. Daniel Tyler, "Mexican Indian Policy in New Mexico," *New Mexico Historical Review* 55 (Apr., 1980), p. 102.

106. Lorenzo Cancio to D. Juan de Pineda, June 11, 1768, DHM, Serie 4, Tomo II.

107. As one of many examples, the widow of Francisco Tomogua, an Opata auxiliary for twenty-two years, asked for a pension, indicating in her petition that among the accomplishments of her late husband were numerous military campaigns and the destruction of Indian dams. Pedro Corbalan to Jacobo Ugarte, Aug. 23, 1787, AGI, Audiencia de Guadalajara, 287.

area in which water holes might be a hundred miles apart, the poison-
ing or polluting of a well was an excellent means of ending a pursuit or
even bringing the enemy to his knees. It was not necessary to seek out
some exotic venomous substance. A dead animal or a dead person
could be thrown into a well or a watering hole.[108]

Even well-fortified presidios were vulnerable to Indian attack
which was directed at the water supply.[109] The problem was especially
acute at the Texas presidio of San Sabá, where a thick groundcover
along the irrigation ditch provided a natural camouflage for Indians
interested in cutting off the water supply.[110] The best-known example
of the water supply being used as a weapon was an incident which
occurred during the Pueblo Rebellion in New Mexico in 1680. With
the outbreak of the rebellion, the Spanish residents of the province
took refuge in Santa Fe. They were able to hold off Indian attacks
until the Pueblos cut the two main acequias flowing through the city.
The ensuing thirst proved more effective than thousands of Indian
arrows. The Spaniards had to withdraw from the city and retreat to
the more secure environs of El Paso del Norte, some two hundred
miles to the south.

The Spaniards quickly learned that peace treaties, if they were to
be lasting, necessarily had to assure the conquered Indians a sure and
adequate water supply. When the Spaniards came to terms with the
Apaches in Sonora in 1786, they realized that the peace would not
endure unless the Apaches were forced to adopt a more sedentary life.
This realization, in turn, meant that they had to be assured of access to
both land and water. The treaty thus included the following provision:

> The above-mentioned populations should be situated on the most
> fertile lands and those with the best irrigation that are found
> unoccupied at the present. To move them onto dry land would be
> to leave them in the same undisciplined freedom that they now
> enjoy. They would never be able to subsist by means of their own
> work and effort.[111]

---

108. "A Campaign Against the Moqui," p. 211.

109. An eighteenth-century military report from the presidio at Espíritu Santo in
Texas spelled out the vulnerability: "... y silos Yndios Enemigos de la Nacion
Carancaguaz, Comanches, Apaches, y Lipanes apodereran como les fuera facil de los
Bajaderos ai Rio se Podia Perecer de Sed." Real Presidio de la Bahia de el Espiritu
Santo, Jan. 12, 1780, BA, Reel 13.

110. Nicolas de Laffora to Marques de Rubi, Aug. 12, 1767, AGI, Audiencia de
Guadalajara, 511.

111. Pedro Garrido y Duran to Viceroy, Jan. 31, 1787, AGI, Audiencia de Guadalajara,
287.

Similarly, when the Seris on Tiburón Island were defeated by Spanish troops in the 1770s, and plans were made to move them to the mainland of Sonora, Carrizal was rejected as a possible location "because it is a salty site with a lot of sand and without water." Even though the Seris were not an agricultural people, the Spaniards believed that the area around Pitic (Hermosillo) held out much more hope for a lasting peace settlement. They had to be relocated "onto land best suited to the cultivation of crops. These newly reduced people must be made to understand the importance of living on land that has a water supply."[112] Coahuila followed the same pattern when local Indians were guaranteed a water supply in the Mesilla de Salinas in return for laying down their arms.[113]

It is clear that the water supply exerted a major influence on how people thought, how they earned a living, and how they related to one another in the desert regions of northern New Spain. At the most basic level, water was the single most important factor in the constant struggle between a spartan diet and starvation. But it also penetrated society in many other ways. It was more than a symbol of power. In many cases it was the very incarnation of power. Control of the water supply by Spaniards, whether rural or urban, whether religious or secular, whether civilian or military, was an effective means of preventing the social pyramid from eroding at its base. It helped assure those in power of continued dominance over the Indian population. Had the need for water not made the Indians vulnerable to Spanish domination, the conquerors would have found other means of social and political control, just as they did everywhere from South America to central Mexico, but they were not bound by precedent. Given the nature of the physical environment and the native population encountered, water control seemed most appropriate to the tasks at hand. Certainly it was effective.

In spite of the perceived exigencies of frontier society, the Spaniards did not enjoy total license with respect to water use. In conflict resolution, Spaniards as well as Indians were subjected to the judicial

112. Antonio María de Bucareli to Julian de Arriaga, Jan. 27, 1773, AGI, Audiencia de Guadalajara, 513. Further information is found in Pedro Corbalan to Viceroy, Mar., 1773, AGN, Provincias Internas, Vol. 98, Exp. 1, and Juan Antonio Meave to Pedro Corbalan, Mar. 4, 1773, AGN, Provincias Internas, Vol. 98, Exp. 1.
113. Guillermo Porras Muñoz, *La frontera con los Indios de nueva vizcaya en el siglo xvii* (Mexico: Fomento Cultural Banamex, A.C., 1980), pp. 221–222.

mechanisms of the state. Their familiarity with the system, as well as with those who administered it, gave them a decided advantage when they appeared before the law in water litigation against Indians. But the law itself recognized the problem, and special legislation was enacted not only to afford the Indians protection but to maintain a modicum of equilibrium between the competing interests. The legal system was complex, but it too left social imprints that would not easily be erased.

PART II

Spanish Colonial and Mexican Water Law

CHAPTER 5

Sources of Water Law

Although some aspects of Spanish American legal history have commanded much scholarly attention, little substantive research has been undertaken on the subject of Spanish colonial and early nineteenth-century Mexican water law.[1] Most of the commentary on water law is, in essence, little more than extrapolations from general treatises on Spanish colonial law or adaptations from what we know of land usage and land ownership. Both approaches leave much to be desired. Furthermore, the overwhelming mass of the legal studies are theoretical to a fault. Resting almost entirely upon an examination of the legislation, they do not proceed subsequently to analyze the application of the laws in specific water controversies.

Because of their theoretical focus and methodological limitations, these studies cannot take account of the important maxim *obedezco pero no cumplo*, "I obey but do not comply," an information mechanism by which judges, like other officials, could resist laws considered unjust in a given circumstance and in the process engage in a kind of civil disobedience. The legislation is extremely important, but studies rely-

1. Two of the most useful water studies for New Spain are William B. Taylor's "Land and Water Rights in the Viceroyalty of New Spain," *New Mexico Historical Review* 50 (July, 1975), 189–212, and Greenleaf, "Land and Water," pp. 85–112. Although they are both only summary statements, I have relied on them heavily in the formulation

ing upon it exclusively are not always able to address the central issues and, when they attempt to do so, they are often in error.[2]

The Spanish legal system as we know it today began to develop in the fifth century A.D., shortly after the fall of the Roman Empire. The Iberian Peninsula fell victim to a series of invasions, most from the north (Vandals, Alans, Suevians, and Visigoths) but one extremely important one from the south (the Moors). Each group that entered the peninsula left permanent imprints of its culture, its heritage, and its ethos. It is not surprising then that the system of jurisprudence that emerged in the following centuries was something of an amalgam of Roman, Germanic, and Moorish law. While some of the respective legal contributions were compatible, others clashed with one another.

Spanish regionalism, fostered by cultural differences, poor communication networks, and the fragmentation of geographic isolation, left a strong juridical legacy. Each Iberian region developed its own administrative and judicial customs; these were converted into accepted legal norms by means of the *fueros*, a series of local privileges granted to each area. Local legal autonomy, guaranteed by the fueros, certainly served parochial interests well, but the fragmentation became excessive and worked against any broadly conceived and rational system designed to promote judicial equity and administrative order.

To harmonize and bring some semblance of reason to what had become an unwieldy judicial structure, in the thirteenth century King Alfonso X, a ruler of remarkable intelligence who distinguished himself in science, mathematics, and poetry, ordered that Iberian law be codified. He believed it crucial, if the law was to have meaning, that a basic reference or encyclopedia be compiled. It was to include not only the written law, but legal custom and practice as well. Only if the law were codified could litigants expect uniform and impartial application. Centralizing the legal system, and in the process eliminating many of the regional fueros, became an integral part of the entire process of national unification, which culminated with the emergence of Spain as a nation-state at the end of the fifteenth century. The famous study commissioned by Alfonso X was completed in 1265 under the title of *Las siete partidas*.[3] Initial public reaction was negative

---

2. Examples abound in the documentation. If one reads only the legislation, he could conclude that royal taxes were not diverted by local officials for community projects. If a new acequia had to be constructed as part of a water settlement, the funding would have to be raised locally. In practice, however, the tobacco tax and revenues from other royal monopolies were used for constructing local dams and other waterworks as a part of the settlement of disputes.

3. *Las siete partidas del rey don Alfonso el Sabio*, 4 vols. (Madrid: n.p., 1789).

and sometimes violent as the independent municipalities saw their judicial discretion limited as never before. Gradually the opposition was worn down.

King Alfonso's great codification is not only a reference or compendium for the study of Spanish law, but upon receiving official sanction eighty-three years later under the terms of the Ordenamiento de Alcalá, it became a major source of Spanish law and indeed formed the basis for much of the legal system later to be introduced in the New World. As Helen Clagett noted so perceptively, unlike so many historical antiques the *Siete partidas* "refused to become useless and gather dust."[4]

The preparation of the *Siete partidas* occupied Spain's leading jurisconsults, including the king himself, for the better part of nine years. Although traces of Germanic and Arabic influences are certainly to be found, the study is much more obviously an adaptation of Roman law, especially Justinian's *Corpus Juris Civilis*, and Canon Law to a medieval Iberian reality.[5] It not only compiled and gave order to the huge corpus of Iberian law, but also offered philosophical and theological rationale for legal doctrine. Narrative rather than analytical, it recognized that competition should be kept within reasonable bounds and cooperation should be encouraged. Unlike the Germanic legal tradition, which sought to institutionalize the law of custom, the *Siete partidas* emphasized the universal ideals toward which a just society must strive.

Like any judicial system, the Spanish legal code, within the context of medieval absolutism, concerned itself with balancing the interests of small groups with those of the larger community and with protecting the traditional rights of the individual as well as the newly perceived prerogatives of society. For the first time in Spanish history, clear distinctions were made between public and private property. Property rights were recognized as absolute, *propiedad perfecta*, as long as they did not infringe upon the rights of others, in which case they

---

4. Helen L. Clagett, "Las Siete Partidas," *The Quarterly Journal of the Library of Congress* 22 (Oct., 1965), p. 341.

5. An excellent brief introduction to the evolution of Spanish law is found in Colin M. MacLachlan, *Criminal Justice in Eighteenth-Century Mexico* (Berkeley: University of California Press, 1974), pp. 1–14. A more comprehensive theoretical treatment is contained in Guillermo Floris Margadant S., *Introducción a la historia del derecho mexicano* (Mexico: Universidad Nacional Autónoma de México, 1971). For the actual application of general legal theory to the Mexican scene, the best study is María del Refugio González, *Historia del derecho mexicano* (Mexico: Universidad Nacional Autónoma de México, in press). In her analysis of legal practices in New Spain, Professor González distinguishes between Meso-America and what she calls arid-America or the northern frontier.

were considered *propiedad imperfecta*. Because of the vagaries of nature, dominion over water was considered more temporary than permanent, and its use was subject to the intervention of the state. Water could be owned privately but, in times of need, it was more susceptible than land to what later became known as eminent domain. A man might allow his crops to rot in the field while his neighbor went hungry and contravene no principle of property law, but he could not waste his water if his neighbor's fields were dry.

Because of the disparate invasions of the Iberian Peninsula following the collapse of Rome, the rulers of Spain, long before the discovery of America, were familiar with the problems inherent in trying to reconcile the interests of different races and different cultures, as well as in juxtaposing the demands of conquerors with the concerns of the conquered. Their solutions to the vexing questions of judicial equity found their way into the *Siete partidas*. Although some sections of the *Partidas* were subsequently amended as newer laws were incorporated, the codification itself was never superseded. In matters of both legal theory and judicial practice, the body of law which Spain later used to govern her New World colonies was the direct heir of the *Siete partidas*.

In the late fifteenth and early sixteenth centuries, Spanish legal institutions were transplanted to the American possessions. From the very outset the laws to be followed were those of the Crown of Castile as they had been codified and subsequently amended in the *Siete partidas*. The judicial system seemed appropriate to the task when Spanish possessions in the New World numbered only a few small colonies in the Caribbean. Adaptation of the *Partidas* was not difficult. But by the end of the sixteenth century the frontiers of Spanish dominion had been extended throughout most of South America, all of Central America and Mexico, and part of what later became the United States. Spain found herself in possession of one of the largest empires the world had ever known. Administration of this huge, diverse area became exceedingly complex.

At the macrolegal level, Spanish philosophers and jurisconsults debated lofty notions such as the right of conquest and the application of the Aristotelian doctrine of natural slavery to the Indian population of the New World. But at the microlegal level, specific legislation was needed to incorporate the Indies into the Spanish world, to govern the daily activities of its inhabitants, and to control its economic output. Thousands of unexpected problems arose as Spaniards attempted to define relationships with groups of Indians diverse from one another in language, religion, culture, and legal tradition. Newly conceived schemes to defraud the Crown of its royal income had to be countered. The increasingly large colonial bureaucracy had to be instructed in His Majesty's will. Political officials from the viceroy, at the top of the political hierarchy, to municipal councillors of the cabildo, at the bottom, sent thousands of suggestions to Spain for the resolution of specific problems. The legislation became voluminous.

By the middle of the seventeenth century, almost 400,000 royal pronouncements concerning the New World had been issued by the Royal Council of the Indies and the kings of Spain. Arranged simply in chronological order, these laws were of almost no use. In the resolution of a specific dispute, a royal councillor could always find an applicable law, but it was not always the most appropriate one. Many of the ordinances quickly became obsolete, and countless others were contradictory. Without some systematization the reign of law in the New World became a shambles. As it became increasingly obvious that the legal system was becoming inoperative, the Spanish monarchs ordered a compilation and codification of New World law similar in scope to the famous *Siete partidas*. Commissioned by the Royal Council of the Indies, the project employed some of the best minds in Spain, including Diego de Encinas, Antonio León Pinelo, Juan de Solórzano Pereira, and Fernando Jiménez de Paniagua.[6] The result was the famous *Recopilación de leyes de los reynos de las Indias*, published in four volumes in 1681 (fig. 5.1).[7] The *Recopilación* is the second major source of what legal historians call *derecho indiano*, or the law of the Indies.

Divided into nine books (*libros*), each with chapters (*títulos*) and subsections (*leyes*), the *Recopilación* organizes and reproduces 6,377 laws in force at the time of publication. Each of the laws contains three elements: the title, which in essence is a summary of the law; the monarch under whom the law was enacted and usually where it was enacted; and the text or body of the law itself. Many of the laws have applicability throughout the Spanish American empire, but a few pertain only to specific areas. Although the organization is far from perfect, although there are contradictions even within the codification, and although many of the laws are not expressed with the legal precision lawyers might desire, it is nevertheless a remarkable testament to Spanish jurisprudence and a comprehensive guide to Spanish colonial law. Immediately after publication, two hundred copies were

6. The work of codification and the problems encountered are described meticulously in Juan Manzano, *Historia de las recopilaciones de Indias*, 2 vols. (Madrid: Ediciones Cultura Hispánica, 1956).

7. All quotes from the *Recopilación* are taken from a facsimile edition of the 1681 volume. *Recopilación de leyes de los reynos de las Indias*, 4 vols. (Madrid: Ediciones Cultura Hispánica, 1973).

RECOPILACION
DE LEYES DE LOS REYNOS
DE LAS INDIAS.
MANDADAS IMPRIMIR, Y PVBLICAR
POR LA MAGESTAD CATOLICA DEL REY
DON CARLOS II.
NVESTRO SEÑOR.
VA DIVIDIDA EN QVATRO TOMOS,
con el Indice general, y al principio de cada Tomo el Indice
especial de los titulos, que contiene.

TOMO PRIMERO.

En Madrid: POR IVLIAN DE PAREDES, Año de 1681.

En Madrid: POR EDICIONES CULTURA HISPÁNICA, Año de 1973.

Figure 5.1   Title page of the original edition of the Recopilación, *published in 1681.* Photograph by Helga Teiwes, courtesy Arizona State Museum

sent to New Spain for distribution to the various governmental units. Additional copies could be purchased for thirty pesos.[8]

The *Recopilación* did not pretend to cover all Spanish American legislation. It was much more comprehensive on administrative law than on criminal law. The *Recopilación* was supplemented by other decrees and ordinances, also important sources of colonial law, but these were valid only if they did not contravene the processes set down in the *Recopilación* itself. Laws previously promulgated which ran contrary to the document were considered null and void. Moreover, if proper legal guidance in a specific matter could not be found, the user was directed back to the *Siete partidas* and other laws of the kingdom of Castile.[9]

Spain's imperial experiment in the New World lasted for a century and a half following the publication of the *Recopilación*. Voluminous legislation began to build up once again, but no new colonial codification was completed. Subsequent editions of the *Recopilación* did not contain learned commentary which might have served to bring it up to date. The general laws of Spain, however, were brought together one time more at the beginning of the nineteenth century. The renewed work of legal compilation was entrusted to Juan de la Reguera, who managed to complete a monumental effort in 1805. Consisting of twelve books, the *Novísima recopilación de las leyes de España* is the fundamental source of Spanish law as it existed at the end of the colonial period.[10] Its general application to the Spanish empire in America has never been established to the satisfaction of all legal historians, but it is cited repeatedly in the absence of specific Spanish American legislation on issues of major importance.

Another major source of Spanish colonial law is the five-volume study by Juan de Solórzano Pereira entitled *Política indiana* and published in Latin in 1647.[11] Spain's most distinguished juridical scholar of the seventeenth century, Solórzano had served as an oidor in the audiencia of Lima and subsequently as a member of the Royal Council of the Indies. He had worked on the *Recopilación*, but his treatise on Spanish jurisprudence is so magisterial in conception and compelling in logic that it has become a basic source of Spanish law. The teachings

---

8. Ernst Schäfer, *El Consejo Real y Supremo de las Indias*, 2 vols. (Seville: Imp. M. Carmona, 1935), I, 319.

9. *Recopilación*, Libro II, Título 1, Ley 3.

10. *Novísima recopilación de las leyes de España*, 6 vols. (Mexico: Galván, 1831).

11. Juan de Solórzano Pereira, *Política indiana*, 5 vols. (Madrid: Compañía Ibero-Americana de Publicaciones, 1930).

of other "masters" of Roman law and canon law were also fundamental sources, but none approached the stature of Solórzano's great work.

Specific ordinances and royal decrees (*autos, bandos, pragmáticas, cédulas,* and *decretos*) and a variety of commissioned studies must be consulted, as they too are basic sources of Spanish law. The large number of these documents precludes simple recapitulation. They have never been compiled in a single source, but they are available in the Spanish and Mexican archives.[12] An extensive sampling was published in three volumes in nineteenth-century Mexico by Juan N. Rodríguez de San Miguel under the title of *Pandectas hispano-mexicanas.*[13]

Three of these documents, none of which are included in the *Pandectas*, are of utmost importance to the history of Spanish colonial water law. First are the regulations for water measurement prepared by Lasso de la Vega in 1761 and endorsed and circulated by the viceroy of New Spain, Joaquín Monserrat, the Marqués de Cruillas.[14] These regulations are the most comprehensive statement of water practice and water law to be found in any colonial documentation. The second of these important sources is the set of detailed instructions given to northern judicial officials in 1786.[15] They specify how water law was intended to be implemented and how disputes were intended to be resolved. Finally, the Plan de Pitic, the founding document for the town of Hermosillo, is of transcendent theoretical importance as it states specifically that the provisions it contains (including the water provisions) are to have applicability not only in the town that prompted its promulgation, but throughout the provincias internas.[16]

Local legislation is every bit as important as royal legislation as a source of water law. At the theoretical level all local laws had to be ratified by the Crown. This process understandably was slow and cumbersome. As a practical matter the laws went into effect as soon as they were issued by the municipal cabildo or the provincial governor.

12. Voluminous legislation for certain topics, such as mining, was codified, but never the ordinances relating specifically to water law.

13. The most recent edition, Juan N. Rodríguez de San Miguel, *Pandectas hispano-mexicanas*, 3 vols. (Mexico: Universidad Nacional Autónoma de México, 1980), contains a superb introduction by María del Refugio González.

14. "Reglamento General de las Medidas de las Aguas," in Mariano Galván Rivera, *Ordenanzas de tierras y aguas: O sea formulario geometrico-judicial* (Mexico: n.p., 1849).

15. Instruccion que deberan guardar las Justicias Subalternas de esta Yntendencia y Govierno por lo respectibo a la Administracion . . . y gobierno politico y economico de q^e depende el aumento y felicidad de los Pueblos, May 20, 1786, AHP, Reel 1787a.

16. Plan de Pitic, AGN, Tierras, Vol. 2773, Exp. 22, and Año de 1796, Californias, UT WBS 9.

Most were never ratified by higher authority, but they remained in force nevertheless. In practice only a denial of ratification by the Crown invalidated them. Royal invalidation of local legislation did occur, but infrequently.

In the last analysis the most revealing, but least studied, source of colonial water law in the Mexican north is not the legislation (either royal or local) but the water cases themselves. Buried innocuously in diverse sections of a dozen archives, these litigations are the only reliable record of what the law meant when it finally filtered down to the lives of people who found themselves engaged in water conflict. The conclusions one might draw from a single water case are precarious, as aberrations did occur. Studied in the aggregate, however, they offer reliable testimony on both water law and water practice.

It would be difficult to overemphasize the role of law in the Spanish administrative system. It dominated all other functions of government. Legislation was, of course, important, but it was the interpretation of this legislation, a judicial function, that gave the Spanish empire in America its unique contours. The emphasis on judicial solutions to the problems of government was so strong that a leading scholar of Spanish administration on the New World, J. H. Parry, concluded: "The principal task of government was considered to be that of adjudication between competing interests, rather than that of deliberately planning and constructing a new society."[17] The planning and construction of a New World society did take place, but it occurred as an outgrowth of the judicial preoccupations that the Spanish Crown considered paramount to the role of government.

17. J. H. Parry, *The Spanish Seaborne Empire* (New York: Alfred A. Knopf, 1967), p. 194.

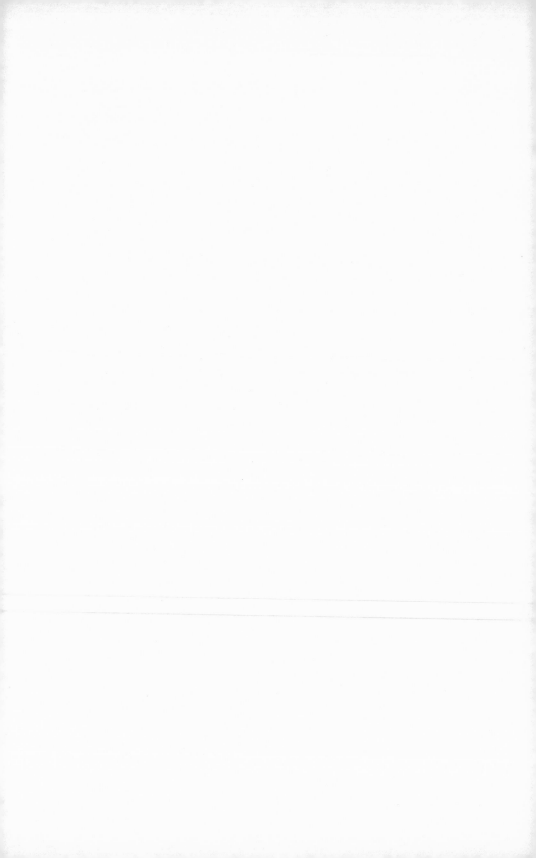

CHAPTER 6

The Legal Relationship of Land to Water

Spanish conquerors, explorers, and settlers had been in Mexico for more than 160 years before the first copy of the *Recopilación* arrived. During that initial period, notions of water rights and land-water relationships gradually evolved, based on the officials' best under-standing of what Spanish jurisprudence entailed, on what local condi-tions seemed to dictate, and on ordinances recently arrived from Spain. Those colonial officials in Mexico best versed in Spanish law found little to surprise them when the first copies of the *Recopilación* were distributed. In most respects the codification was in complete harmony with the *Siete partidas,* Solórzano Pereira's *Política indiana,* subsequent Spanish law, and their contemporary application in New Spain. The main beneficiaries were those who were not well ac-quainted with the legal tradition and who did not know where to look for legal guidance.

The arrival of the Spaniards in Mexico in the early sixteenth century did not occasion any immediate large seizure of Indian land. In the 1520s, 1530s, and 1540s, Mexico held out promises of quick wealth more lucrative than land: native treasure, mining production, and Indian labor. But in the second half of the sixteenth century the situation changed. The original booty was gone, and the catastrophic decline in native population left previously occupied lands vacant and reduced the potential revenues to be derived from Indian labor. The acquisition of land, therefore, assumed a new importance, and the Spaniards availed themselves of various means, both legal and illegal, of securing control. The crassest method was simply usurpation—the forceful take-over of native property. In most cases, however, legal niceties were followed and the land was acquired by purchase or grant, an action sometimes preceded by the resettlement of Indians into *congregaciones*. These new communities of Indians were initiated theoretically to facilitate their conversion. They were significant in land acquisition history because the lands previously occupied by the groups, often very good lands with a ready water supply, were left vacant and became *realengos* (royal lands) or *baldíos* (vacant or public lands).[1] Spanish land acquisition under the congregación policy became such an abuse that King Philip II ordered it stopped in 1560.

The most controversial aspect of early Spanish colonial land policy, and the one which would subsequently precipitate not only historical debate but also much litigation, was the decision to extend to certain individuals the right to make land grants to deserving colonists. As early as 1523 Hernán Cortés, as governor of New Spain, was given this right.[2] Not long afterward, others, including the audiencia, viceroys, various governors, and alcaldes mayores, possessed it as well. Even newly established communities were empowered to make land grants to the recently arrived and to the already established citizens who wanted more. By the late eighteenth century, individual presidio commanders in the Southwest had been given the power to make grants of land.[3] Once all of the legal provisions of the land grant were met, it could be revoked only in the most unusual of circumstances. The land was private property to be passed on to the heirs of the grantee.[4]

The original land grants (*mercedes*) were theoretically of two types: *peonías* (about twenty acres or the amount that one man would work in one day) for the conquering foot soldiers, and *caballerías* (about one hundred and five acres) for the noblemen.[5] In practice, however, because land seemed so plentiful and few Spanish settlers considered themselves less than noble, the peonía was rarely used in New Spain.

1. The congregaciones are examined in Howard F. Cline,"Civil Congregations of the Indians of New Spain, 1598–1601," *Hispanic American Historical Review* 29 (Aug., 1949), 349–396.

2. *Novísima recopilación*, Libro 3, Título 5, Ley 1.

3. The authorization to the presidio commanders came in a dispatch from Commandant General Pedro de Nava on March 22, 1791. Quoted in Leonidas Hamilton, *Mexican Law: A Compilation of Mexican Legislation* (San Francisco: n.p., 1882), pp. 99–100.

4. See G. Micheal Riley, *Fernando Cortes and the Marquesado in Morelos, 1522–1547* (Albuquerque: University of New Mexico Press, 1973), pp. 57–58.

5. José M. Ots Capdequí, *El régimen de la tierra en América Española durante el Período Colonial* (Ciudad Trujillo: Universidad de Santo Domingo, 1946), pp. 61–64.

By the middle of the sixteenth century, the most common pattern that emerged was for an individual to be granted a *vecindad*, which consisted generally of a lot upon which to build a house, a garden area, two or three caballerías of harvest land, and some pasture land.[6] A common feature in many grants was the proviso that the land should be cultivated within a year and should not be allowed to lie fallow for more than four consecutive years. Flagrant violation could prompt revocation of the grant.

The early Spanish land grants in Mexico did not automatically contain water rights. This fact did not prevent the owners from irrigating their land. They did so illegally, however, realizing that if their water use was brought into question, they could later acquire water rights by grant, purchase, or various other means.[7] In the early postconquest period, for example, thirty-two settlers at Celaya were awarded vecindades. Later, water for irrigation was added to their grants.[8] This situation was not unique, although sometimes many years passed before water rights were added.

The reasons for not automatically extending water rights with land grants reflected long-established Iberian water traditions. Water had to be carefully regulated in the interest of the entire community. Land grants in medieval Spain were made granting irrigation rights (*terre in regadivo*) or withholding them (*terre in seccano*).[9] The *Siete partidas* stated that water was the thing man could least do without. Therefore, following the principles set forth in the Code of Justinian, it could be used in common by all persons for certain purposes: drinking, fishing, navigation, docking and repairing of boats, and unloading of merchandise. No special permission was needed for these activities. Significantly, water for irrigation or for harnessing its motive energy for industrial purposes was not included in the category of common use of water.[10] The *Siete partidas* did address the question of irrigation, as the issue was of major significance in arid Iberia. But water in large amounts, such as for irrigation or for powering mills, could not be treated as any other water "because it

6. The most comprehensive discussion of Spanish land policy in New Spain is contained in François Chevalier, *La Formation des grands domaines au Mexique: Terre et société aux XVIe–XVIIe siècles* (Paris: 1952). The English condensation without the copious footnotes was published under the title *Land and Society in Colonial Mexico* (Berkeley: University of California Press, 1970).

7. The acquisition of water rights is discussed in chapter 7.

8. Chevalier, *La Formation des grands domaines*, p. 63.

9. Thomas F. Glick, *Irrigation and Society and Medieval Valencia* (Cambridge, Mass.: Harvard University Press, 1970), p. 13.

10. Partida 3, Título 28, Leyes 3 and 6.

would not be wise that the benefit of all men be hindered by the interest of some individuals."[11] The same distinction between kinds of water was made in New Spain. Lasso de la Vega's water regulations were clear:

> . . . because all public rivers are, as a matter of fact, for public and common use, it should not be presumed that they are public and common with regard to their flow; they can be used publicly only for personal domestic needs.[12]

The decision to extend or withhold water rights in a land grant was generally a calculated one. Water use was defined in relationship to land classification, and there were many different classifications of land. At the time of its discovery of the New World, the Spanish Crown declared its ownership of all the land in the Indies. Book III, Title I, Law I of the *Recopilación* states:

> By grant of the Apostolic Holy See[13] and other just and legitimate titles, we are Lords of the West Indies, Islands and Tierra Firme of the Ocean Sea, discovered and to be discovered, and these are incorporated in our Royal Crown of Castile. And because it is our will and because we have promised and judged it fitting these lands shall always remain united for their maximum perpetuity and strength, we prohibit their alienation.[14]

Juan de Solórzano Pereira stated the same phenomenon even more clearly in his classic study, *Política indiana:*

> Except for the lands, meadows, pastures, woodlands and waters that by particular concession and grant have been made . . . all the rest of this land, and especially that which is yet to be plowed and cultivated, is and should be of the Royal Crown and Dominion.[15]

Land, water, and mineral wealth were all part of the royal patrimony and could be alienated from Crown ownership only by the Crown itself or by properly designated authority. (*Idque a Principe conceditur alii nulli competit jus aque dandae.*) If the royal patrimony were

11. Partida 3, Título 28, Ley 8. Spanish American water law still distinguishes between water for domestic purposes, such as human consumption or bathing, and water for industrial or irrigation purposes. See Ana Hederra Donoso, *Comentarios al código de aguas* (Santiago: Editorial Jurídica de Chile, 1960), pp. 3–4.

12. "Reglamento General de las Medidas de las Aguas," in Galván Rivera, *Ordenanzas de tierras y aguas,* p. 159.

13. This is a reference to the papal bulls of Pope Alexander VI made in 1493: *Intercaetera* and *Dudum Siguidem.*

14. *Recopilación,* Libro III, Título 1, Ley 1.

15. *Política indiana,* Libro VI, Capítulo 12, numero 3.

not alienated or privatized in some way, it was considered to be for the benefit of all. Book IV, Title 17, Law 5 of the *Recopilación* speaks to this point:

> We have ordered that the pastures, woodlands, and waters shall be held in common in the Indies ... and this shall be observed wherever there shall be no title or authority from ourselves by which a different disposition be made.[16]

Generally consistent with the *Siete partidas*, water on Crown lands (realengos) in New Spain could be used for certain purposes by the public: for drinking, bathing, recreation, and even for watering domesticated animals. Spanish citizens were well aware that no special permission was needed for these domestic uses, and in their correspondence they made the proper distinctions between irrigation water and common or domestic water.[17] A map of the water system at the Presidio de Santa Rosa in the jurisdiction of Coahuila (fig. 6.1) indicates the important legal distinction made on the basis of land classification. The six acequias running through the settlement were designed for domestic usage, and no permission was needed to draw water from them. The two acequias outside the presidio were for irrigation purposes, and it was necessary for water rights to be conveyed to the individual users. But water law in northern New Spain was not an exact replica of the system defined centuries earlier in the mother country. Adaptation to a different reality placed new restrictions even on the use of common water. In Spain anyone could fish in public waters, but in eighteenth-century Texas special permission was needed.[18] Similar restrictions were placed on free navigation of rivers. Persons in early nineteenth-century Texas who wanted to initiate a canoe charter service on several Texas rivers found out that they, too, required special authorization.[19]

There were no riparian rights for agricultural or industrial uses in

---

16. *Recopilación*, Libro IV, Título 17, Ley 5.

17. A 1731 document from Texas, for example, claims that the right to a certain water source was not only for domestic use but also for irrigation: "para gozar sus benefisios tanto en las tierras de labor en las casas." Juan Leal Goras to Juan Antonio Perez de Almazan, July 27, 1731, AGN, Provincias Internas, Vol. 163, Exp. 3. The distinction between common water and irrigation water is corroborated in Joseph W. McKnight, "The Spanish Heritage in Texas Law," (Address to the Dallas Historical Society, May 6, 1970), reprinted in *El Companario* 4 (Sep., 1973), p. 2.

18. Bartolomé Rosales to Governor Manuel Muñoz, Mar., 1791?, BA, Reel 21; Man¹ Flores de Valdes to Governor Muñoz, Feb., 17, 1791, BA, Reel 24; Governor Muñoz to Flores de Valdes, Feb. 17, 1791, BA, Reel 24; Félix Herrera to Governor Muñoz, Nov., 1793, BA, Reel 24.

19. Nemesio Salcedo to Antonio Cordero, Mar. 6, 1809, BA, Reel 40.

New Spain. The grant of a piece of land fronting on a river entitled the owner, without additional authorization, to use the water for domestic purposes, but for nothing else. The water was still royal patrimony to be disposed of at the discretion of the Crown or its designated authorities. The only automatic alienation of water with a land grant was for water that originated on the piece of land. A spring or a well became the property of the owner of the land where it rose, a tradition deeply engrained in medieval Spanish water law.[20] The distinct ownership pattern between surface and subsurface water is not easy to explain. Water originating from rain was considered common property,[21] but knowledge of aquifers was very rudimentary. Maybe the water in springs and wells came from subterranean sources; maybe it had just always been there; the supply certainly seemed limitless.[22] There was little or no appreciation that underground water also originated from precipitation, or that depleting an underground reserve on a given piece of property could have a direct impact on the water supply of a neighbor. Given this imperfect understanding, a person could pump water from a well or channel spring water to his fields without special permission. The only limitation on the use of water originating on private property was that it could not be used maliciously simply to deny its access to a neighbor.[23]

Relatively few water disputes emerged on Crown land because the concept of royal patrimony was well understood. Water conflict was much more recurrent on land that was held by a community or by private individuals. Land could be alienated from the Crown to community or private ownership in various ways and in different degrees of privatization. Some realengos were simply deeded to new towns in the founding document of the new community. These lands passed from Crown ownership to communal ownership as they became *tierras*

---

20. Burns, "Irrigation Taxes in Early Mudejar Valencia," p. 561.

21. "Las cosas que comunalmente pertenecen a todas las criaturas que biuen en este mundo, son estas; el ayre, e las aguas de la lluuia, e el mar, e su ribera. Ca qualquier criatura que biua, puede usar de cada vna destas cosas, segun quel fuere menester." Partida 3, Título 28, Ley 3.

22. In 1674 French scientist Pierre Perrault established that springs were fed by earthly precipitation, not by some wondrous subterranean source, but the discovery never quite caught up to Spanish jurisprudence.

23. Partida 3, Título 32, Ley 19. The clearest definition of subsoil water rights is contained in Escriche's legislative dictionary. "El propietario de una heredad puede disponer á su arbitrio del agua de una fuente que nace en ella, y desviarla de la heredad de su vecino por donde solia pasar; porque el manantial hace parte del fundo en que nace, y pertenece por tanto en propiedad al dueño de este. Mas deberá decirse lo contrario, si el propietario del fondo en que está el manantial no apartase o mudase el curso del agua en beneficio suyo sino solo por hacer mal a su vecino. . . ." Escriche, *Diccionario razonado de legislación*, p. 408.

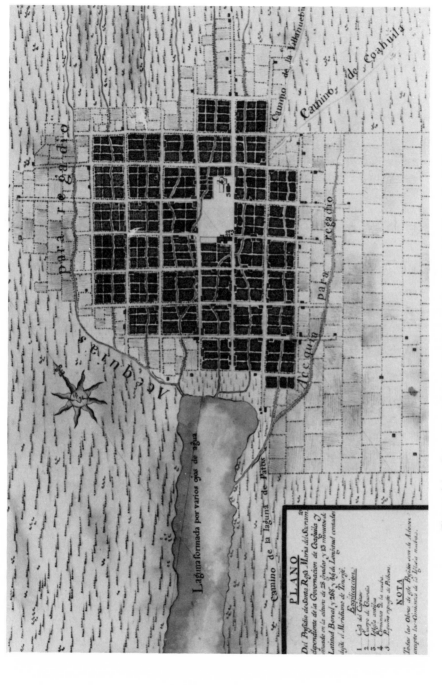

Figure 6.1   Domestic and agricultural acequias at the Presidio de Santa Rosa. By permission of the British Library, courtesy Arizona State Museum

concegiles, administered by the local governing body for the pueblo as a whole. Part of the tierras concegiles was retained as common land for the benefit of the entire population, part of it was retained for the future growth of the community, and part of it was privatized as it passed legally into the hands of individual settlers. The water on land held by the community, as water on royal land, was for communal use and was administered by the cabildo, which exercised the corporate right. It could be used for domestic purposes and, at least on some occasions, to irrigate a farm plot held by the town in common.[24] Individuals, however, could not use this common water to irrigate their private fields. The *Recopilación* provided for a fine of 5,000 pesos of gold for persons who used Crown water or common water for personal gain.[25] When Lasso de la Vega prepared his *General Regulation for the Measurement of Water*, he reiterated that "no one without permission of the prince can conduct public waters to his lands for irrigation, especially in this New Spain."[26] This important provision was enforced throughout northern New Spain, and there are examples of fines and arrests for those who broke the law.[27]

The Spanish legal system provided different classifications of private land ownership. Cattle ranchers, for example, could receive a *merced* for a *sitio de ganado mayor* (approximately 4,338 acres), or sheep raisers a *sitio de ganado menor* (approximately 1,928 acres), but generally only a small percentage (a few *caballerías* of 105 acres each) would be designated as *labores* or *labranzas* (small agricultural plots).[28] There are examples of grazing grants permitting the owner to irrigate as much of the land as the available water permitted, but these cases are extremely rare and probably reflect inordinate influence on the part

---

24. Francisco Domínguez y Company states that common land held by the village could not be cultivated. In northern New Spain, however, it was often cultivated. See Domínguez y Company, "Funcciones económicas del cabildo colonial Hispano-americano," in Altamira y Crevea, *Historia municipal,* pp. 165–167.

25. *Recopilación,* Libro IV, Título 17, Ley 5.

26. "Reglamento General de las Medidas de Agua," in Galván Rivera, *Ordenanzas,* p. 158.

27. See, for example, Autos e ynformacionez echas contra Fran[co] Montes alias el Pintor de Nacion Pima, a pedim[to] del el comun pueblo de Cucurpe, Año de 1723, AHP, Reel 1723B, and Auto del Alcalde Mayor Francisco Bueno de Bohorques y Concuera, Santa Fe, July 16, 1720, SANM, II, 317a.

28. Medidas de tierras y modo de medirlas que estan en uso segun las ordenanzas, AGN, Archivo Histórico de Hacienda, Temporalidades, Leg. 1165. Smaller càttle and sheep ranches were called *criaderos de ganado mayor* (1,084 acres) and *criaderos de ganado menor* (864 acres), and they too contained only a small percentage of cropland. See, as an example, Amparo de posesion de tierras a favor de Joseph de Torres y Vergara, Nov. 12, 1717, AGN, Mercedes, Vol. 70, Fol. 52.

of the petitioner.[29] More common is a huge grant made to Joseph Eugenio de la Garza Falcón in Coahuila in 1734. Garza Falcón was awarded 113 sitios de ganado mayor (490,194 acres), but only eight caballerías (840 acres)—a minuscule percentage—carried water rights.[30] The Jesuit hacienda of Tabaloapa in Chihuahua embraced fourteen and three-quarters sitios (almost 64,000 acres), but only six caballerías (630 acres), or less than one percent, were cropland.[31] Smaller grazing grants permitted a slightly higher percentage of the land to be irrigated, but seldom did this right exceed five to ten percent of the total acreage. The same general criteria applied to the large communal grants, whether they be Spanish towns or Indian pueblos. For example, when the Tlaxcalan Indians were given land and water for the new community of San Estéban de la Nueva Tlaxcala in the district of Saltillo, they received three square leagues of land (13,014 acres) of which twenty caballerías (2,100 acres) were designated as labores.[32] This was an unusually generous grant of irrigated cropland and no doubt reflects the favorable position which the Tlaxcalans enjoyed throughout the colonial period because of their assistance to the Spaniards during the conquest and subsequent pacification of New Spain.[33] The more common pattern was for a pueblo in the north to receive about one square league with five or fewer caballerías designated as labores.

In making land grants and determining water usage, distinctions were made on the nature of the request and the land usage intent of the granting agency. The *Recopilación*, in law after law, is very clear on the distinct classification of land. For example, Book IV, Title 7, Law 14 distinguishes between *tierras de pasto* (pasture) and *labor* (cropland); Book IV, Title 12, Law 8 distinguishes between *tierras* (lands) and *tierras para ingenios* (land for mills); Book IV, Title 12, Law 13 makes a distinction between *tierras que hiviere de regadio* (irrigation land) and

29. V Exᵃ aprueba las diligᵃˢ . . . al Regᵒʳ Dn Franᶜᵒ Manˡ de la Puente, Apr. 11, 1752, AGN, Mercedes, Vol. 76, Fol. 154.

30. Confirma la composicion de las tierras que se espresan hecha por el Señor Juez Privativo de Ventas y composiciones, Sep. 18, 1734, AGN, Mercedes, Vol. 73, Fol. 99. Subsequent grants made to the Garza Falcón family increased their water rights on the Sabinas River. See Harris, *A Mexican Family Empire,* p. 9.

31. H. Bradley Benedict, "The Sale of the Hacienda of Tabaloapa: A Case Study of Jesuit Property Redistribution in Mexico, 1771–1781," *The Americas* 32 (Oct., 1975), p. 177.

32. Thomas de Uribe Bracamonte to Sor Fiscal, Dec. 20, 1702, AGN, Tierras, Vol. 1427, Exp. 13.

33. Tlaxcalan colonization in Coahuila can be traced in part in Testimonio de Autos Fhos sobre Providencias y Conberziones de la Provinzia de Coaguila, Año de 1712, AGI, Audiencia de Guadalajara, 142.

tierras de ganados (cattle land). Differing land classifications are perhaps most apparent in Book VI, Title 3, Law 8, which stipulates that
when towns are founded they should have water, land, and cropland.
If these land distinctions were made only in the *Recopilación* or in other
royal statutes, one could well question their validity as operative principles. But the same distinctions appear repeatedly in actual grants of
land and in the resolution of specific disputes throughout northern
New Spain. A few examples will suffice.

A 1649 water dispute pitted the Indians of Santa Cruz del Río
Nazas (in present-day Durango) against the owner of a neighboring
cattle hacienda. The details of that case are not of great importance
here, but the settlement made clear distinctions between land and
irrigation land.[34] The land grant made to Sandía Pueblo in New
Mexico in 1747 distinguished between land and cropland.[35] A land
inheritance case in the upper Río Grande valley of New Mexico in
1772 made the necessary distinction between cropland and unplowed
land.[36] The land grant to the Canary Islanders who settled San
Antonio, Texas, was equally clear that some of the grant was for tierras
de regadío and some for tierras de pasto.[37]

The different classifications of land ownership are extremely important to Spanish colonial water law because some of them carried
water privileges while others did not. The grants of a sitio de ganado
mayor or a sitio de ganado menor did not carry water rights for
irrigation or industrial purposes. The same is true for smaller grazing
grants or *tierras de agostadero*. When Bartolomé Lobato asked for a
grant of grazing land in 1714, he requested that water rights be
included with it.[38] He was awarded the grant, but the water was to
remain common water.[39] In most cases, those requesting grazing land
knew that they could not receive water rights with it and asked for the
land only for the purposes of grazing their herds.[40] The grants them-

34. Santa Cruz del Rio Nazas contra Don Phelipe de la Cueba Montano, July 12, 1649,
AHP, Reel 1653B.

35. Viceroy Count Revillagigedo to Governor Codallos y Rabal, Mar. 16, 1747, SANM,
I, 1347.

36. Juana Benavides to Ignacio Alori, Mar. 23, 1772, SANM, I, 45.

37. Real Despacho. D. Juan de Acuña, Marqués de Casafuerte, Mar. 12, 1731, AGN,
Provincias Internas, Vol. 163, Exp. 3.

38. Bartolomé Lobato to Governor Juan Ygnacio Flores Mogollón, 1714, SANM, I,
433.

39. Merced to Lobato from Governor Flores Mogollón, Aug. 27, 1714, SANM, I, 433.

40. Examples abound throughout northern New Spain. See, for example, Ignacio
Roybal to Governor, n.d., SANM, I, 1339; Edmund Quirk to Lieutenant Governor,
May 13, 1803, BA, Reel 31; Nemesio Salcedo to Antonio Cordero, June 3, 1806, BA,
Reel 34; Juan Ant° Saucedo to Muy Illstre Ayntam^to, Nov. 8, 1823, BA, Reel 75;

selves, on occasion, specified that water rights were not included. The 1768 grant from New Mexico Governor Pedro Fermín de Mendinueta to Baltasar Baca, for example, read in part, "and this grant I do make to father and son in equal shares, for them and their successors, for the pasturage of their herds of stock, and not in any case for planting. . ."[41] The more common pattern, however, was for the grant to indicate simply that it was made for the purpose of grazing.[42] No mention of planting or irrigation water is made and therefore no water rights can be properly implied. Grants of a sitio de ganado mayor or de ganado menor did often specify that watering holes (*aguajes*) for the cattle, horses, mules, or sheep were included within the grant. When Mariano de la Riva was awarded a sitio de ganado mayor in Baja California in 1769, his grant read that he had been awarded a square league "so that he and his successors would possess and enjoy it with all of its pastures, watering holes, paths, entrances, and exits."[43] The phraseology was the same in the Baja California grazing grant made to Cristóbal Geraldo the following year,[44] and similar phrases appear in grazing grants authorized elsewhere in northern New Spain.[45] The inclusion of watering holes was simply a formality, because Spanish law provided that animals could be watered without special permission in common water. Some grazing grants did not specify that they included watering holes,[46] but this oversight did not result in controversy. The law was clear.

The question of water rights on grants of farmland is not so easily

---

Expediente formado por Dn Francisco de la Fuente, vecino de la villa de Saltillo, sobre que sele despache titulo de confirmacion de unas tierras, 1789, AGN, Tierras, Vol. 1186, Exp. 2.

41. Myra Jenkins, "The Baltasar Baca Grant," *El Palacio* 68 (Spring, 1961), p. 55.

42. Merced to Ignacio Roybal from Marques de la Nava de Brazinas, Governor and Captain General of New Mexico, Mar. 4, 1704, SANM, I, 1339.

43. Consesion del sitio de ganado mayor nombrado Palmarrito, sito en la Jurisdiccion de Todos Santos hecha por el Real Visitador Conde de José de Galves a favor de Mariano de la Riva, Apr. 8, 1769, AHBCS, Leg. 2, Doc. 9.

44. Consesion del sitio de ganado mayor nombrado Angel de la Guarda sito en el municipalidad de San Antonio hecha por el juez privativo de tierras, Don Manuel García Morales a favor de Cristobal Geraldo, Feb. 3, 1770, AHBCS, Leg. 2, Doc. 23.

45. VE Aprueba y confirma la merced ynserta hecha al Capitan Don Thomas de la Garza Falcón, Feb. 1, 1707, AGN, Mercedes, Vol. 74, fols. 109–110.

46. Examples are found in Concesion del sitio de ganado mayor nombrado San Simon sito en la municipalidad de San Antonio hecha en 22 de Mayo de 1789 por el Sargento teniente de justicia y comisionado de D. Luis López a favor de Juan de la Crus y Osio, AHBCS, Leg. 2, Doc. 98, and Concesion del Sitio de Ganado Mayor nombrado San Bernardo sito en la municipalidad de Sr. José del Cabo hecha en 11 de Noviembre de 1800 por el gobernador D. José Joaquín de Arrillaga a favor de Juan Antonio Lucero, AHBCS, Ley 2, 153.

resolved. Many farm grants were made with a provision that they carried with them the water necessary for their cultivation. The land grants made to the founders of San Antonio, Texas, for example, specified that "within the limits of their suerte . . . they will enjoy the benefits of the waters from the . . . Arroyo and Rio San Antonio."[47]

Those persons most knowledgeable about the Spanish legal system specifically requested that water rights be extended with their farm land. When Joseph Ramón de Noriega requested a land grant in Baja California in 1770, he asked that irrigation rights be extended with it.[48] Similarly, in 1671 Juan González, a citizen of Saltillo, asked for two caballerías of land and specified that he be granted "the merced including the water contained on that land."[49] In early nineteenth-century Texas, José Antonio Saucedo asked that favorable action be taken on "the land and water" he asked for in his petition,[50] and José Manuel Granados asked that he be awarded "two days' water right" with his land grant.[51] Others specifically asked that grants of water be added to their farming grants. If all necessary requirements were met, the requests would be honored.[52]

The problem to be addressed, however, is that in innumerable cases, water is not mentioned in the grant of farmland nor is it subsequently added by other kind of legislative or judicial action. In her study of Spanish water law in Texas, Betty Dobkins argues against an implied right: "Spanish law did not simply assume that waters were granted with the land."[53] But others disagree. In his examination of several thousand land grants made in central and southern Mexico during the second half of the sixteenth and early seventeenth centuries, William Taylor found that the majority of them did not contain explicit water provisions. Because of this fact and other information, Taylor concluded that "land ownership carried with it an implied right to available water."[54] My own reading of the documentation suggests

47. Real Despacho, D. Juan de Acuña, Marques de Casafuerte, Mar. 12, 1731, AGN, Provincias Internas, Vol. 163, Exp. 3.

48. Joseph Ramón de Noriega to Juez Comisionado de Tierras y Poblaciones, Mar. 15, 1770, AHBCS, Leg. 2, Doc. 24.

49. Fernando de Villanueva to Governor, Apr. 4, 1671, AGN, Tierras, Vol. 1427, Exp. 13.

50. Juan José Hernandes, Mig.ᵗ Arciniega, and Ramón Musquiz to Ayuntamiento [de Béxar], Jan. 8, 1824, BA, Reel 76.

51. José Manuel Granados to Jefe Político, Dec. 27, 1823, BCA, MR–S.

52. Merced to Capⁿ Diego Arias de Quiros by Governor Juan Ygnacio Flores Mogollón, July 30, 1715, SANM, I, 8.

53. Dobkins, *The Spanish Element in Texas Water Law*, p. 130.

54. Taylor, "Land and Water Rights," p. 207.

that there is certain merit in Professor Taylor's hypothesis, but to be useful it requires some qualification. Certainly there was no implied right to water in the grazing grants, the sitios de ganado mayor, de ganado menor, and tierras de agostadero. Equally certain is that in the grants made to a community (either Spanish or Indian), some of the land was designated as pasture land, and some as woodland. There was no implied grant of water for these lands. Even the case of farmland must be qualified.

The Spanish legal system recognized at least three kinds of farm-land: *tierras de pan sembrar; tierras de pan coger*; and *tierras de pan llevar*. The first classification causes no definitional problem: tierras de pan sembrar were clearly designated for dryland farming. On occasion they are also labeled as *tierras de trigo de aventurero*. As the phrase itself suggests, only the most adventurous would bother to plant on them. These farmlands carried no water right.[55]

Tierras de pan coger, more commonly called *tierras de temporal* in the documentation for northern New Spain, have precipitated much legal debate, as they have been defined in different ways. Virtually all scholars agree that these lands are dependent upon the rainy season (the *temporal*) for their water source. But their legal susceptibility to irrigation has caused controversy. Some legal historians have defined them as "not irrigable," others as "not requiring irrigation," and still others (perhaps misinterpreting the word temporal) as "temporarily irrigable."[56] Although the documentation is far from clear on this matter, the evidence at least suggests strongly that they are not legally irrigable. I have seen no actual land grants which indicate that they are intended to be irrigated, and at least some land grants imply strongly that they are not irrigable. In 1768, for example, Salvador de Castro was awarded two suertes of land, one of them designated as *de riego*, or irrigated land, and the other as *de temporal*.[57] If tierras de temporal were intended to be irrigated, the distinction in the grant would have been meaningless.[58] Similarly, an 1824 Texas document

---

55. The Spanish Royal Academy dictionary defines *trigo de aventurero* in Mexico as meaning grain grown on unirrigated land. Real Academia Española, *Diccionario de la lengua española* (Madrid: Editorial Espasa Calpe, S.A., 1970), p. 147.

56. An excellent discussion of this problem is found in Dobkins. *The Spanish Element in Texas Water Law*, pp. 124–127. Dobkins concludes that tierras de temporal are arable land which could be irrigated following rains. I presume she is speaking of lands that, following rains, might be physically irrigable but not necessarily legally irrigable.

57. Concesion . . . a favor de Joseph Salvador de Castro, Nov. 8, 1768, AHBCS, Leg. 2, Doc. 13.

58. In their book on agriculture in Mesoamerica, Angel Palerm and Eric Wolf also distinguish between "agricultura de temporal o secano y de regadio." *Agricultura y civilización*, p. 26.

describing José de Sandoval's land and water rights states that "in addition he also held temporal land."[59] The issue is more clearly addressed in article 13 of the Plan de Pitic, which states that tierras de temporal "do not enjoy the benefit" of the acequia.[60]

The most authoritative source on land and water classifications, Manuel Galván Rivera, specifies only tierras de pan llevar as irrigable.[61] Nothing in the *Recopilación*, subsequent ordinances, judicial decisions, or land grants leads one to believe that Galván Rivera was incorrect. Although tierra de pan llevar has sometimes been defined as wheatland, it is more properly defined as irrigable land.[62] The first constitutional legislature of the state of Chihuahua, enacting ordinances for the new political entity, agreed with Galván Rivera and defined only tierra de pan llevar as irrigable.[63]

In the three major classifications of cropland, it is safe to assume that the implied water right can be extended only to tierras de pan llevar.[64] When Manuel Castillo asked the governor of Texas for "un terreno de pan llevar"[65] he was asking for both land and water. If he was granted a piece of tierra de pan llevar, even if water was not specified, the implication is strong that he was granted the water that went with it.

Although this refinement of the implied right to water helps in some cases, in numerous others it does not, as none of the three legal classifications of cropland is mentioned, nor is water specified. In many small grants the land awarded is classified as suertes or as labores (or labranzas). The suerte, a garden plot, was theoretically

59. Gaspar Flores to José de Sandoval, Dec. 31, 1824, BCA, MR 63.

60. Plan de Pitic, UT WBS 9. Article 13 states: ". . . formara el Comisionado un prudente calculo de todo terreno util y fructifero que por medio de la Azequia contruida puede regarse y del restante que sin tener este beneficio conduze aproposito para siembras y Cosechas de Temporal. . . ."

61. Galván Rivera, *Ordenanzas de tierras y aguas,* p. 91.

62. François Chevalier translates *pan llevar* as wheatland. See his *Land and Society in Colonial Mexico,* p. 66. Because of the great emphasis of the Crown on increasing wheat production, it is likely that irrigable acreage in central New Spain was more apt to be devoted to wheat than elsewhere in the viceroyalty. On the northern frontier, however, crops other than wheat were grown legally on tierras de pan llevar. These lands carried water rights.

63. "Las tierras de pan llebar son: las cultivadas y que se riegan por medio de aguas preparatorias á voluntad." *Colección de decretos y ordenes dictados por el honorable Congreso Primero Constitucional de Chihuahua, en sus sesiones ordinarias desde 1° de julio hasta 30 de setiembre de 1827* (Chihuahua: Imprenta de Gobierno del Estado, 1828), p. 60.

64. The concept of implied water was used in medieval Spain. A grant for *terre in regadivo* entitled the owner to irrigation water even though water might not have been specified in the grant. See Glick, *Irrigation and Society,* p. 13.

65. Manuel Yuirri Castillo de sor. Gefe del Departamento de Texas, July 4, 1825, BA, Reel 82.

equal to one-fourth of a caballería, or about twenty-six acres.[66] In practice, many were smaller and at least some were larger.[67] The labor was generally a small agricultural plot (one or two caballerías or between 105 or 210 acres). The actual size varied from time to time and from place to place. As a general rule, they were larger in the north than in central and southern Mexico. The kind of population pressure so prevalent in many areas of the south did not apply to the north, and northern aridity dictated more generous allotments.

Land grants made in suertes did not necessarily carry water rights.[68] When Gerónimo Chino, a resident of Baja California, asked for three suertes, he was awarded them, but his grant specified that only one of them carried water rights (*suerte de regadío*) while two of them did not (*suertes de temporal*).[69] Similarly, Felipe Romero received two suertes with water rights and two without,[70] and José Antonio Munguía received two suertes, both without water rights.[71] A similar distinction in types of suertes is found in the Sonora and New Mexico documentation as well, both before and after Mexican independence. When Antonio de los Reyes, the Bishop of Sonora, developed a plan to improve the missions of the region in 1774, he suggested that the Indians each be given two suertes of land, one with irrigation water and one without.[72] In the 1830s, New Mexico settlers were awarded suertes on the San Joaquín grant; one-third of them carried water rights, and two-thirds of them did not.[73] In those many cases in which suertes were awarded without mention of water, the case for implied rights is very weak unless there is some independent indication in the documentation that the land in question is intended to be irrigated.

66. Galván Rivera, *Ordenanzas de tierras y aguas*, p. 75.

67. The use of the word *suerte* ("luck") in this land designation derives from the fact that these garden plots were drawn by lot. The original Canary Island settlers of San Antonio, Texas, for example, seem to have received suertes of about fifty acres. See Dobkins, *The Spanish Element in Texas Water Law*, p. 114.

68. In his legal history of San Francisco, John Dwinelle defines suertes as "cultivable lots of land," but does not treat the issue of their relationship to water. *The Colonial History of the City of San Francisco* (San Francisco: Towne and Bacon Book and Job Printers, 1863), p. 8.

69. Concesion de tres suertes . . . a favor de Geronimo Chino. . . . Aug. 30, 1768, AHBCS, Leg. 2, Doc. 5.

70. Concesion de cuatro suertes . . . a favor de Felipe Romero, Aug. 30, 1768, AHBCS, Leg. 2, Doc. 6.

71. José Antonio Munguia and José María Lasso to José de Galvez, Oct. 16, 1768, AHBCS, Leg. 2, Doc. 10.

72. ". . . tendran dro a dos suertes de trra de dos cientas varras en quadro, una de riego y otra de temporal. . . ." Noticia delas Prov^as de Sonora, Apr. 20, 1774, AGI, Audiencia de Guadalajara, 586.

73. Ebright, "The San Joaquin Grant," p. 19.

On occasion, part of the suerte is designated as a *huerta*, or family garden. The huerta, by definition, was an irrigated plot and therefore carried water rights.[74] The remaining portion of the suerte could not be irrigated unless the water right was extended in some way.

The case for implied water in grants specified as labores or labranzas is much stronger.[75] In his study of ranching in colonial Mexico, William H. Dusenberry concluded that labores always included water rights.[76] Although the statement may be too absolute, a strong case can be made in its support. The labor was designed for intensive agriculture and orchards needed to feed the local nonagrarian population and to provide excess agricultural production for missions and Indian communities. A surplus could not be produced in the arid north without access to water. Furthermore, the juxtaposition in the legislation of labores or labranzas with the need for intensive agriculture provides additional circumstantial evidence for the implied water right.[77] When Juana Benavides in New Mexico asked the alcalde mayor to confirm her right to her dead son's land, "unas de lavor y otras hiriaza," she was claiming the part of his land that carried water rights.[78] When the Canary Islanders of San Antonio found themselves disputing water with neighboring missions, they pleaded that, when Viceroy Marqués de Casafuerte made them grants of tierra de labor, he was granting them the right to two water sources (*dos ojos de agua*) as well.[79] Their claim was ultimately sustained.[80] When the Jesuit hacienda of Tabaloapa was surveyed and appraised for sale after the expulsion of the Jesuits, the phrases *caballerías de labor* and *de pan llevar* seem to have been used synonymously.[81] There are occasions when a labor or part of a labor is made without water

---

74. Palerm and Wolf, *Agricultura y civilización*, p. 54.

75. Elsewhere in Spanish America the labores are most commonly referred to as *chacaras*.

76. William Dusenberry, *The Mexican Mesta: The Administration of Ranching in Colonial Mexico* (Urbana: University of Illinois Press, 1963), p. 101n.

77. See, as examples, *Recopilación*, Libro IV, Título 3, Ley 8; and Libro IV, Título 5, Ley 9; Libro IV, Título 7, Ley 14; and Libro VI, Título 3, Ley 8. An example of the same juxtaposition in the contemporary documentation can be found in Testimonio de dilixencias y derrotero practicado en virtud de Superior Horn . . . por el Gral. Don Pedro de Rabago y Theran . . . Año de 1748, AGN, Historia, vol. 52.

78. Juana Benavides to Alcalde Mayor Manuel Garita Pareja, Mar. 3, 1772, SANM, I, 29.

79. Juan Real Goras to José Antonio Perez de Almazán, July 27, 1731, AGN, Provincias Internas, Vol. 163, Exp. 3.

80. Pedro de Rivera to Viceroy, Dec. 1, 1731, AGN, Provincias Internas, Vol. 163, Exp. 3.

81. Benedict, "The Hacienda of Tabaloapa," p. 176.

rights,[82] but the case for implied water rights, in the absence of specific denial, is strong.

The location of land on a water source was an important consideration in water usage. Downstream landowners on a natural water course (a river or a stream), if they held water rights, were protected against damming or diversion by their upstream neighbors. But downstream owners on an artificially constructed water course (an irrigation ditch or canal) did not have water rights unless they were specified in formal agreement with the upstream users. For example, if a farmer or group of farmers tied into the lower end of a ditch constructed by others, they had no legal right to passage of the water unless the upstream owners extended that right.[83] Except in cases of extremely bad relations between neighbors, right to such usage was commonly granted. If it were not, the downstream users were entitled to build their own acequia across their neighbors' land or even place a dam on it, and in the process deny him important crop acreage.[84]

The relationship between land and water was very complex and not always precise. It is clear, however, that water was granted or withheld on the basis of land classification. The case for implied water right can be carried too far. The absence of water provisions in certain land grants cannot be attributed simply to oversight. Not all land grants, not even all farming grants, were intended to convey water rights. If they were, there would have been no need for the addition of water rights to land grants already held. Just as a land merced did not automatically convey subsoil rights, neither did it automatically extend water rights. In some limited cases it did, but in many others it did not.

82. After the Texas mission of San José was secularized, its land was divided. Among those who were granted a plot was José María Escalera, who received part of a labor without water. "A d. Jose Mᵃ Escalera se le ha mercenado y posesionado de un rincon de labor sin agua en las tierras. . . ." Gaspar Flores, Dec. 31, 1824, BCA, MR 91.

83. "Reglamento General de las Medidas de las Aguas," in Galván Rivera, *Ordenanzas de tierras y aguas,* p. 166.

84. Caytano Trevino to Governor Francisco Bruno Barreros, June 9, 1818, AGN, Tierras, Vol. 1419, Exp. 3.

CHAPTER 7

Water Rights and Their Acquisition

How did one acquire water rights under Spanish colonial law? These rights could be obtained in different ways. As indicated in the preceding chapter, in some cases the request for the land grant also included a request for water, and, in the absence of mitigating considerations, both requests were honored. In other cases, water rights could be added to a land grant already made through a *merced de agua*. The granting official would make a determination if the water in question was located on royal land. If it was, and if the grant would not prejudice the rights of others, he would make the award. This process occurred in Santa Fe in 1715. Captain Diego Arias de Quiros asked for a water grant to accompany a land grant made previously. The governor examined the request to determine if it was on Crown land and then made his decision: "being in the royal patrimony, as it is, I make you a grant in the name of His Majesty of the above-mentioned spring of water."[1]

Many land grants were vague and subject to different interpretations on the matter of water. In these instances, it was possible to have the water rights clarified through the process of *composición*.[2] Composición was not a title to water or land but a mechanism for receiving one. It embraced a complicated judicial method used to cleanse,

---

1. Merced to Cap^n Diego Arias de Quiros by Governor Juan Ygnacio Flores Mogollon, July 30, 1715, SANM, I, 8.
2. The legal basis for composición is found in *Recopilación,* Libro IV, Título 12, Ley 6.

authenticate, and even alter original grants.³ In most cases it legit-imized a fait accompli. A special commission or an individual ap-pointee would examine the claims, the documents, and the circum-stances surrounding the grant and then render a decision. A favorable decision almost always assured a clear title, and the nature of the decision seems to have been strongly influenced by the amount paid to the person or persons undertaking the procedure. Francisco Baes Trevino, a wealthy landowner from Monterrey, paid 250 pesos for a water composición in the middle of the eighteenth century. His rights to the water were confirmed.⁴

A 1754 royal ordinance ordered officials in New Spain to simplify the process and make it easier for the Indians to avail themselves of it.⁵ But because the legal steps involved in a composición were often lengthy and the costs high, few landowners, either Spanish or Indian, used the process to request legitimization of their water rights unless they were forced to do so by circumstance. The process was known in northern New Spain and was applied to some water cases, but not frequently.⁶ Once a composición was effected, it constituted a legal document almost as good as a legal title itself. In one eighteenth-century water dispute in Coahuila, the litigant, unable to produce an original title which justified his water use, won a clear victory over an opponent with a legal title because he had been awarded his water right in an earlier composición. The judge issued his decision indicat-ing that "although Dn Juan Nepomuceno Larralde has not presented his original merced . . . he has produced his composición, which counts as a title and establishes the validity of the original grant."⁷ The composición was an important legal mechanism which helped water users whose legitimate rights were called into question because of the failure to meet some insignificant legal technicality. But they were also

3. The process of composición is skillfully analyzed in Greenleaf, "Land and Water," pp. 88–91. See also Julio Cesar Montenegro, *Aspectos legales del problema de la tierra, época colonial* (Mexico: Academia Nacional de Historia y Geografía, 1978), pp. 82–86, and François Chevalier, *Land and Society in Colonial Mexico*, pp. 270–277.
4. Desp. de Composición de Tierras a Dn Francisco Baes Trevino, Sep. 25, 1745, AGN, Mercedes, Vol. 75, Fol. 35v.
5. Real instrucción de 15 de Octubre de 1754, cited in Galván Rivera, *Ordenanzas de tierras y aguas*, pp. 28–35.
6. Examples of composición in the north can be found in Bartolomé Baca to Alcalde Constitucional de Almeda, Apr. 27, 1824, UNM SC; confirma el Desp. de Composi-cion de Tierras a Dn Francisco Baes Trevino, Sep. 25, 1745, AGN, Mercedes, Vol. 75, Fol. 35v; and VE Aprueba y confirma el Depacho librado . . . June 12, 1745, AGN, Mercedes, Vol. 77, Fol. 38.
7. Luis Galiano to Governor Melchor Vidal de Lorca y Villena, Nov. 25, 1778, AGN, Tierras, Leg. 1018, Exp. 3.

a source of potential abuse, as they could be used by the affluent and influential to blur distinctions between cropland and grazing land and to convey water rights for purposes not originally intended.

A much more common method of acquiring water rights through the judicial mechanism of the state was the *repartimiento de aguas*. Water disputes in the north were as constant as were periods of drought. If neighbors could not agree among themselves upon an equitable distribution of water from a single source, whether it be from a river, a stream, a reservoir, a spring, or an acequia, one or both could submit the dispute either to a water judge or to the appropriate court of first instance. The judicial official to whom the case was directed had wide latitude in the process of decision-making. He was encouraged to exercise his own discretion, but a well-defined body of legal principles gradually emerged that helped him reach a decision.[8] There were occasions when the rights and needs of one litigant so clearly surpassed those of his competitor that he was awarded all of the water in contention. These cases were clearly exceptions, however. In the vast majority of instances, the water was divided in repartimiento.

The legal basis for the repartimiento de aguas, contained in the *Recopilación*, was part of the attempt of the Spanish Crown to assure that Indians would be treated fairly in the allotment of water. Book IV, Title 17, Law 5 states: "We decree that the audiences name judges, unless it is the custom for the viceroy, or president, or cabildo to do so, who shall apportion waters to the Indians for the irrigation of their farms, orchards, and cultivated fields, and to water their cattle, in such a way as to offend no one."[9] But the system was used not only in settling water disputes between Indians and non-Indians, but among Indians themselves and Spaniards themselves.

The concept of dividing available water was fundamental to the repartimiento. The very word *repartimiento* (from the Spanish *repartir* and the Latin *partiri-partio*) suggests that in the case of dispute an equitable solution be found on the basis of a division of what was available. And if the lessons of etymology escaped the judges, the law in the *Recopilación* stated that repartimientos are to be made "such as to offend no one." Sometimes the nature of the repartimiento was spelled out with great specificity.[10] Water amounts in surcos or *bueyes* (a buey conveyed 2,596.9 gallons per minute) were allocated to the

---

8. The criteria used for making decisions in water disputes are discussed in chapter 8.
9. *Recopilación*, Libro IV, Título 17, Ley 5.
10. Juan Antonio Lobato, Oct. 30, 1823, SANM, I, 1292; Auto de Declara[on] de la agua y su repartimiento, July 13, 1731, AGN, Provincias Internas, Vol. 163, Exp. 3.

contending parties. At other times, the litigants were ordered simply to share the water. In a long and complicated water controversy between Pablo Montoya and the Indians of Santa Ana, both sides were ordered simply to work the irrigation ditch together.[11] On occasion, when the relationship of the land to the water source demanded it, water divided in a repartimiento was split into separate channels. The more common pattern, however, was to allocate the entire flow to the contending parties for fixed periods of time.

Apportionments of water made by judges in repartimientos came to have legal status. If one party to the partition took more than the share he had been awarded, he could be fined or subjected to other penalties. In one eighteenth-century New Mexico case, the Salazar family refused to abide by the terms of a repartimiento and lost their full rights to the water in question.[12] In most cases, however, the terms of the repartimientos were carried out, and in the process both parties gained legal water rights. Their rights to the water were not permanent, as Spanish jurisprudence appreciated that few conflicts were resolved so wisely that future abuse could not stem from a decision at one time just. A changing set of circumstances could occasion a new distribution in different proportion. In some cases, water repartimientos specified that they would expire at the death of the contending parties.[13] A new repartimiento would then be adjudicated.

Original water grants and subsequent water repartimientos were elastic, both expansive and contractive. In individual cases, an increase in the size of a family, or, in communal grants, an increase in size of a town, could prompt additional water allocation. The 1775 land allocation to the citizens of San Gabriel de las Nutrias, New Mexico, stipulated that the number of tierras de labor could be expanded in the future to accommodate increases in the number of families.[14] Because tierras de labor carried irrigation rights, an increase in water is strongly inferred. Similarly, an additional allocation of tierras de

11. ". . . an hallado p' justicia que D. Pablo Montoya trabaje ala sequia en union de todo el pueblo. . . ." Testimonio, Bernalillo, July 18, 1829, UNM SC. Additional examples of water repartimientos are found in Taylor, "Land and Water Rights," pp. 200–205; Nicolás León, "Bibliografía mexicana del siglo XVIII," *Boletín del Instituto Bibliográfico Mexicano* 4 (1903), 28–29.

12. ". . . no usen de la dicha acequia y ni del agua que por ella corre por aver perdido por su Ynovedencia a lo por mi mandado y sentenciado. . . ." Governor Pedro Fermín de Mendinueta to Teniente Salvador García, Feb. 15, 1770, SANM, II, 657.

13. Juan Nepomuceno de Larralde to Sr. Gov. y Comandante Gral, 1775, AGN, Tierras, Vol. 1018, Exp. 3.

14. ". . . que de tierras de Labor se les hizo, y las mas que pueda haver para las creces que las dhas familias tengan. . . ." Revalidation of Merced to San Gabriel de las Nutrias by Governor Thomas Vélez Capuchín, Dec. 15, 1755, SANM, I, 645.

pan llevar was given to the residents of Las Trampas, New Mexico, because the town had grown rapidly.[15] When the water repartimiento of the Canary Islanders and the San Antonio missions was implemented, one-fifth of the supply was left unassigned in anticipation of future growth.[16]

Water rights could also be obtained through purchase of several kinds. A landowner needing water could buy it from a neighbor who held legitimate rights to it. He could also buy land from someone who held water rights to the land, and the water could be included in the purchase. On other occasions, local cabildos could sell allotments of common water. In the latter case, the sales were generally made for only a fixed period of time, and, once that period of time expired, the right of acquisition expired with it.[17] Not all Spaniards understood the mechanisms of sale. When Carlos Rodríguez found himself contending for water rights with his neighbor, Joseph Saenz, he admitted that Saenz had purchased his water from an official appointed by the cabildo, the subdelegado de ventas y composiciones de tierras. But he argued that this official had no right to make the sale "because the law holds that rivers are common property."[18] What he failed to recognize was that river was common only until it was privatized, and sale by the government was a legitimate form of privatization.

One of the least known but most important methods of acquiring water rights was the special compact made between two individuals or between individuals and the state for *sobras*, also called *demasías* or *remanientes*. Sobras were water in excess of the amount needed or wanted by someone holding the primary right to that water. They could be a source of extra income to the water owner, or they could be the means by which a water owner allowed others to use a water source once his own water needs had been satisfied.[19] Sometimes formalized

15. ". . . no ser suficientes esta porcion de tierras de pan llebar por la multiplicacion de estas familias. . . ." Merced to Santo Thomas Apostol del Rio de las Trampas, by Governor Thomas Vélez Capuchín, Santa Fe, July 5, 1751, Microfilm of New Mexico Land Grants, Surveyor General Records, Reel 16, Report No. 27.

16. Auto de Declara[on] de la Agua y su repartimiento, July 13, 1731, AGN, Provincias Internas, Vol. 163, Exp. 3.

17. Examples of different kinds of water purchases are contained in José Gerónimo Huizar to Gefe Político, Jan. 5, 1824, BA, Reel 76; Fran[co] del Prado y Arze to Juan Bau[ta] Elquezabal, Apr. 8, 1805, BA, Reel 33; Aviso al Público, Monclova, June 4, 1834, BA, Reel 6, and En el Real y Minas de Sr José del Parral, Nov. 25, 1783, AHP, Reel 1783B.

18. Carlos Rodríguez to Senor Alc[e] Mayor y Cap[n] Gral, Oct. 23, 1767, AHP, Reel 1767.

19. The concept of sobras or demasías was also used in land acquisitions and resulted in no shortage of litigation as the compacts constituted legal titles that the courts were bound to recognize. See Ots Capdequí, *El régimen de la tierra*, p. 60.

by a written document, more often they were informal agreements reached by neighbors. On occasion no agreement was reached at all, but an individual who had used sobras over a period of years with the knowledge and forbearance of the owner could later claim a continued right to use them. The silence and toleration of the water owner was recognized as a tacit consent. *Sobrante* compacts became so common in the Hispanic Southwest that even the courts began to make use of the concept in formal water repartimientos.

In northern New Spain, requests for sobras were generally made by destitute members of society—people broken of spirit who claimed that, without the acquisition of this water right, they would be unable to support their families.[20] There is a pathetic quality to these requests for water, and in many cases sobrante rights were extended on the basis of dire need. The use of sobrantes became an integral part of water law in New Mexico during the colonial period and was used to divide water not only between Indians and non-Indians, but among different groups of Indians.[21] Because the user, having only secondary rights, was more at the mercy of annual variations of snow cover and rainfall, reservoirs were constructed whenever possible to trap the sobras. These reservoirs constituted a kind of insurance policy against seasonal drought that otherwise could kill the harvest.[22]

The nature of the individual sobra compact determined the extent of the water right. In one eighteenth-century New Mexico case, sobrante rights were extended only at the discretion of the woman holding primary rights and only after her needs were satisfied.[23] Because the holder of the primary rights was given discretionary powers in the sobra compact, she was entitled to alter and expand her water rights at the expense of the holder of the sobrantes. A Mexican-period case in California was similar. Encarnación Sepúlveda was

20. See, for example, the petition of Martín Fernández to Govern^r y Cap^n Gral for "Sobras del Difunto Xptobal de Lazerna. . . ," 1724, SANM, I, 217; Petition of José María Gallego to Diputación Territorial for "lo sobrante de las tierras valdias de las naturales de Pecos," 1825, SANM, I, 338; and Petition of Bartholome Lobato to Governor Juan Ignacio Flores Mogollon, 1714, SANM, I, 433.

21. The New Mexico pueblos of Acoma and Laguna disputed the water of the Río Gallo for two centuries, as Acoma held primary rights and Laguna had rights only to the sobras. For additional information, consult Edward D. Tittmann, "The First Irrigation Lawsuit," *New Mexico Historical Review* 2 (Oct., 1927), 363–368.

22. Sobrante reservoirs can still be found in certain areas of the Tewa region of northern New Mexico.

23. The pertinent portion of the document states that the petitioners have no rights at all to the water, ". . . salbo que la ya mencionada Viuda voluntariamente quiera permitirles el uso de la agua sobrante de sus menesteres." Governor Pedro Fermín de Mendinueta to Teniente Salvador García, Feb. 26, 1770, SANM, II, 657.

given sobrante rights to public waters "in case the public does not desire to use its water."[24] In other cases, however, sobrante rights were protected against new or expanded uses by the grantee holding priority rights. In the notable case of Taos and San Fernando de Taos versus Arroyo Seco,[25] the Pueblo of Taos' primary rights were confirmed, but San Fernando de Taos and Arroyo Seco were guaranteed sobrante rights.[26] After the Pueblo took its share, San Fernando de Taos was entitled to sobrantes, because its water claim antedated that of Arroyo Seco. But even Arroyo Seco was awarded sobrante rights of one surco when water was abundant and a lesser proportion when it was scarce.

In most cases, sobrante rights were not as absolute as those defined in the Taos-Arroyo Seco repartimiento. A more common pattern is that revealed in the decision in the eighteenth-century case of Juan Nepomuceno Larralde versus José Lozano:

> Larralde is entitled to use and take the water from the above-mentioned Río de las Savinas in preference to Lozano. He may take that which is necessary to irrigate four caballerías of land . . . and afterwards, if the water lasts, the Hacienda of Lozano can take the same amount for the cultivation of its labranzas. The order of preference will be maintained.[27]

There was good reason for Spanish officials to have delineated two kinds of sobrante rights, one which was absolute and one which was conditional. The poor farmer wanting to break new ground for a family garden plot would have as much information as possible concerning his water source. In the first instance, he knew that in time of drought he would be entitled at least to some water, or in the second instance he would know that he was at the mercy of those holding primary rights. This procedure was designed to help him make the best possible decision as to how he should proceed.

The relationship between primary and sobrante rights rests with the practice of usage. Those persons holding primary rights were entitled to first use of the water, and those holding sobrante rights to secondary or tertiary use. In some cases, priorities were established for a series of graduated sobrante rights with one individual ultimately

24. Cited in John Caughey's testimony for the court in *Los Angeles versus San Fernando*, p. A135.
25. This case is discussed in chapter 3.
26. Juan Ant° Lobato, Oct. 30, 1823, SANM, I, 1292.
27. Sentenᵃ del Gobernador Dn Melchor Vidal de Lorca y Villena, Apr. 14, 1779, AGN, Tierras, Vol. 1018, Exp. 3.

given the last sobrante water.[28] Once extended, however, sobrante rights were protected by the law. If a landowner entered into a compact for sobrante water, he could not be denied subsequent use of that water unless the compact itself specified that his sobrante rights were made conditional upon the whims of the holder of the primary right.[29] Sobrante rights were so thoroughly engrained in the Spanish colonial and Mexican judicial systems that the concept was adopted by United States courts and applied to water disputes in those territories ceded to the United States at the end of the Mexican War.[30]

Did Indians, by virtue of ethnicity, enjoy water rights different from those of their Spanish counterparts? Many laws in the *Recopilación* direct themselves to the protection of Indian property rights, including water. For example, Book VI, Title 10, Law 1 states: "Do not permit . . . the Indians . . . to be aggrieved in their persons or property. . . . "[31] Book IV, Title 12, Law 5 is even more specific, as it provides that, when land and water grants are made to Spaniards, "the Indians must be protected in their lands, cultivated fields and pastures. . . . "[32] And Book IV, Title XII, Law 14 states that, when land grants are made, special care shall be given to protecting Indian rights, "giving to the Indians that which they need to work their fields and grow their herds, confirming what they presently have and granting them anew what may be necessary."[33] Many other laws in the *Recopilación* could be cited to show special concern for Indian rights. William Taylor asserts that the *Recopilación* reveals a "paternalistic preoccupation with the well-being of the indigenous population" and concludes that this concern "contributed to a special, sometimes preferential, status for Indians under Spanish rule."[34] The assertion is certainly correct but available documentation permits qualification and refinement. With considerably less restraint, Betty Dobkins car-

28. ". . . tres dulas ultimas sobrantes. . . ." Gaspar Flores to D. José de Sandoval, Dec. 31, 1824, BCA, MR 63.

29. The Aztecs in the Central Valley of Mexico had a similar notion of sobrantes or *altepetlalli*. See Alba, *Derecho azteca*, p. 42.

30. For the application of the sobrante concept by the District court for the Third Judicial District of New Mexico in the 1857 case between Acoma and Laguna, see Tittmann, "The First Irrigation Lawsuit," pp. 363–368.

31. *Recopilación*, Libro VI, Título 10, Ley 1.

32. Ibid., Libro IV, Título 12, Ley 5.

33. Ibid., Libro IV, Título 12, Ley 14.

34. Taylor, "Land and Water Rights," p. 191. A similar conclusion, also based on the laws contained in the *Recopilación*, is found in Vlasich, "Pueblo Indian Agriculture," p. 73.

ries the argument further and states that "the *Recopilación* was a charter of privileges for the Indian."[35]

If one reads certain laws to the exclusion of others, it is possible to conclude that Indians were to enjoy a privileged position before the law. But a more impartial sampling of the 6,400 laws in the *Recopilación* indicates that this contention is conceptually flawed. Each example of preferential treatment for Indians can be countered with an example of prejudicial treatment against them. Unlike Spaniards, they could sell their land only with express permission of competent authority;[36] they could not be sold arms;[37] they could not purchase wine;[38] they could not hold dances without the permission of the governor;[39] they could not live in a village other than their own;[40] they had to pay part of the salary of an official designated to protect them, even though they had no choice in his selection;[41] and not even Indian caciques could use the title "Señor."[42] If one reads only these laws to the exclusion of others, it is easy to build a strong case for the special status of Spaniards. This approach would be conceptually flawed as well.

There is a better way of approaching the issue of Indian rights before the law without engaging in the Hispanista versus Indigenista or Black Legend versus White Legend debate. There is no doubt that throughout the entire colonial period the Spaniards had everything working in their behalf against a largely powerless Indian population. Specific laws incorporated into the *Recopilación* and judicial decisions favoring Spanish interests are often no more than testimony to the influence and leverage that individual Spaniards exerted at the Spanish court and in countless New Spanish courtrooms. Of equal importance, the special status of the Indians, while indeed in some respects special, should not be construed as synonymous with preferred status. In some instances it was preferred, in many others it was less than preferred, but in most instances it was simply different. Spanish

---

35. Betty Eakle Dobkins, "Indian Water Rights Under Hispanic Law: A Historical Perspective," (unpublished manuscript prepared for *The State of New Mexico vs. R. Lee Aamodt, et al.*, 1974), p. 52.
36. *Recopilación*, Libro IV, Título 12, Ley 16.
37. Ibid., Libro VI, Título 1, Ley 31.
38. Ibid., Libro VI, Título 1, Ley 36.
39. Ibid., Libro VI, Título 1, Ley 38.
40. Ibid., Libro VI, Título 3, Ley 18.
41. Ibid., Libro VI, Título 6, Ley 2.
42. Ibid., Libro VI, Título 7, Ley 5.

paternalism was a double-edged sword. The fact that Indians could sell their land only with the express permission of competent authority reflects no doubt a paternalistic desire to protect them, but it also constitutes but one of many factors that made the Indians less free than their Spanish neighbors.

The debate over who had preferred status, Spaniards or Indians, is as pedantic and esoterically academic as it is insoluble. The remarkable and emulative aspect of the *Recopilación,* and many of the court decisions that stemmed from it, was not simply that it sought to protect a conquered and abused population (although that alone might have made it remarkable), but that in a dynamic and sometimes chaotic post-conquest society, it sought justice for all persons. That such a laudatory goal was not attained, no serious scholar would deny.

The protective legislation put on the books for Indians was not placed there for the purpose of affording them preferred status under the law. It must be read not only as a guide to what men ought to do, but also as an indication of what they actually did. If a special law was enacted to limit the weight an Indian *tameme* (carrier) could carry on his back, it is clear that, prior to the enactment of such a law, he was being forced to carry more. Because no similar law was specified for Spaniards by no means suggests a preferred status for the Indian. Because the Indians were abused, because they were cheated, because they were not familiar with the intricacies of the Spanish judicial system, because they were seldom in the position to pay handsome bribes, and because there were virtually no Indian lawyers to guard their interests, they obviously needed extra protection. If they were to survive, much less prosper, they needed an official such as the Protector of the Indians charged with the function of defending them. In the limited sense, it can be argued that this protection constitutes preferred status, but, in the larger sense, the object was not to assure them a special legal standing in the community; rather it was the attempt to assure that they would not be at such a decided disadvantage at the hands of those who wielded such enormous power and who often wielded it capriciously.

As an example of the Indian's different relationship to the courts, the *Recopilación* provided that if a Spaniard committed a crime against an Indian, he would be punished more severely than if he committed the same crime against another Spaniard.[43] Was this preferred status for Indians? Theoretically, at least, they could anticipate a more stringent punishment for crimes committed against them. But why was

43. Ibid., Libro VI, Título 7, Ley 5.

such a law needed? There would be no reason for such a law if many Spaniards were not maltreating Indians. Because of some of the mental and psychological baggage the Spaniards brought to the New World and carried along with them to the northern reaches of New Spain, an inexcusably large number considered it unimportant if an Indian were maltreated. This intolerable situation was further exacerbated when Spaniards believed that they could engage in illegal or immoral activity with impunity. The purpose of the more stringent punishment was clearly to curtail an oppressive abuse, not to give the Indians preferred status. A statute which superficially seems to provide preferred status for Indians is, in reality, an attempt on the part of the Spanish Crown to assure equal status under the law. It is the attempt to establish an equilibrium among the competing interests that were anything but equal.

Moving from the general to the particular, the water disputes studied and analyzed do not reveal that Indians, by virtue of their ethnicity, were to have preferred status in the allotment of water. The *Recopilación* and other Spanish legislation gave them certain guarantees with respect to land and water. It also gave Spaniards certain guarantees. Water was a means to an end, and it was not to be distributed on an ethnic basis. The general principle was fully consistent with the Spanish judicial tradition which held that not only Iberians, but foreigners, were entitled to use the waters of Iberian rivers.[44] This concept was given specific applicability to the residents of the northern desert. Judicial officials in northern New Spain were instructed "to try by all means possible to assure that both hacendados and Indians enjoy surface and subsurface water for the irrigation and fertility of their fields."[45] The Plan de Pitic, in Article 6, expounded the same principle,[46] as did the ordinances issued at the time other towns were founded and when land and water grants were made.[47]

44. "Los Rios, e los Puertos, e los caminos publicos pertenecen a todos los omes comunalmente; en tal manera que tambien pueden Vsar dellos los que son de otra tierra estrana como los que moran, et biuen en aquella tierra. . . ." *Siete partidas*, Partida 3, Título 28, Ley 6.

45. Instrucción que deberan guardar las Justicias Subalternas. . . . May 2, 1786, AHP, Reel 1787a.

46. Plan de Pitic, Article 6, UT WBS 9.

47. After the Pueblo Rebellion of 1680 and the southern retreat of the Spanish settlers to El Paso, new grants of land and water were made in the El Paso area. These grants specified that the grantees were to receive "the land necessary for cultivation and the necessary water from the river to irrigate them, for both Spaniards and others who were forced to retreat from those provinces (New Mexico) and found themselves in the vicinity of the Paso del Río del Norte and for all other peaceful Indians." See Testimonio del Noveno quaderno de los Autos sobre las Pretensiones del Capⁿ Dⁿ Antonio de Valverde de Cosio . . . Año de 1703, AGI, Audiencia de Guadalajara, 142.

Indian rights to water were not held in higher legal esteem than the rights of Spaniards to water, but neither were they held in lower legal esteem.[48]

48. For the opposing point of view, skillfully argued, see Taylor, "Land and Water Rights," pp. 191–194. Support for the concept of theoretical judicial equality between Indians and Spaniards is found in Antonio Muro Orejón, "La igualdad entre Indios y Españoles," *Estudios sobre política indigenista española en América* 1 (Valladolid: Universidad de Valladolid. 1975), pp. 366–386. François Chevalier agrees with Muro Orejón and argues that the purpose of incorporating Indian institutions into Spanish peninsular jurisprudence was to encourage "eventual equality." See *Land and Society in Colonial Mexico*, p. 190.

CHAPTER 8

The Adjudication of Water Disputes

From both a legal and a historical perspective, one of the most interesting and least studied aspects of colonial water law concerns the judicial criteria upon which legal disputes were resolved. The principles are varied, complex, and to some extent carry with them the possibility of internal contradiction. But, as Plato observed, and a score of philosophers subsequently echoed, justice would be a simple matter if only men were simple. The residents and judges of northern New Spain were not generally distinguished by their formal schooling, but even less were they notable for their simplicity. Spanish citizens, mestizos, and Indians learned quickly how to play the legal game. Judges recognized as a practical matter the need to reconcile the disharmony of man and nature in a hostile environment, and they also knew that they would be held accountable if they ventured too far from the spirit and intent of Spanish law.

When a water dispute occurred, the contesting parties almost always tried to work out the problem themselves. On occasion, they would call upon the local priest to serve as an informal mediator.[1] It is difficult to ascertain how many disputes were resolved informally, because these resolutions generally are not incorporated into the surviving documentation unless the agreement in question precipitated a subsequent dispute.

1. See, for example, Don Juan Tepeguan, Casique del Pueblo de Santa Crus to Gran Senor y tlatoani mayor de nuestras tierras. . . , July 12, 1649, AHP, Reel 1653B.

When water controversies were carried to the appropriate governmental authority, the litigants were first asked to produce a just title for land or water.[2] During most of the sixteenth century, when land and water seemed plentiful and the Spanish population was small, local units of government made grants, and some of them large grants, as they saw fit, with little interference from higher officials. In the process, many Indian properties were abused, and there was great confusion even among titles to Spanish properties. By the late sixteenth century, the situation had gotten out of hand, and the Crown sought to tighten up granting procedures and clarify what had already been done. Recognizing the beauty inherent in order, in 1591 a royal cédula authorized the viceroys and governors to demand titles whenever a dispute occurred.[3] Solórzano Pereira stressed the importance of this decree when he published his *Política indiana* some fifty-six years later and added that proof of just title could be demanded at any time by the viceroy and his representatives.[4]

From the time of the 1591 cédula, legal titles were extremely important in New Spain. If they were not prepared in the proper form, with the correct corresponding signatures of the granting authority, the witnesses, and the scribe, and with a description of the physical act of possession, they could be declared null and void. If all of the prerequisites were met but the documents were not prepared on official paper, their legitimacy could be called into question.[5] The

---

2. The phrase ordering the title varied. "Hagan demonstraciones delos titulos y mercedes." "Exhibe los titulos y papeles." ". . . notifique haga presente ante mi de los titulos y papeles que tiene." ". . . y trairia lo escritura de las tierras referidas." ". . . haga exibir antesi las mercedes o titulos." "instrumento auttentico de esa posesion. . . ." But no matter what the specific phraseology, the message was clear. The litigants were placed on notice that they had to present proper documentation to support their claims. For examples, see Testimonios de los Autos formados sobre el Repartimiento de Tierras en la Colonia del Nuevo Santander Perteneciente alas Misiones de Californias, Año de 1770, AGI, Audiencia de México, 1369; Auto de Alfonso Real de Aguilar, Santa Fe, June 14, 1715, SANM, I, 7; and Juan Pérez Hurtado to Ignacio Roybal, Santa Fe, Sep. 18, 1704, SANM, I, 1339; Thomas Vélez Capuchin to Philipe Tafoya, Feb. 4, 1763, SANM, I, 1351; Escripto de Gabriel de Vergara, Viseprefecto y Presid^te de las Misiones de co Sta crus de Queretaro, May 31, 1731, AGN, Provincias Internas, Vol. 163, Exp. 3; Auto de Don Melchor Vidal de Lorca, Gobernador y Com^te Gral por S. M. De este Nuevo Reyno de León; Mar. 21, 1778, AGN, Tierras, Vol. 1018, Exp. 3.

3. Ots Capdequí, *El régimen de las tierras*, pp. 68–69.

4. *Política indiana*, Libro VI, Capítulo XII, 9.

5. Many official documents from throughout the Southwest were not prepared on paper bearing the official royal seal because local officials often ran out of it. The danger of invalidation was there, however, as the law was clear. "Papel sellado. El que está señalado con las armas del rey ó nación, y sirve para autorizar las escrituras públicas, las diligencias judiciales y otros instrumentos, que si se hiciesen nulos en papel común." Escriche, *Dicionario razonado de legislación*, pp. 491–492.

new emphasis on just titles was one of those attempts on the part of the Spanish Crown to protect Indian interests. In the eighteenth century, when the intendant of the Provincias Internas, Henrique de Grimerest, ordered that titles be examined, he specified that it was the protection of the Indians he had in mind.[6] But, like so many other attempts to guard Indian interests, this one backfired. If Spaniards had to produce their titles, Indians did also, and they were even more unlikely to have them, or, if they did, to have them in proper form.

Four of the Tewa pueblos of New Mexico needed their titles in the nineteenth century, but in all four cases the Indians were unable to produce the documents because they had been lost previously. In the case of Tesuque, Indian witnesses testified in 1856 that their torn and tattered title was taken by a Mexican government official for copying and never returned. The case of the San Ildefonso title is similar. The local priest reputedly carried the document to Santa Fe for copying, and the Indians never saw it again. The Pojoaque title was allegedly used in a lawsuit tried before the alcalde of Chimayo, Bautista Vigil, and never returned to the pueblo. And the Nambe document was turned over to an acting governor of New Mexico to be used in pending legislation and never again seen by the Indians.[7]

Spanish petitioners for land and water on Indian property quickly learned that the just-title ploy could work in their benefit. Unscrupulous Spaniards hoodwinked Indians to turn over their titles to them; subsequently they would be bought and sold and even used as collateral for loans. Time after time, Spanish litigants demanded that authorities require the Indians to present their title, and in many cases they could not.[8] The 1736 case of Baltasar Trujillo is a typical example. The Indians of the pueblo of San Ildefonso, in the upper Río Grande valley, charged that Trujillo was using their agricultural lands, their acequia, and their water without permission. An extremely complicated litigation followed. The Indians claimed that many years before they had lent Matías Madrid a piece of land so that

---

6. Henrique de Grimerest to Antonio Portier, Sep. 13, 1790, AGI, Audiencia de Guadalajara, 288.

7. Testimony of Governor of Tesuque, Carlos Vigil, et al., Taken before Surveyor General of New Mexico, June 14, 1856, Microfilm of New Mexico Land Grants, Pueblo Grants, Reel 7; Testimony of Governor of San Ildefonso, Acencio Pena, et al., Taken before Surveyor General, June 28, 1856, Ibid.; Testimony of Governor of Nambe, Juan Rosario Padilla, et al., Taken before Surveyor General, Sep. 29, 1856, ibid.

8. "Suplico . . . que muestren los titulos. . . ." Fran[co] García to Cap[nn] Xbtobal ponse de leon, June 9, 1688, AHP, Reel 1692A.

he could build a house on it.[9] Through an entire series of inheritances
and sales, the property, located in the middle of the Indian *labores*,
ultimately fell into the hands of Baltasar Trujillo. By means of carefully presented testimony Trujillo was able to establish that earlier
Spanish officials had certified the inheritances and the sales; Trujillo
therefore held the property legally even if it had not been Madrid's to
sell. But then Trujillo used his trump card. "The Indians of the said
pueblo," he argued, "have not exhibited the title to their land."[10] The
governor of New Mexico upheld his claim to the land and water and in
the process demonstrated the significance attached to just title. Other
land and water disputes in which just title assumes a major role
abound in the surviving documentation.[11]

A second consideration was the doctrine of prior use or prior
appropriation, a concept generally argued on the basis that the water
in question had been used *de tiempo immemorial*, or *de costumbre immemorial*.[12] The doctrine of prior use is almost invariably misunderstood.
It was not an absolute concept that overshadowed all other factors in
the distribution of water.[13] It did not mean that whoever had used a
water source first was entitled to continuing use without regard to the
well-being of others. It was, however, a very important consideration in
the allocation of water and one which the Indians of northern New
Spain used to their advantage in water disputes. It could help sustain a
water right in the absence of title or other legal documentation and
could help assure a favorable allocation in a *repartimiento de aguas*.

The Spanish concept of prior use in water disputes dates back at

9. Philipe Tafoya, to Senor Govr y Capp[n] Graal, 1763, SANM, I, 1351.

10. Gervasio Cruzat y Góngora, Governor of New Mexico, Apr. 7, 1736, SANM, I,
1351.

11. Los Ciudadanos Juan M[a] Moquino, Andrés de la Candelaria y Ant[o] de la Cruz,
Año de 1829, AGN, Justicia, Tomo 48, Exp. 19; Juan Nepomuceno to Sr. Gov. y
Comandante Graal, 1775, AGN, Tierras, Vol. 1018, Exp. 3; Testimonios de los Autos
Formados sobre el Repartimiento de Tierras en la colonia del Nuevo Santander
Pertenecientes a las misiones de Californias, AGI, Audiencia de México, 1369.

12. Other variations of the same concept are embodied in the phrase "costumbre tan
antigua de q[e] no hay ya memoria en los hombres." José María Ortuño to Sor Fiscal de
lo Civil [de Monterrey], AGN, Tierras, Vol. 1395, Exp. 11.

13. A typical misunderstanding and exaggeration of the doctrine is voiced by James
M. Murphy, who states that "the law, in effect, said the water was public property, and
whoever got there first and used it had prior rights over all others." See Murphy, *The
Spanish Legal Heritage in Arizona* (Tucson: Arizona Pioneers' Historical Society, 1966),
p. 15 ff. Murphy's treatment of the application of Hispanic water law to Arizona after
the Treaty of Guadalupe-Hidalgo is very helpful. The weakness of his analysis,
however, rests with the fact that it merely juxtaposes the riparian tradition of common
law with the prior-appropriation tradition of Roman law, not recognizing that the
latter is only one of many important water considerations in the Spanish and Mexican
legal systems.

least to the thirteenth century. The *Siete partidas* does not develop the doctrine with any degree of specificity but leaves no doubt that prior use was an established legal principle. The *Partidas* first define usage as that which evolves "from what men say and what men do continuously for a long period of time and without being obstructed."[14] The issue of no obstruction was crucial to the principle, as the Spanish did allow early objection to a new usage by a process called *denuncia de obra nueva*.[15] The doctrine is subsequently made directly applicable to water disputes.

> If a man has been awarded the right to conduct water, to irrigate his property, from a source that rises on another's property, and if later the owner of the source wishes to give that right to another person, he will not be permitted to do so without permission of the person who *first* [emphasis mine] was extended that right.[16]

The prior-use doctrine was mutated with the passage of time. As the legal doctrine developed, it became apparent that prior use was not synonymous with oldest use. When Joseph Miguel Losano of Nuevo León found himself disputing water ownership with his neighbor, Juan Nepomuceno de Larralde, in 1778, he argued that the law should not only respect but should give priority to the length of time that contending parties had held their titles.[17] He clearly believed that the longer a title was held, especially if it was uncontested, the more secure it became before the law. The argument he put forth was an old one but not as persuasive as that of his opponent, who conceded that Losano's right antedated his but who turned the prior-use argument in his own favor. His water right was a newer one, but it was granted with the full realization that Losano held an older right. The newer right should, therefore, prevail.[18] In this case it did. Larralde won his water and made clear that a firmly established newer use was a type of prior use that was taken into account in water conflict. Many Spaniards, and after independence many Mexicans, incorporated the

14. Partida I, Título 2, Ley 1.

15. Escriche, *Diccionario razonado de legislación*, p. 181.

16. Partida 3, Título 31, Ley 5. Similarly, the *Siete partidas* authorized the use of running water for purposes of powering a mill only if the water was not diverted from the owner of an already established mill. Partida 3, Título 32, Ley 18.

17. "La ley deve atender la anterioridad de tiempo en el título." Joseph Miguel Losano to Governor Melchor Vidal de Lorca, Mar. 1778, AGN, Tierras, Vol. 1018, Exp. 3.

18. When Losano argued "que el que es primero en tiempo deve ser perferido en dro," Larralde countered with "que el que es primero en dro deve ser preferido en tiempo." See Juan Nepomuceno de Larralde to Governador Vidal de Lorca, 1778, AGN, Tierras, Vol. 1018, Exp. 3.

phrase *de tiempo immemorial* in the adjudication of their water contro-versies.[19] Sometimes it helped them, sometimes it did not.

In an unusually perceptive study, William Taylor characterizes prior use as "a type of superior right, but it did not usually serve to establish exclusive rights for the oldest user, especially if there were surplus waters."[20] This conclusion is, without question, correct, and at least one New Mexico water case between Indians and non-Indians, *Taos versus Arroyo Seco*, suggests forcefully that prior use could not sustain a claim to exclusivity even when water was scarce.[21] Prior use was a carefully controlled legal principle. Spanish jurisprudence rec-ognized that it held within it the seeds of contradiction and conflict. In its legal definition, therefore, it spelled out the conditions necessary for judicial application:

> Use is the custom, general practice, or modus operandi that has been imperceptibly introduced and has acquired the force of law. Prior use is founded on the tacit consent of the public that ob-serves it, of the courts that conform to it, and the legislator that permits its application. . . . Prior use contrary to reason or to good custom can never acquire the force of law, because in such a case it can be considered no more than an old mistake, being less a use than an abuse and an infraction of law: *Mala enim consuetudo, non minus quam perniciosa corruptela, abjicienda est et vitanda: quod contra bonos mores esse dignocitur, omnino abolendum est.*[22]

A third fundamental criterion was need. This concept is a signifi-cant factor in water legislation, as a number of laws in the *Recopilación* and elsewhere call for a distribution on the basis of what is needed to sustain a family.[23] Article 20 of the Plan de Pitic appoints a special water judge so that the available water will be distributed in propor-tion to the needs of the respective plantings.[24] Other municipal ordi-nances specified that if any individual was not using water granted to

19. The phrase is common in water litigation. See, for example, Petition of Manuel Lucero, Pablo Lucero, Rafael de Luna et al., Aug. 4, 1836, SANM, I, 628.

20. Taylor, "Land and Water Rights," p. 203. Taylor's conclusion is repeated in Vlasich, "Pueblo Indian Agriculture," p. 80.

21. Juan Eusevio García de la Mora to Governor Antonio Narvona, Apr. 26, 1826, Santa Fe, SANM, I, 389; Decision of Juan Anto° Lobato, Oct. 30, 1823, SANM, I, 1292.

22. Escriche, *Diccionario razonado de legislación*, p. 686.

23. See, for example, *Recopilación*, Libro III, Título 2, Ley 63, and Libro IV, Título XII, Ley 14.

24. "Para que estos disfruten con equidad y justicia el beneficio de las Aguas, a proporcion de la necesidad que tuvieren sus respectivas siembras, se nombrara anualmente por el Ayuntamiento un Alcalde. . . ." Plan de Pitic, Article 20, AGN, Tierras, Vol. 2773, Exp. 22.

him, and others needed the water, the original grant should be re-voked.[25] Even in the case of a spring or a well originating on a piece of private property, the most privatizable kind of water supply, the owner could not deprive his neighbor of its use simply by wasting that which he did not need.[26] Need is also incorporated into many petitions for water mercedes and composiciones, and it is invariably included in requests for sobras.[27]

A typical example is the early nineteenth-century petition of Francisco Xavier Ortiz and his two sons, José and Juan Antonio, for land and water from the sobras of the Indian pueblo of San Ildefonso. Ortiz argued to the jefe político that he had served the Crown for years without salary. Neither he nor his sons had anything with which to sustain themselves. And then he made his final appeal. "Nobody more than you knows that need in which we find ourselves."[28]

As important as need was in requests for water, it was even more important in the adjudication of subsequent water disputes. Guidelines for the settling of water controversies promulgated in Santa Fe in 1720 ordered that water judges "divide the water always verifying the greatest need . . . and giving to each one that which he needs."[29] This order was scrupulously followed. Not only is need one of the criteria upon which water decisions are made,[30] but, in some cases at least, it is clearly the most important factor. In the water dispute between the Pueblo Indians of Taos and the Spaniards of Arroyo Seco, the latter had a very weak case to plead except for the fact that they needed the water. In the decision handed down, they received their water allotment almost entirely on the basis of need.[31] Similarly, when Margarita de Luna, an eighteenth-century New Mexico widow, disputed water with her neighbors, she built her case on the doctrine of need. A

25. Bandos de Policia y Hordenes de buen govierno [San Antonio de Béxar], Jan. 10, 1802, BA, Reel 30.

26. *Novísima recopilación*, Libro III, Título 28, Ley 31. The doctrine of need might well be traceable to the Moorish legal tradition. The Koran taught that the withholding of surplus water from a neighbor who needed it was a sin against Allah.

27. Petition of Martín Fernandez to Govern.r y Capp.n Graal for Sobras del Difunto Xptobal de Lazerna..., 1724, SANM, I, 217; Petition of José María Gallego to Diputación Territorial, 1825, SANM, I, 338; and Petition of Bartholomé Lobato to Governor Juan Ignacio Flores Mogollón, 1714, SANM, I, 433.

28. Francisco Xavier Ortiz to Sor. Gefe Político, Feb. 19, 1824, SANM, I, 1293.

29. Nombram.to y Orden de Juezes para el Repartimien.to de lagua, Santa Fe, July 16, 1720, SANM, II, 317A.

30. See, for example, Manuel Martinez to Jefe Político, July 3, 1823, SANM, Reel 15; La Comisión Encargada del Asunto de los Senores Vigiles. . . . Aug. 28, 1836, SANM, I, 628; Juan Eusevio García de la Mora to Governor Antonio Narvona, Apr. 25, 1826, SANM, I, 389.

31. Juan Antonio Lobato, Oct. 30, 1823, SANM, I, 1292.

representative of the alcalde mayor confirmed her dire situation and reported his findings with a bit of attempted humor: her crops had dried out to such an extent "that not even if she irrigated them with Holy Water could they be saved."[32] Ultimately, she won her case.

The protracted and litigious acequia dispute between Pablo Montoya and the Indians of Santa Ana also found the doctrine of need occupying a prominent role. The final resolution of the case by the court in Santa Fe is dated August 1, 1838. It states that Pablo Montoya's crops were dying for lack of water, that he was in possession of documentation establishing his right, and that he needed the water. In one of the strongest declarations ever of the doctrine of need, the court held that "even if he didn't have legal right, need is supreme to all laws."[33]

Related to need, but different in its application, was a fourth criterion, the concept of injury to a third party. The roots of this legal principle are found in Iberian legal history, but it was applied to Mexico as early as 1535.[34] Because of the doctrine of royal patrimony, the Spanish Crown was the first interested party in any water allocation and the person making the request was the second, but Spanish law was clear on the need for protecting the interests of any third party. The concept has within it the germs of the law of equal freedom developed in the nineteenth century by Herbert Spencer: "Every man has freedom to do all that he wills provided he infringes not the equal freedom of any other man." Spanish jurisprudence recognized not only the equal rights of legal contenders but also the potentially competing interests of the state.

The special phraseology of the doctrine of injury to third party varies from document to document. A typical rendition is contained in the 1707 grant made to Captain Tomás de la Garza Falcón in Coahuila: "I make this grant without prejudice to the Royal Patrimony nor to any third party who might have a better right."[35] When water

32. Margarita de Luna to Governor Pedro Fermín de Mendinueta, Feb., 1770, SANM, I, 657.

33. ". . . le de el agua al enunciado Montoya pues v save q^e aun Cuando no tubiera Dro La Nesecidad hes la supprema de todas las leyes. . . . Salvador Montoya to Alcalde de Santa Ana, García Montoya, Aug. 1, 1838, UNM SC. The pace of justice in this case was intolerably slow, as more than twenty-five years passed between the original contention and the final resolution. The interminable delays were not unusual. A similar case in New Mexico between Indians from Sandía and a neighboring Spaniard lasted from 1829 to 1841. See Los Ciudadanos Jose Mª Moquino, Andrés de la Candalaria y Antº de la Cruz, AGN, Justicia, Tomo 48, Exp. 19.

34. Cédula dirigida al Virrey de la Nueva España en que se le permitió . . . ciertas tierras, Encinas, *Cedulario indiano*, I, 65.

35. VE Aprueba y confirma la merced ynserta hecha al capital Don Thomas de la Garza Falcón, Feb. 1, 1707, AGN, Mercedes, Vol. 74, Fols. 109–110.

grants were made to Spaniards in Indian areas, the no-prejudice clause often singled the Indians out for protection. Thus, when Pedro Cano asked for a water grant in the Tarahumara region of Chihuahua in 1672, he specified that such a grant would not be "in prejudice to the Indians, who live quite a few leagues away, nor to any other third party who might have a better right."[36] Similarly, when a water diversion project was planned for El Paso, the petition argued that the project would be implemented "without prejudice to the Indians or any other third party."[37]

Requests for water or for additional water were almost always subjected to the third-party test, and the test took many different forms. Witnesses could be summoned to testify on the probable impact of a water grant. If testimony were inconclusive, the granting authority would commission independent experts, called either *peritos* or *veedores*, to make an on-the-spot analysis and a recommendation.[38] The inspection process was known as a *vista de ojos*, a *vista ocular*, or a *reconocimiento*. The steps are revealed in a 1744 account from Sonora.

> In the Royal Presidio of San Pedro de la Conquista on the nineteenth day of the month of July in the year seventeen hundred and forty-four, I, the said Alferez Don Salvador Martín Bernal, together with official measures and witnesses, went out to study the water outlet that the documentation in my possession refers to. Having examined the bank of the River from this Royal Presidio to a rocky hill that is located about a half a league distant from the east bank of the River, I could not discover any other place where the outlet could be made to irrigate the said fields and even this outlet will be costly. Finding that it would not cause prejudice to any third party, I designated this place as the outlet and entered it in the document which I signed with the above-mentioned official measures and witnesses and to which I attest with full faith and credit.[39]

If injury to a third party was demonstrated, either by testimony or by the vista de ojos, the request would be denied.[40] But the third-party

36. Pedro Cano to Joseph García, Nov. 10, 1672, AHP, Reel 1671A.

37. Testimonio de Diligencias . . . capitulo veintte, Año de 1754, ALPC PE-51.

38. Declaracion de todas las Tierras de Lavor, July 8, 1731, AGN, Provincias Internas, Vol. 163, Exp. 3.

39. Reconocimiento de Salvador Martín Bernal, July 19, 1744, AGN, Provincias Internals, Vol. 247, Exp. 3.

40. Examples of water requests being denied because of injury to third parties are contained in Juan Bauptista Montano to Governor Pedro Fermín de Mendinueta, 1767, SANM, I 573, and Xptobal Torres, Alcalde Mayor de la Villa Nueva de Santa Cruz to Xptobal Tafolla, June 10, 1724, SANM, I, 942.

test had other ramifications as well. Not only could it be used to sustain or deny a water request, it could also influence the specific nature of a water grant. In 1715, for example, Diego Arias asked for a water grant near Santa Fe. Some of his neighbors protested that, if the grant was extended, a pond lower on the stream would be denied its water. The governor of New Mexico, Juan Ignacio Flores Mogollón, recognized that the lower users might indeed be prejudiced. He decided to make the grant, but with conditions. The size of Diego Arias' new pond was to be limited to six varas square (a little less than 36 square yards), its depth was regulated, and, finally, if these conditions did result in injury to third parties, the Arias pond would have to be opened so that sufficient water could flow downstream.[41]

A variation of the principle of no injury to third party was the notion of least injury to third party. Access to water often required that the outlet (the *saca de agua* or *toma de agua*) and the acequia be located on another person's land. Spanish law stipulated clearly that water access in these areas superseded rights to private domain. The outlet could be used because the banks of rivers were considered part of the river, and thus belonged to the royal patrimony. The acequias could cross another person's land because of the law of *servidumbre del aquaducto*, which was defined by Lasso de la Vega as "the right to conduct water through others' property to irrigate one's own, or someone else's, as provided for in the law of right-of-way."[42] In either case, however, the outlet or the acequia had to be constructed in such a manner as to cause least injury to the third party.[43]

A fifth important criterion was intent. Why did a petitioner or group of petitioners want more water? How did they intend to use it? Were their goals in harmony with those of the larger community? Most importantly, what was the intent of governing officials with respect to this water?

In the absence of strong competing reasons, water for mining operations was generally approved because the government intent was to increase Crown revenue from the mining tax, the *quinto*. It was not unusual that Felipe de la Cueva Montano, in contending with Indians for water he needed for a silver mine, reminded authorities "of the considerable sum paid to His Majesty in quintos each year."[44] When a

41. En la Villa de Santa Fe de la Nueva Mexico, en 30 de Julio de 1715 años, SANM, I, 8.
42. "Reglamento General de las Medidas de las Aguas," in Galván Rivera, *Ordenanzas de tierras y aguas*, p. 161.
43. Galván Rivera, *Ordenanzas de tierras y aguas*, pp. 95–96.
44. Petition of Felipe de la Cueva Montano, July 19, 1649, AHP, Reel 1653B.

new mining code was adopted in 1783, special provisions were in-cluded to guarantee an adequate water source for all mines in New Spain.[45] Similarly, water to irrigate wheat always carried high priority because this grain was in high demand in northern New Spain. Land and water for presidios, where the intent was to increase national defense, also ranked very high.[46] Local military officials were some-times empowered to alter existing water distributions in the interest of national defense.[47] In the case of presidios, government intent for water usage came very close to bordering on the doctrine of eminent domain. In eighteenth-century Coahuila, for example, Teodoro de Croix, the first commandant general of the Provincias Internas, seized the property of a privately owned hacienda so that its land and water could be used to establish a new presidio, badly needed to guard against Indian attacks.[48]

Government intent was not a constant throughout the colonial period. It varied with perceived needs from time to time and from place to place. In the 1780s, officials in Mexico City decided that New Spain needed cloth from Texas. They ordered local authorities to make water available to the mission Indians for the express purpose of hemp cultivation.[49] The order was carried out.

Petitions for water often tried to anticipate government intent. Missionaries asking for water seldom forgot to remind granting au-thorities that the king intended the Indians to be relocated in missions and converted.[50] When Captain Diego de Quiros asked for water for his Chihuahua mine, he reminded the governor of Nueva Viscaya, Joseph García de Salcedo, that the king was very interested in the mining tax.[51] The grant was made. Similarly, Captain Andrés López de Gracia wanted a grant of land and water in the Valle de San Antonio de Casas Grandes in Nueva Viscaya. Knowing that it was the

45. Ordenanzas del Tribunal General de la Minería de Nueva España, May 22, 1783, in Beleña, *Recopilación sumaria*, II, 214–292.
46. Pedro Antonio de Albares to Governor, June 14, 1740, AGN, Californias, Vol. 80, Exp. 28.
47. Diego de Borica to Senor Caballero de Croix, Oct. 20, 1778, AGI, Audiencia de Guadalajara, 270.
48. Teodoro de Croix to Jose de Galvez, Dec. 28, 1778, AGI, Audiencia de Guadalajara, 270.
49. Decreto del Presidente de la Real Audiencia, Mar. 15, 1785, BA, Reel 1.
50. Escripto de Gabriel de Vergara, Viseprefecto y Presidente de las Misiones de Co Sta Crus de Queretaro, May 31, 1731, AGN, Provincias Internas, Vol. 163, Exp. 3. In this document the missionaries argue for water on many grounds, including "a la propaga-sion de la rreligion christiana."
51. ". . . muy interesado en sus R^S Quintos. . . ." Petition of Diego de Quiros, Parral, June 24, 1674, AHP, Reel 1671A.

government intent to develop this area, he buttressed his request with the caveat that, if the grant was made, "the royal roads will be protected and a large number of Indians will come to know the Catholic faith."[52] Government intent having been properly anticipated, the grant was extended.

A sixth criterion was legal right, a phenomenon not well understood in Spanish colonial water law. To be sure, when water controversies were carried to the courts, the contending parties were asked to defend their legal rights with proper documentation.[53] But there was a variety of legal rights, and they did not weigh equally on the Spanish colonial and Mexican scales of justice. In its conceptualization of legal right, Spanish law first distinguished between municipal or corporate rights on the one hand and individual or private rights on the other. After independence, Mexican law did the same. The municipal tradition was strong in Spain prior to the conquest of America, even though some of it fell victim to the Crown's centralization of authority during the Reconquest. The local cabildos were given wide latitude in the distribution of water and in the resolution of water disputes.[54] In original distribution, the water needs of the town were to take precedence over those of individual colonists.[55] If a cabildo inadvertently awarded too much of the available water to individuals at the expense of the community as a whole, these individual water grants would be rescinded.[56] If a local governing body sought royal funding for a water project, it invariably included in its request the idea that the entire community needed the dam or the irrigation ditch.[57] There is no question that in the Spanish and Mexican judicial systems the

52. Petition of Andrés Lopez de Gracia, Parral, Dec. 24, 1671, AHP, Reel 1671.

53. For example, "rrepresentar el dro que pertenzia a dha mision con especialidad al ojo de agua mensionado. . . ." José Antonio Almazán, July 27, 1731, AGN, Provincias Internas, Vol. 163, Exp. 3.

54. The municipal water tradition is developed in William B. Taylor, "Colonial Land and Water Rights of the New Mexico Pueblo Indians with Special Reference to the Tewa Region" (unpublished manuscript for the case of *New Mexico vs. Aamodt*, 1979). See also Encinas, *Cedulario indiano*, I, 63, and Rafael Altamira y Crevea et al., *Contribuciones a la historia municipal de América*. (Mexico: Instituto Panamericano de Geografía e Historia, 1951). The fueros of medieval Cataluña, Navarra, and Granada all recognized the corporate preference to water and subjugated private rights. See written testimony of William B. Stern, "The Water Rights of the Pueblo of Los Angeles," in *Los Angeles vs. San Fernando*, p. B26.

55. Ynstrucion practica que hande obserbar los comisionados para el repartimiento de tierras. . . , Jan. 25, 1771, AGN, Historia, Vol. 16, Exp. 8.

56. Real Cédula de 18 de Noviembre de 1803. Rodríguez de San Miguel, *Pandectas*, II, 304.

57. Testimonio de Diligencias executadas en virtud de despacho del Sr. Don Tomas Vélez Capuchín . . . a fin de que se execute el arbitrio . . . para la preza y vocasequia de este Rio del Norte, . . . Año de 1754, ALPC PE-51.

rights of the corporate community weighed more heavily than those of the individual. As Betty Dobkins has stated: "To look at the Spanish [water] system through the lens of individualistic property concepts is to miss its *raison d'etre*."[58] The principle is perhaps best synopsized in an 1832 water controversy in New Mexico. When a Mexican landowner in the vicinity of San Juan Pueblo asked for water rights, he was turned down by the governor because the pueblo's right as a community was stronger than his. The governor noted in his letterbook that "the common [right] of the pueblo is without doubt more deserving than that of a single man."[59]

The water retained by the Spanish American town was held in trust for the benefit of the entire community. It was not the property of the inhabitants of that town, either individually or collectively, but rather was the property of the corporate body itself.[60] The judicial personality of that corporate body was vested in the cabildo, which held legal authority to make all judgments concerning local water usage. The community preference to water under Spanish colonial and Mexican law has figured prominently in the legal history of the United States and forms the basis of the so-called Pueblo Rights Doctrine. A series of California and New Mexico water decisions has held that "Mexican colonization pueblos should have a prior and paramount right to the use of so much of the water of streams or rivers flowing through or along or beside such pueblos as should be necessary for the use of such pueblos and their inhabitants. . . . "[61] The idea behind the Pueblos Rights Doctrine is sound, but its use in United States courts has been inappropriately rigid and absolute.

Spanish water law was far from simplistic. The issue of corporate or individual preference is one case in point. The water advantage that the corporate community enjoyed over the individual, on the basis of legal right, was by no means absolute. Spanish law also addressed the rights of the individual. As early as 1573, when King Phillip II issued his famous ordinances on the founding of new towns, he spec-

---

58. Dobkins, *The Spanish Element in Texas Water Law*, p. 98.

59. Governor's Letterbooks to Alcaldes Constitucionales, May 8, 1832, MANM, Reel 14.

60. A. William Hall, *Irrigation Development* (Sacramento: California State Office, 1886), p. 368.

61. Robert Emmet Clark, "The Pueblo Rights Doctrine in New Mexico," *New Mexico Historical Review* 35 (October, 1960), p. 266. The article demonstrates that the California Pueblo Rights Doctrine was made applicable to New Mexico in the decision of *Cartwright et al. vs. The Public Service Company of New Mexico (66 N.M. 64. 343 P. 2d 654, September 3, 1959)*. The decision was subsequently appealed by the plaintiff and upheld by the New Mexico Supreme Court.

ified that grants of land and water should be made in such a way as to result in no prejudice to existing Indian towns, existing Spanish towns, "nor to individual persons."[62] It is instructive that the corporate rights of the community, whether it be Indian or Spanish, were not to infringe upon, much less invalidate, the rights of the individual. Two hundred years after the ordinances of Phillip II, the Plan de Pitic reaffirmed exactly the same principle. Article 2 of the Plan specifies that, when a new town is planned, its boundaries should not result in injury to established Indian towns or to individuals. The principle of individual rights is stated even more forcefully in Article 19, which admonishes water judges not to give anyone in the town more than his fair share in order to protect the rights of individuals not residing in the town.[63] A royal decree issued by King Ferdinand VII on the eve of Mexico's separation from Spain clearly protected individual rights to water, for it even authorized tax exemptions for both communities and individuals opening up new irrigation canals.[64] The protection of individual rights vis-à-vis those of the corporate community did not change with Mexican independence. In December of 1841, just a few years before war broke out between the United States and Mexico, Guadalupe Miranda was given a water grant in New Mexico. It specified that it was made without prejudice to either the common good or the individual good.[65]

The concern of Spanish water law with individual rights can be traced in a number of disputes, but the principles are most clearly enunciated in an 1808 controversy between Andrés Feliu y Fogones, dean of the church of Monterrey, and the cabildo of the same city. Fogones had inherited an orchard of ten solares with water rights from his predecessor at the church, Fray Rafael José Rengel. Rengel had puchased his water rights, had constructed the acequia madre with his own funds, and had planted the largest orchard in Monterrey. He had regularly donated trees to the city for its beautification and had allowed the city poor to have his sobrante water at no cost. After Rengel's death, Fogones continued the same policies, but the city decided to construct a new acequia madre, diverting the water before

62. ". . . que sea en parte a donde no pare perjuicio a cualesquier pueblos despañoles o de indios que antes estubieren poblados, ni de ninguna persona particular." "Ordenanzas de su Magestad hechas para los nuevos descubrimientos, conquistas y pacificaciones," in *Colección de documentos inéditos. . . , XVI, p. 167.*

63. Plan de Pitic, AGN, Tierras, Vol. 2773, Exp. 22, and UT WBS 9.

64. Decreto 30 del Rey Don Fernando VII, August 31, 1819. Cited in Written Testimony of William B. Stern, *Los Angeles vs. San Fernando*, p. B45.

65. Report of the Water Commission, Santa Fe, Dec. 23, 1841, SANM, II, 629.

it reached the existing ditch. The city claimed it needed the water as an income-producing source (*propios*) and planned to charge individuals ten to twelve pesos a day for its use. Fogones was furious. He charged the local government with committing a violently despotic act. He was giving water free to the poor, and the city now wanted to charge them.[66] Fogones' lawyer, José María Ortuño, made a strong case against the city. They were taking water legally held by an individual, and in the process were prejudicing not only the owner, but the many poor people to whom he allowed free use. "Who would have presumed, even remotely," he continued, "that water, a product of nature, common and necessary to all living things, would be converted into a saleable commercial product?" Worse, they planned to sell it to whomever could pay the most for it.[67] The city refused to budge, and the case eventually reached the Audiencia de Guadalajara. The high court found that Fogones' arguments had merit and ruled against the city. Individual rights to water could withstand unjustifiable corporate claims.[68]

Spanish and Mexican protection of individual water rights should not be misinterpreted. The rights of the community were certainly guarded as well and, indeed, in some respects were held in preference, but the individual rights to water and land were not wantonly subjected to those of the corporate community.

The question of legal right presents one additional problem to the study of Spanish colonial water law. It derives from the issue of historicism. Most guides to historical method wisely admonish the researcher to resist the understandable temptation of superimposing the cultural values of one world upon another. If a country's history is to be understood on its own terms, cultural empathy must rest with the society being studied, not the society to which the scholar belongs. This principle is especially important to the study of institutional history and legal history, in which there is a strong and almost natural tendency to view the relationship of the individual and the state through the cultural prisms of a later age.

In many contemporary societies, if a dispute over water should occur, the fundamental question to be asked is: Who has legal right to the water? In the Spanish colonial legal system this was not the basic

66. Dn Andres Feliu y Fogones to Governor, Feb. 4, 1808, AGN, Tierras, Vol. 1345, Exp. 11.
67. José María Ortuño to Sor Fiscal de lo Civil, Mar. 1808, AGN, Tierras, Vol. 1395, Exp. 11.
68. Audiencia to Ayuntamiento de Monterrey, May 9, 1808, AGN, Tierras, Vol. 1395, Exp. 11.

question. It was an answer to a still more fundamental inquiry. Litigants in water disputes knew that the court might not decide the issue on the basis of legal right and tried to cover themselves by incorporating other arguments that would support their cases. When Juan Nepomuceno de Larralde found himself disputing water with his neighbor, José Miguel Losano, in Nuevo León, he told the judge specifically that, if the case was not decided on the basis of legal right, the court should consider the fact that Losano already had two water outlets and he had only one.[69]

In the previously mentioned water case of *Santa Ana versus Angostura*, need was placed above legal right in the water distribution.[70] The identical principle was enunciated in an 1832 New Mexico water decision which declared that need was superior to all rights.[71] The well-documented water dispute between the Canary Islanders who settled San Antonio and the five surrounding missions affords another example. The missionaries developed a strong and erudite judicial treatise, at proper times interspersing the text with Latin phrases (*conservatio et continuata productio*) and citing principles of Roman law, Spanish law, and specific legislation from the *Recopilación* in support of their legal right.[72] The counterclaim of the settlers was much simpler. The king had asked them to come to New Spain and had promised them land and water. The commander of the presidio compromised, giving both sides some of the water, but in his decision took the occasion to indicate that, even if the Islanders could muster no laws in support of their legal right, they were still entitled to the water because the king had indeed ordered their migration.[73] But the clearest statement of the role of legal right in water distribution came in the New Mexico case of *Taos versus Arroyo Seco*. Even though the Indians of the pueblo of Taos had total right (*derecho total*) to the water, the Spanish settlers of Arroyo Seco were awarded a share in the repartimiento.[74]

At least one other student of Spanish and Spanish American water practices has been troubled by our imperfect understanding of

69. Larralde to Gobernador Vidal de Lorca, 1, 1778, AGN, Tierras, Vol. 1018, Exp. 3.

70. Salvador Montoya to Alcalde de Santa Ana, García Montoya, Aug. 1, 1838, UNM SC.

71. Manuel Martínez to Jefe Político, July 3, 1832, MANM, Reel 15.

72. Escripto de Gabriel Vergara, Viseprefecto y Presid^te de las misiones de Co Sta Crus de Queretaro, May 31, 1731, AGN, Provincias Internas, Vol. 163, Exp. 3.

73. "Y quando no huviere ley . . . que los favoresca en esta parte sera muy bastante la Real Cédula en la que mande Su Mag^d saliessen de sus tierras para que poblassen las de aquella provincia." Pedro de Rivera to Viceroy, Dec. 1, 1731, AGN, Provincias Internas, Vol. 163, Exp. 3.

74. Juan Ant° Lobato, Oct. 30, 1823, SANM, I, 1292.

legal right. Thomas Glick, after an extensive study of Spanish irrigation in medieval Valencia, turned his attention to the irrigation system of San Antonio, Texas. Among his provocative conclusions is the assertion that legal rights to water have been overstressed in the legal history. Glick argues persuasively that water practices, conditioned by local circumstances, are sometimes more important than legal rights themselves.

> Water rights are a society's idealized assessment of the best way to utilize water resources, according to the objectives most highly valued by that society. There is a subtle interplay between rights and practice, between the ideal and the real, and there has been a tendency to overstress the importance of rights in the overall picture. . . . At best the legal structure provides a framework in which arrangements are worked out. If subsequent practice proves, however, that the idealized assessment of resource utilization was incorrect, or inappropriate to the situation, the rights are altered—often with resistance—to meet the exigencies of the environment.[75]

Professor Glick's conclusion has much to recommend it. The documentary evidence from throughout the Southwest suggests strongly that, when a controversy over water surfaced, the underlying inquiry centered on the issue of how the water was to be divided. Who had the legal right was no more than one answer to this essential question. Judicial decision, in effect, came to the aid of custom. Legal rights, whether they be corporate or individual, did not constitute a single, overbearing consideration in the adjudication of water disputes.[76]

A seventh criterion upon which water disputes were resolved was the doctrine of equity and the common good, extremely important theoretical principles in Spanish colonial and Mexican law. Spaniards, no less than others, appreciated that an enviable jurisprudence should focus on the good of the whole. Because equity did not recognize ethnicity and made no distinctions between wealth and poverty, it was the major goal of the administrative system established in the New World.[77] After hearing all of the evidence and, in some cases, receiving the reports of independent experts, the judge charged with mak-

---

75. Thomas Glick, *The Old World Background to the Irrigation System of San Antonio, Texas* (El Paso: Texas Western University Press, 1972), pp. 50–51.
76. The *Recopilación* itself provided an important role for local custom in water allocations. See, for example, Libro II, Título 1, Ley 4, and Libro IV, Título 17, Ley 11.
77. See, for example, Mario Góngora, *Studies in the Colonial History of America* (Cambridge: Cambridge University Press, 1975), p. 72.

ing a water determination would ask himself what was equitable for the litigants, what was equitable for other individuals, and what was equitable for the larger community, *el bien y pro comun*.[78] He would concern himself not only with the question of who stands to gain what, but, more importantly, with the question of who stands to lose what. Ultimately, he would resolve the case with some form of compromise, a solution that seldom pleased anyone, but, more significantly, did not cause irreparable damage to anyone.

The common good was not necessarily synonymous with the water preference of the corporate community over the individual. The latter was a narrowly conceived legal concept; the former a broad principle much akin to what later became known as the Benthamite doctrine of the greatest good for the greatest number. An individual serving the common good with his water source could defeat even the corporate community in water litigation if that community was shirking its responsibility to the citizenry.[79] Although the corporate right of the community was generally weighted more heavily than the right of the individual, it did not follow that the corporate right was held in higher esteem than an aggregate of individual rights if, for example, the nonincorporated population using a water source approximated or even outnumbered the population of the corporate community. Spanish and Indian pueblos in northwestern New Spain were often small, and it was not unusual for the surrounding population to outnumber the population of the town itself. In addition, two corporate communities or two unincorporated populations could dispute water. In instances such as these, as well as many others, the doctrine of equity and the common good would assume an important role.

The relationship between equity and the common good is clear in the documentation. Equity is the means, and the common good the end. Water judges were constantly reminded that only through equity could they promote the happiness of the community and the common good.[80] In 1768, for example, the governor of New Mexico instructed the alcalde mayor of Santa Fe that, in a pending allocation of waters, he should divide the resource "with equity."[81] Some forty-six years

78. *Novísima recopilación*, Libro VI, Título 24, Ley 1.

79. This was one of the issues resolved in the case of *Fogones vs. Monterrey* cited above. See Expediente Promovido por el Dn Andres Feliu y Fogones . . . sobre que los Regidores de Aquella ciudad impiden de su uso del agua. . . , AGN, Tierras, Vol. 1395, Exp. 11.

80. ". . . el aumento y felicidad de los pueblos. . . ." Instrucciones que deberan guardar las Justicias subalternas, May 21, 1786, AHP, Reel 1787A.

81. Governor Don Pedro Fermín de Mendinueta, Mar. 12, 1768, SANM, II, 637. The commander of the presidio of Altar gave exactly the same instruction to his water judges. Caballero de Croix to don Joseph Gálvez, Dec. 23, 1780, AGI, Audiencia de Guadalajara, 272.

later another New Mexico governor ordered the alcalde mayor of Taos to settle a complicated water dispute by combining "equity and justice."[82] The Plan de Pitic based its entire water distribution formula on the principles of "equity and justice."[83] It is clear from the juxtaposition of these two phrases in a number of documents that a distinction is made between justice, which is a legal principle, and equity, which is an ethical assertion. A water distribution could be just (satisfying all legal requirements) without being equitable (promoting the common good). As William Stern stated in his expert testimony in the water controversy between the cities of Los Angeles and San Fernando, the litigation of water disputes under Spanish law concerned itself more with "doing the best for the common good" than it did with the explanation of the law itself.[84]

In actual decisions, judges were at pains to indicate to their superiors that their verdicts had been rendered with the common good in mind. In the water repartimiento of Nicolás Ortiz the judge indicated with some redundancy that his decision had been conditioned in part by "the common good of everyone."[85] When the Santa Fe Water Commission made a grant to Guadalupe Miranda, one of the reasons specified was that, because he helped travelers with water and supplies, the grant would be "in the common good."[86] Other examples abound. The water judges of northern New Spain were not convinced that an aggregate of unbridled individual ambitions would produce a harmonious society.

The doctrine of equity and the common good encompassed lofty and perhaps unattainable ethical goals. But those judges who proclaimed the doctrine with enthusiasm in their decisions were doing more than genuflecting toward a utopia or paying lip-service to a vague and meaningless notion. As it established itself as a working principle of Spanish law, the doctrine provided the moral mechanism for bridging the gap between the self-interest of individuals and the larger interest of society. It mitigated against any attempted water monopoly and provided one of the few avenues for a more contemplative kind of justice. Incapable of categorical definition, it also gave judicial officials tremendous flexibility in rendering decisions. The

82. Decree of Governor Alberto Maynez, Santa Fe, Apr. 15, 1815, SANM, I, 1357.
83. Plan de Pitic, Article 20, AGN, Tierras, Vol. 2773, Exp. 22.
84. Stern, "The Water Rights of the Pueblo of Los Angeles," in *Los Angeles vs. San Fernando*, B27.
85. ". . . en el vien comun de todos." Auto de cabesa de causa criminal contra el Cap[n] Nicolás Ortiz, July 13, 1723, SANM, II, 317A.
86. ". . . por el bien procummunal." Report of the Water Commission, Santa Fe, Dec. 23, 1841, SANM, II, 629.

geographic isolation of the north and inadequacy of transportation and communication made it unusual to seek advice in Guadalajara or Mexico City. Because decisions had to be made locally, flexibility was extremely important. Certainly the same flexibility left ample room for abuse, but it also provided a basis for discretionary judgment when local conditions seemed to dictate that title, legal right, or prior use should be subordinated to more immediate environmental exigencies. A legal right was firmly etched, but the common good could change with the passage of time. In short, the doctrine facilitated the matching of water allocations and water need as it made the Spanish struggle for justice less wooden and mechanical.

As part of Spain's colonizing endeavor in the New World, the Hispanic Southwest exhibited many characteristics common to the entire empire. But this frontier region was not merely a mirror of Spanish undertakings elsewhere; it emerged with a unique historical experience. The natural environment dictated that water would exert an influence unusual in the Spanish-speaking world. The availability or scarcity of water determined man-land relationships, conditioned patterns of human adaptation, helped define sexual and clan roles within certain groups, molded the nature of ethnic interactions, and even bequeathed a special kind of value system. Politically, economically, religiously, and militarily, water was a crucial ingredient in the historical potpourri which helped differentiate the Mexican north from other areas of New Spain.

Prior to the initial Spanish contact, Indian tribes in the northern desert appreciated that the manipulation of water could help free them from privation but, by subjecting them to more stringent measures of social control, could enslave them nevertheless. Most of those Indians who had resisted the temptations of becoming sedentary agriculturalists prior to the arrival of the Spaniards gradually succumbed to a war of attrition in the eighteenth and nineteenth centuries. History soon vindicated their fear that social control would lead to social abuse. The scenario was played out on a grand scale in the centuries following the initial Spanish settlement of the north.

The Spanish conquest of the northern frontier followed patterns not unfamiliar to students of sixteenth-century Spanish America, but the system of post-conquest control was more novel than in other parts of the empire. It did not take long for the conquerors, soldiers, missionaries, and colonists to realize that dominion over water not only meant control of the land it washed, but, more importantly, domination of those who resided on it. The Spanish motivations ranged across a broad spectrum, from personal aggrandizement and the desire for power to the more benevolent spiritual concerns of the clergy. But in all of these cases domination of the native population was the goal, and manipulation of water an important weapon to be employed. Had water not been so crucial in controlling the Indians, the Spaniards undoubtedly would have disputed water among themselves, because it was both necessary and scarce. But Spanish competition for water had an added incentive. Clergy, soldiers, and individual colonists could not easily control the Indian population for their own purposes if their Spanish neighbors monopolized the nearest water source. The contests for water were thus heated, whether they pitted Spaniard against Spaniard or Spaniard against Indian.

Had the Mexican north been an area of great material wealth or the home of large concentrations of Indians, officials in Mexico City, stimulated by the prospects of gain, would have taken greater interest in it. But great distance from the center of power and general apathy combined to insulate the region. Local and provincial officials both before and after Mexican independence, by default enjoyed wide latitude of action. Municipal water ordinances seldom were ratified by higher authority and, unless they were egregious in disregard of general legal norms, seldom were denied ratification. They remained in full force at the pleasure of the local elites. In the provincial capitals of the north an active governor could serve as a counterbalance to the cabildo, but in most towns the cabildo's word was law and seldom challenged with success.

In a system of exaggerated local control, abuse in water allocation was constant, and when it became intolerable the judicial mechanisms of the state were called into place. The kinds of water disputes which both Spaniards and Indians carried to the courts of northern New Spain are an excellent reflection of the society in which they lived, and the judicial doctrines upon which they were to be resolved an eloquent statement of the goals envisioned for a just society. The actual decisions reached reveal much about the local power structure in the colonial period and early nineteenth century.

It is true that Spanish officials seemed more devoted to the letter of the law than to its application, especially when it threatened to work against the best interest of the local elites. But what is surprising about the adjudication of water conflicts is that the elites did not exert more influence than they actually did. To be sure, influence helped. The wealthy and the powerful won more cases than they lost and in the process often trampled on the rights of others. Local officials could be bribed, and they sometimes were. Networks of family ties and compadrazco could suborn the safeguards of the judicial system, and sometimes they did. But there are enough examples of Indians, mestizos, and poor Spaniards coming out of the courts with more water than when they entered to conclude that the voluminous legislation designed to protect the interests of the disadvantaged, both before and after Mexican independence, was not completely in vain. Compromise and concern for the common good were not merely lofty goals rejected cavalierly in the courts of the Hispanic Southwest. They were not simply guises making possible the cohabitation of the judge with his conscience. They were fundamental principles brought to bear even in the most complex of water adjudications and even when the status of one of the litigants would have suggested that his opponent stood no chance in the impending case.

Less obvious than those heated contests which pitted man against his fellow man were those struggles between man and his environment. Few appreciated that innocent tampering with the delicate desert ecosystem, especially with its natural water reserve, might portend fundamental, permanent change. Legal restrictions on the use of water were defined largely in an ecological vacuum. Admirable in their concern for equitable distribution, only occasionally did they address the need for conservation. The price to be paid for demanding a quick profit from the earth's resources was never imagined, much less assessed. The short-term benefits of ecolturation often yielded to long-term liabilities which could manifest themselves either suddenly and violently or subtly and gradually. While floods certainly antedated the arrival of man in the Southwest, to natural occurrences were added the inevitable retributions to thoughtless manipulation. The aftermath of flooding provided only the most graphic illustrations of the permanent impact of ecolturation. In countless other ways the desert land did not remain indifferent to its exploitation.

For three centuries, from roughly 1550 to 1850, water exerted an amazingly constant influence in the Mexican north. Spanish settlement, with its attendant demographic and economic shifts, exacerbated water scarcity, but, once this new reality came to dominate the life cycle of northerners, the water history of the region underwent few dramatic changes. The major alterations in the religious organization (the expulsion of the Jesuits) and political structure (the organization of the Provincias Internas and subsequently Mexican independence from Spain) made little difference. The economic dislocation and human suffering caused by a drought or a flood, or the opportunity afforded a poor Indian to redress a water grievance in the courts, were about the same in the middle of the nineteenth century as they had been in the middle of the sixteenth.

The continuities of water history in the north were, of course, determined in part by cycles of precipitation. Interethnic tensions rose during dry years and lessened during wet ones. But not all the continuities were predetermined or inevitable. If eighteenth- and nine-teenth-century settlers had learned irrefutable water lessons from earlier generations of colonists, such as the consequences of constructing buildings in the floodplain of an arroyo, basic changes in social patterns would have emerged with the passage of time, and these, in turn, could have lent themselves to the formulation of a new periodization. But this type of change did not occur. Later settlers in the north, for better or for worse, were prisoners not of history but of certain cultural predispositions. The lure of constructing buildings under the shade of trees found in the floodplain was more seductive than the lessons of dozens of previous villages being destroyed by floods. These eighteenth- and nineteenth-century settlers not only refused to accept the lessons of precedent, but remained impervious to the laws of nature.

The struggle for water in the Hispanic Southwest was above all a microcosm of the entire spectrum of competing human values. While the native American populations of the desert viewed the precious liquid as the medium of life, the conquerors, missionaries, and settlers viewed it as an instrument of control, a source of power, and most importantly as the fount of accumulated wealth. Even in the aftermath of the physical subjugation of the Indian there was only a mixing, never a blending, of ideas concerning the accommodation man ultimately must make with the earth's natural bounty.

Afterword

More than a decade has passed since the original publication of *Water in the Hispanic Southwest*. The historiography of Hispanic water law has matured greatly in those intervening years. The major stimulus to the scholarship in the United States has been continuing litigation in state and federal courts where judges and special masters, using expert witnesses' reports, depositions, and testimony, have sought to better comprehend the nuances of the obligations the United States assumed in 1848 when it ratified the Treaty of Guadalupe-Hidalgo. The process has been evident throughout the states that share a common border with Mexico, but it has been most apparent in Arizona and New Mexico, as those two states began a general adjudication of water rights, and some litigants (heirs or successors in interest to original grantees) found it important to exert their rights under Spanish and Mexican law.

Experience has shown me that many of my friends and colleagues in Mexico do not readily understand why Hispanic water law continues to be of such interest to the United States court system. Many friends and colleagues in the United States are equally incredulous, and their astonishment increases when I explain that it is not today's Hispanic water law but rather that water law of the eighteenth and nineteenth centuries that has captivated water lawyers and crowded United States court dockets in the 1980s and 1990s. The basic explanation for this seeming anomaly is found in international law, treaty law, and United States case law.

If the political maps of the world remained forever constant, there would be no need for the law of nations to focus on the problems of state succession. Since the advent of the nation state, however, revolutions for independence, peaceful cessions, sales and trades, wars of conquest, and major and minor boundary adjustments have occasioned changes in territorial sovereignty. History has shown repeatedly that an area can belong to one country on one day and to another on the next. In more recent times, cartographers have been kept extremely busy as the former Soviet Union and Yugoslavia fell apart while East and West Germany fell together. Invariably, changes in territorial sovereignty have bequeathed an unbelievably perplexing legacy of legal quandaries. They concern not only abstract principles of diplomacy and international law but also, and more important, groups of people whose lives have been disrupted by the actions of others: residents and nonresidents; rich and poor; newcomers and those long established—all with vested interests of one kind or another.

The law of state succession, an international law construct, has as its major goal the curtailing of the most egregious impacts of territorial change. It rests on the fundamental legal principle, endorsed by the most distinguished legal scholars throughout the world, that property and other vested rights previously acquired under a former sovereign must be respected by the successor state.[1] After an extensive review of the scholarly literature, Professor D. P. O'Connell, in his seminal two-volume study on state succession, concludes that when a change of territorial sovereignty occurs, "private property rights, and rights deriving from judicial decisions remain unchanged. . . . [T]he successor state is entitled to exercise the predecessor's rights and is obliged to discharge the predecessor's duties, because international law so directs."[2] The principle that acquired rights (*droits acquis*) survive the incident of state succession is, in fact, "one of the most well-established norms in the field."[3]

---

1. For a sampling of international endorsement of this principle, one can consult J.H.W. Verzijl, *International Law in Historical Perspective,* vol. 7 of *State Succession* (Leiden: A. W. Sijthoff, 1974); Amos S. Hershey, *The Essentials of International Public Law and Organization* (New York: Macmillan Company, 1927); Ernest Nys, *Le droit international: Les principes, les theories, les faits* (Paris: Librarie des Sciences Politiques Sociales, 1912); Herbert A. Wilkinson, *The American Doctrine of State Succession* (Westport, Conn.: Greenwood Press, Publishers, 1975); Emanuel Ritter von Ullmann, *Völkerrecht* (Tubingen: J. C. B. Mohr, 1908); Carlos Calvo, *Le droit international: Theorique et pratique,* 6 vols. (Paris: A. Rousseau, 1887–1888); Wesley L. Gould, *An Introduction to International Law* (New York: Harper, 1957); Coleman Phillipson, *Termination of War and Treaties of Peace* (London: T. F. Unwin, 1916); and Friedrich August Heydte, *Völkerrecht* (Cologne: Verlag für Politik und Wirtschaft, 1907).

2. D. P. O'Connell, *State Succession in Municipal Law and International Law,* 2 vols. (Cambridge: Cambridge University Press, 1967), p. 32.

3. Michael John Volkovitzch, "Righting Wrongs: Towards a New Theory of State Succession to Responsibility for International Delicts," *Columbia Law Review* 92 (December 1992), 2203.

In the absence of some international covenant to the contrary, a successor state can subsequently alter acquired rights, but legislation to change or abrogate them must be explicit and precise. As O'Connell establishes, "[U]ntil a successor State legislates to terminate acquired rights, . . . these remain in existence as facts."[4] In those rare instances when an ownership pattern in a cessionary state is completely inconsistent with the concept of property in a successor state (for example, the "ownership" of a slave in a nation without slavery), then it is necessary that steps be taken "in order to indemnify the holder of the right for its loss under the new legal order."[5] International covenants provide additional protections, making the alteration of acquired rights difficult or impossible. World history is replete with international treaties expressly protecting vested rights during changes of territorial sovereignty. A small sampling would include the treaty between Sweden and Great Britain (1719), France and the Bishopric of Liège (1772), France and Austria (1814), the Congress of Vienna (1815), Hanover and Prussia (1827), France and Prussia (1829), Greece and Turkey (1881), Bolivia and Brazil (1903), and Serbia and Turkey (1914).[6]

The principle that an area's change of sovereignty alters its public law but leaves intact its private law, including property law, also has deep roots in the United States historical experience. In 1803, when the United States acquired Louisiana from France, former citizens of Louisiana continued to enjoy their property as before. The Florida acquisition treaty of 1819 (the Adams-Onís Treaty) guaranteed acquired rights as well. When a test case reached the United States Supreme Court in 1833, Chief Justice John Marshall concluded that the property guarantees that are afforded individuals apply equally if the territory in question was acquired amicably or by conquest.

> It may not be unworthy of remark, that it is very unusual, even in cases of conquest, for the conqueror to do more than displace the sovereign and assume dominion over the country. The modern usage of nations which has become law would be violated . . . if private property rights should be generally confiscated and private rights annulled. The people change their allegiance; their relation to their ancient sovereign is dissolved; but their relations to each other and their rights of property remain undisturbed.[7]

Throughout the nineteenth century, dozens of cases in state and federal courts articulated the same principle. The decisions clearly

4. O'Connell, *State Succession*, p. 265.
5. Verzijl, *International Law in Historical Perspective*, vol. 7, p. 74.
6. Ibid., p. 78.
7. *United States v Percheman*, 7 Pet. 51, at 86.

indicate that the courts did not always have good evidence upon which to assess the nature of acquired rights under the laws of prior sovereigns. Even so, whether they were perfectly or poorly understood, there was little debate on the applicability of the laws themselves. While the United States court system sought to protect foreign citizens, or nationalized citizens, in the United States, the Department of State vigilantly sought to assure the same protections for United States citizens living abroad who suffered the consequences of changes of territorial sovereignty. The United States courts did recognize that it was possible to alter acquired rights but only to the extent that they were not specifically protected by United States treaty obligations. This principle was most succinctly affirmed in *Delassus v United States,* which held that "the conqueror may deal with the inhabitants and give them what law he pleases, unless restrained by the capitulation, but until alteration be made the former laws continue."[8]

In 1848, at the conclusion of the war between the United States and Mexico, the Treaty of Guadalupe-Hidalgo provided ample protection for the property rights of Mexicans who suddenly found themselves residing in the United States. That document is a classic example of applying the law of prior sovereigns to citizens innocently prejudiced by a change of territorial possession. Article VIII of the Treaty of Guadalupe-Hidalgo states:

> Mexicans now established in the territories previously belonging to Mexico, and which remain for the future within the limits of the United States, as defined by the present treaty, shall be free to continue where they now reside, or to remove at any time to the Mexican Republic, retaining the property which they possess in the said territories, or disposing thereof, and removing the proceeds wherever they please, without their being subjected, on this account to any contribution, tax, or charge whatever. . . . In the said territories, *property of every kind,* now belonging to Mexicans not established there, shall be inviolably respected. The present owners, the heirs of these, and all Mexicans who may hereafter acquire said property by contract, shall enjoy with respect to it guarantees equally ample as if the same belonged to citizens of the United States [emphasis mine].[9]

Article IX provided additional guarantees as it stipulated:

> The Mexicans who in the territories aforesaid, shall not preserve the character of citizens of the Mexican Republic, conformably

8. *Delassus v United States,* 9 Pet. 117 quoted in Wilkinson, *The American Doctrine of State Succession,* p. 39.

9. United States Senate, *The Treaty Between the United States and Mexico,* 30th Cong., 1st sess., Executive Document 52 (Washington, D.C., 1848), p. 47.

with what is stipulated in the preceding article, shall be incorporated into the Union of the United States, and be admitted at the
proper time (to be judged of by the Congress of the United States)
to the enjoyment of all the rights of citizens of the United States,
according to the principles of the Constitution; and in the mean-
time, shall be maintained and protected in the free enjoyment of
their liberty and property, and secured in the free exercise of their
religion without restriction.[10]

The treaty negotiators and the respective congresses could have
limited the kind of property to be encompassed by the broad promise
of protection. Following Hispanic law, they could have confined it to
only *propiedad perfecta* or *propiedad imperfecta,* or only to real property
(*propiedad immueble*) or personal property (*propiedad mueble*). But they
unequivocally included "property of every kind." If the treaty guarantees have sometimes been misunderstood or misrepresented, it is because Article X of the treaty, pertaining explicitly to land grants, was
never ratified by the United States Senate. The significance of the failure to ratify must be viewed in its own historical context and with the
intent of the president and the Senate in mind.[11]

The original draft of the Treaty of Guadalupe-Hidalgo, negotiated
by United States Commissioner Nicholas P. Trist and his Mexican
counterpart, stipulated the following in Article X:

All grants of land made by the Mexican government, or by the
competent authorities, in territories previously appertaining to
Mexico, and remaining for the future within the limits of the
United States, shall be respected as valid, to the same extent that
the same grants would be valid if the said territories had remained
within the limits of Mexico. But the grantees of lands in Texas, put
in possession thereof, who, by reason of the circumstances of the
country since the beginning of the troubles between Texas and the
Mexican Government, may have been prevented from fulfilling all
the conditions of their grants, shall be under the obligation to ful-
fill the said conditions within the periods limited in the same re-
spectively; such periods to be now counted from the date of the
exchange of ratifications of this treaty: in default of which the said
grants shall not be obligatory upon the State of Texas, in virtue of
the stipulations contained in this Article.
The foregoing stipulation in regard to grantees of land in
Texas, is extended to all grantees of land in the territories aforesaid, elsewhere than in Texas, put in possession under such grants;

10. Ibid.

11. In a strictly technical sense, the president ratifies treaties but can do so only with the advice
and consent of the Senate. Failure to receive consent of the Senate means that a treaty, or part
of a treaty, is not ratified. See Samuel B. Crandall, *Treaties, Their Making and Enforcement* (New
York: AMS Press, 1968), pp. 67–82.

and, in default of the fulfillment of the conditions of any such grant, within the new period, which, as is above stipulated, begins with the day of the exchange of ratifications of this treaty, the same shall be null and void.

The Mexican Government declares that no grant whatever of lands in Texas has been made since the second day of March one thousand eight hundred and thirty-six; and that no grant whatever of lands in any of the territories aforesaid has been made since the thirteenth day of May one thousand eight hundred and forty-six.[12]

The Senate's failure to ratify Article X should not be interpreted to suggest that the recipients of land grants, made first by Spanish and subsequently by Mexican officials, were left unprotected by the treaty. The explanatory provisions of the Protocol of Querétaro substantiate this point.

Because the United States government did not ratify the entire treaty negotiated by the United States and Mexican peace commissioners, and because the Mexican government expressed concern with the changes, President Polk found it necessary to send two new envoys to Mexico to explain the reasons for the alterations and, if possible, to secure Mexican congressional approval of the amended document. In the exercise of these tasks the two envoys were also empowered to negotiate an international protocol with the properly designated Mexican official.

President Polk originally chose Senator Ambrose H. Sevier, Chairman of the Senate Foreign Relations Committee and a champion of ratification, to be the United States Envoy Extraordinary and Minister Plenipotentiary to Mexico. Senator Sevier became ill just at the time he was scheduled to depart for Mexico, and because the medical prognosis was unclear, the president made a second appointment, Attorney General Nathan Clifford. Both appointments were approved by Congress, and because Sevier recovered from his illness, both men participated in winning Mexican congressional approval and in drafting the contemplated protocol. The Mexican envoy, Luis de la Rosa, was actually Mexico's Minister of Foreign Relations.

President Polk's instructions to his special envoys were clear.

Sir: You have been appointed by the President, by and with the advice and consent of the Senate, to a most important and responsible mission. The task has thus been assigned to you of consummating the treaty of peace which was signed at Guadalupe Hidalgo, on the second day of February last, between the United States and the Mexican Republic, and which, . . . was ratified by the Senate with amendments.

12. Ibid.

This brief statement will indicate to you clearly the line of your duty. You are not sent to Mexico for the purpose of negotiating any new treaty or changing in any particular the ratified treaty which you will bear with you. None of the amendments adopted by the Senate can be rejected or modified, except by the authority of that body. Your whole duty will then consist in using every honorable effort to obtain from the Mexican government a ratification of the treaty in the form in which it has been ratified by the Senate. . . . For this purpose it may become necessary that you should explain to the Mexican Minister for Foreign Affairs . . . the reasons which have influenced the senate in adopting their several amendments. . . .

Should you find it impossible, after exhausting every honorable effort, to obtain a ratification from the President and Congress of Mexico of the treaty, as it has been amended by the Senate, it may become necessary for you . . . to express an opinion as to what portion of the Senate's amendments they might probably be willing to yield for the sake of restoring peace between the two republics. This will be a very delicate duty; but upon one point at least you will be relieved of all embarrassment. Neither the President not the Senate of the United States can ever consent to ratifying any treaty containing the 10th article of the Treaty of Guadalupe-Hidalgo, in favor of grantees of land in Texas or elsewhere. The Government of the United States do [sic] not possess the power to carry such an article into execution; and, if they did, it would be highly unjust and inexpedient. Should the Mexican government persist in retaining this article, then all prospects of immediate peace is [sic] ended; and of this you may give them absolute assurance.[13]

The instructions were unambiguous. The United States envoys had no authority to negotiate a new treaty or to modify the one already ratified by the United States Senate. Their action, significantly, was to be explanatory. The two United States commissioners were successful in gaining Mexican ratification of the amended treaty. In the course of that effort, and in keeping with their instructions, they offered the reasons for the Senate action on Article X. This explanation formed the basis of Article II of the Protocol:

The American government by suppressing the 10th article of the Treaty of Guadalupe-Hidalgo did not in any way intend to annul the grants of land made by Mexico in the ceded territories. These grants, notwithstanding the suppression of this article of the treaty, preserve the legal value that they may possess and the grantees may cause their legitimate titles to be acknowledged before American tribunals.

Conformably to the laws of the United States, legitimate titles

---

13. James Buchanan to Ambrose H. Sevier, March 18, 1848, *Congressional Globe*, February 19, 1849, p. 495.

to every description of property, personal and real, existing in the ceded territories, are those which were legitimate titles under the Mexican law of California and New Mexico up to the thirteenth of May, 1846, and in Texas up to the 2nd of March, 1836.[14]

Both the Treaty of Guadalupe-Hidalgo and the Protocol of Querétaro make it clear that valid Mexican land grants were protected in the ceded territories. This conclusion is not altered by the failure of the U. S. Senate to ratify Article X, because Article VIII of that treaty also protected Mexican "property of every kind" and Article II of the Protocol of Querétaro offered still additional evidence of intent. While a protocol does not require the consent of the Senate or enjoy the rank of a treaty, it is an accepted mechanism for the peaceful resolution of international disputes and has been used repeatedly in United States history to facilitate the cessation of hostilities,[15] provide a clear statement of intent, and provide the necessary context for another document. Less formal than a treaty, a protocol enjoys the international stature of a covenant, a charter, or a pact, and holds higher international standing than the mere exchange of notes or letters.[16] The Protocol of Querétaro was never rejected or repudiated by the United States Senate or any other branch of the federal government and therefore continues to stand as the correct and official interpretation of the amended treaty.[17]

Because water rights were property rights under Hispanic law, the

14. The Protocol of Querétaro can be found printed in various places, including the *Compilation of Treaties in Force* (Washington: Government Printing Office, 1899), p. 402. The Spanish text is totally consistent with the English text. It reads as follows: "El gobierno americano, suprimiendo el artículo X del tratado de Guadalupe, no ha intentado de ninguna manera anular las concesiones de tierras hechas por México en los territorios cedidos. Esas concesiones, aun suprimiendo el artículo del tratado, conservan el valor legal que tengan; y los concesionarios pueden hacer valer sus títulos legítimos ante los tribunales americanos. Conforme a la ley de los Estados-Unidos, son títulos legítimos en favor de cada propiedad, mueble o raiz, ecsistente en los territorios cedidos, los mismos que hayan sido títulos legítimos bajo la ley mexicana hasta el dia 13 de Mayo de 1846 en Californias y en Nuevo-México, y hasta el dia 2 de Marzo de 1836 en Tejas." The Spanish text can be found in *Tratado de Guadalupe Hidalgo* (México: Secretaría de la Presidencia, Departamento Editorial, n.d.).

15. For example, the United States used similar protocols in 1814 at the end of the War of 1812, in 1898 at the end of the Spanish American War, in 1897 in submitting international claims arbitrations, and in 1910 at the establishment of the International Prize Court at the Hague.

16. An international protocol can be defined as "an international agreement less formal than a treaty. A protocol may be an independent agreement, or it may be supplemental to a convention drawn up by the same negotiators explaining or interpreting the provisions of the convention." James R. Fox, *Dictionary of International and Comparative Law* (Carlisle, Pa.: Oceana Publications, 1992). Various uses of international protocols are traced in Tsune-Chi Yu, *The Interpretation of Treaties* (New York: AMS Press, 1968), passim.

17. This is also the conclusion of Geoffrey P. Mawn in "A Land Grant Guarantee: The Treaty of Guadalupe-Hidalgo or the Protocol of Querétaro," *Journal of the West* 14 (October, 1975), 49–63.

Treaty of Guadalupe-Hidalgo and the Protocol of Querétaro protected water appurtenant to Spanish and Mexican land grants. The present owners of lands originally comprised in those grants, as successors in interest, continue to hold the water rights originally awarded to, or subsequently acquired by, the Spanish or Mexican proprietors. It is this factor that has stimulated the applied history and has contributed in such an important way to the maturation of Hispanic water law historiography.

The inquiries of the "forensic historians" in the last twelve years have focused primarily on three issues: groundwater law; the water rights of municipalities; and the day-to-day management of *acequias* in rural areas. Some of the new studies have been published,[18] but much remains hidden in unpublished reports framed specifically for litigants, potential litigants, or in some cases the courts themselves.[19] Although these subjects cannot be treated in detail here, a summary of recent findings helps to update the previous conclusions proffered in this study.

In the early 1980s, research on Hispanic water law focused almost

18. See, for example, Michael C. Meyer, "The Living Legacy of Hispanic Groundwater Law in the Contemporary Southwest," *Journal of the Southwest* 31 (Autumn, 1989), 287–299; Daniel Tyler, "Underground Water in Hispanic New Mexico: A Brief Analysis of Laws, Customs, and Disputes," *New Mexico Historical Review* 66 (July, 1991), 287–299; Daniel Tyler, *The Mythical Pueblo Rights Doctrine: Water Administration in Hispanic New Mexico* (El Paso: Texas Western Press, 1990); John O. Baxter, *Spanish Irrigation in Taos Valley* (Santa Fe: New Mexico State Engineer Office, 1990); Hans W. Baade, "The Historical Background of Texas Water Law—A Tribute to Jack Pope," *St. Mary's Law Journal* 18 (1986), 1–98; Charles L. Briggs and John R. Van Ness (eds.), *Land, Water and Culture: New Perspectives on Hispanic Land Grants* (Albuquerque: University of New Mexico Press, 1987); Federico M. Cheever, "A New Approach to Mexican Land Grants and the Public Trust Doctrine: Defining the Property Interest Protected by the Treaty of Guadalupe-Hidalgo," *UCLA Law Review* 33 (1986), 1364–1409; Malcolm Ebright, *Land Grants and Lawsuits in Northern New Mexico* (Albuquerque: University of New Mexico Press, 1994); Anastasia S. Stevens, "Pueblo Water Rights in New Mexico," *Natural Resources Journal* 28 (Summer, 1988), 535–583; and Peter L. Reich, "Mission Revival Jurisprudence: State Courts and Hispanic Water Law Since 1850," *Washington Law Review* 69 (October, 1994), 869–925.

19. Some of the unpublished reports include Michael C. Meyer, "Hispanic Water Rights on the San Ignacio del Babocómori: The Treaty of Guadalupe-Hidalgo and the Gadsden Purchase," Tucson, 1993; Michael C. Meyer, "The Water Regimen of New Mexico in 1848 and the Treaty of Guadalupe-Hidalgo," prepared for the Southwest Hispanic Research Institute, University of New Mexico and the Taos Valley Acequia Association, 1994; Daniel Tyler, "Underground Water in Hispanic New Mexico: An Analysis of Laws, Customs and Disputes," report for American Water Development, Denver, Colorado, 1987; Michael C. Meyer, "The Baca Float Number Four Land Grant: An Assessment of Water Rights Under Spanish Colonial and Mexican Law," Tucson, Arizona, 1986; Guillermo Margadant, "Memorandum About Legal-Historical Aspects of the Las Vegas Grant of 1835," report for State of New Mexico ex re. *Reynolds v Lewis* (1986); Guillermo Margadant, "The Pueblo Water Rights in the City of Las Vegas, N.M.," Mexico City, 1985; and G. Emlen Hall, "Shell Games: The Continuing Legacy of Rights to Minerals and Water on Spanish and Mexican Land Grants in the Southwest," paper prepared for the Rocky Mountain Mineral Law Institute, circa 1988.

entirely on surface water law. Relatively little effort had been devoted to groundwater law. Now we are able to document how differently the two categories of water law were treated. The differences begin with the most fundamental issue of all—the manner in which one acquired the right to use the water in question. Water that originated on a piece of land, that ran solely within its confines, or that lay under it was automatically alienated from state ownership with the sale or grant of the land. It was appurtenant to landownership. No special water right or additional permission was required to use it, and no limits were set on the amounts that might be used.

Spanish groundwater law in this respect is thus a direct legacy of its Roman predecessor. In the Roman legal system, water that ran perennially from one property to another (*aqua profluens*) was in the public domain (*res communes*). On the other hand, spring water or percolating water (*aqua viva*) and rainwater (*aqua pluviae*) were considered part of the land. Roman law privatized groundwater to the extent that it could be used exclusively by the owner, even causing damage to a neighbor unless there was a conscious and malicious intent to damage that neighbor.[20] Because it inhered in landownership, the right to continued use of groundwater was in no way dependent upon its regular use. It was not forfeited by reason of abandonment.

The legal inheritance of the Roman tradition was carried into the *Siete Partidas,* in which groundwater and other diffused surface water originating on a piece of land or running solely within its confines (including wells and springs) belonged to the owner of the land on which it rose (Partida 3, Título 32, Ley 19).[21] Rainwater or snowmelt that flowed in an intermittent stream or arroyo could be impounded by the landowner in reservoirs, dams, cisterns, storage tanks, or any other device and put to subsequent beneficial use without permission because it was considered private water.[22] The *Siete Partidas,* in fact,

20. Gallego Anabitarte et al., *El derecho de aguas en España,* vol. 1, p. 416. In this particular matter, at least, the common law and civil law were indeed similar.

21. The basic statement on the private ownership of groundwater reads: "Fuente o pozo de aqua auiendo algun ome en su casa si algun su vezino quissiese fazer otro en la suya para auer aqua e para aprouecharse del: puedelo fazer, e non selo puede el otro deuedar, como quier que menquasse por ende el aqua de la fuente, o del su pozo. Fueras ende si este que lo quisiesse fazer: non lo ouviesse menester más se mouiesse maliciosamente por fazer mal, o engaño al otro con intención de destajar." The English translation is as follows: "Where a man has a spring, or well, on his property and his neighbor wishes to make one on his property, in order to procure water for his use, the latter may do it, and the former cannot prevent him, notwithstanding the water in the first spring or well may be thereby diminished, unless the person wishing to make the new well has no need of it and acts maliciously, with the intention of doing harm to the other." *Siete Partidas,* Partida 3, Título 32, Ley 19.

22. *Siete Partidas,* Partida 2, Título 20, Ley 4.

specified that it was an obligation of all inhabitants to make their land productive, and it further indicated that "man has the power to do as he sees fit with those things that belong to him according to the laws of God and man."[23]

Did the landowner actually own the groundwater, spring water, and intermittent stream water, or did he merely enjoy the use of that water without any additional authorization from the Crown? The best evidence argues forcefully that the landowner's exclusive right to water originating on or underlying his property was not simply to usufruct of that water but rather was a vested right of ownership of the water itself. It was possessed in dominium. While perennially running surface water was *propiedad imperfecta* of which one could enjoy possessory use subject to state control, groundwater was *propiedad perfecta*, the property of the landowner. Moreover, the ownership did not have to be obtained by separate purchase, grant, or judicial decision; it was conveyed automatically by the same title as the surface of the land. In comparison with perennially running surface water, groundwater was at one and the same time more easily privatizable and more totally privatized. One could use it, buy it, sell it, rent it, or even waste it.

Hispanic groundwater law was designed to protect individual rights, to encourage private initiative and entrepreneurship, to stimulate economic development, and even to accumulate personal wealth. This was not Spanish medieval feudalism. This was incipient capitalism, a glorification of the sanctity of private property and a celebration of *laissez faire*. With but very few exceptions, a person could do what he wanted with his groundwater resource even if it prejudiced the interests of his neighbor. Under some circumstances it even permitted the exercise of individual caprice. Groundwater law represented free enterprise with but very few constraints.

Surface water law, on the other hand, offered itself as a necessary counterpoise. It had a more benevolent social purpose. It recognized that unbridled individual ambition would never produce a harmonious society and viewed justice not as a metaphysical abstraction but as an attainable goal. By enshrining the concept of normative restraint, it was clearly designed to check monopoly, limit the influence of irresponsible locals, protect the disadvantaged, and most importantly to encourage equity.

The surface water law and groundwater law were dominated by two different ethics, but together they offered some philosophical symmetry. By placing the rights of the individual at its epicenter, Hispanic

---

23. *Siete Partidas,* Partida 3, Título 28, Ley 1.

groundwater law certainly would have appealed to Kant. Surface water law, on the other hand, by extolling the role of the state over the
individual, would have won the warm endorsement of Hegel. Viewed
holistically, Spanish water law, if not representing the triumph of reason over will, was an ingenious system that provided the moral mechanism for bridging the gap between the self-interest of the individual
and the larger concerns of society. It combined the reasonableness of
private property with the justice of serving the common good.

Municipal water rights under Hispanic law have too long been understood as resting upon the foundations of the Pueblo Rights Doctrine, a legal construct which posited that legally established corporate
communities enjoyed a "prior and paramount right" to all surface waters flowing through or surrounding them.[24] Because the author of
this study never uncovered primary historical evidence detailing such
a "prior and paramount right," and because he was never convinced
of the existence of such a notion, the Pueblo Rights Doctrine received
scant attention in the original edition of *Water in the Hispanic Southwest*.
When it was mentioned, a brief attempt was made to confine its broad
scope. The research of an expert witness in the State of New Mexico's
recent effort to refute the Pueblo Rights Doctrine sustains that such
caution was not misguided and also sheds new light on the true nature
of municipal water rights.[25]

In the original granting and subsequent division of waters, corporate communities enjoyed an advantage over single individuals. The
municipal preference did not stem from statutes establishing a priority
of users but rather from the Spanish understanding of the role of the
municipality in the social order. During the seven centuries of military
activity against the Moors, Spanish towns, as strategic outposts and
bastions of frontier defense, gained considerable autonomy through
the granting of *fueros*. Included in most of the fueros were provisions
granting the municipalities jurisdiction over outlying land and water.[26]
Not even at the end of the fifteenth century were the Catholic sovereigns, Ferdinand and Isabella, able to strip local *ayuntamientos* of their
traditional authority in these matters. In 1573, from the Escorial, King

24. The Pueblo Rights Doctrine was formulated in two nineteenth-century California cases:
Lux v Haggin (1886), 69 Cal. 255, and *Vernon Irrigation Company v Los Angeles* (1895), 106 Cal.
237. The doctrine was accepted and even expanded by the New Mexico Supreme Court in
the 1958 case, *Cartwright v Public Service Company of New Mexico*, 66 N.M. 64.

25. Tyler, *The Mythical Pueblo Rights Doctrine*, passim.

26. See Justiano Rodríguez, *Los Fueros del Reino de León* (León: Ediciones Leonesas, 1981);
Ignacio Jordan de Asso y del Rio and Miguel de Manuel y Rodríguez, eds., *El Fuero Viejo de
Castilla* (Madrid: Imprenta de Don Alejandro Gómez Fuente Negro, 1847); and Galo Sánchez,
ed., *Libro de los Fueros de Castilla* (Barcelona: Ediciones el Albir, 1985).

Philip II decreed a number of highly important royal ordinances concerning the laying out of towns. Among these was the provision that towns were to retain water for domestic and agricultural needs, and they were to apportion it, along with communal land, to the original settlers and those who came later.[27] Although the land became privatized after several years of beneficial use, the water continued to be controlled by the local *ayuntamiento* because future settlement might occasion a different allocation pattern. In a practical sense the corporate community also enjoyed another advantage. Since water disputes generally were adjudicated by the ayuntamiento, or by water judges appointed by it, apportionment schemes seldom worked to the disadvantage of the municipality.

Daniel Tyler addressed the issue of municipal rights in his devastating critique of the Pueblo Rights Doctrine.

> What rights, if any, could communities (pueblos) claim in an atmosphere dominated by the principle of equitable, or proportional, distribution? Unquestionably, the protection of a community's acequia madre and the preservation of a domestic water supply were objectives of both municipal and territorial officials. Pueblo water rights were established in law and maintained in practice, but they were not absolute or limitless. . . . [P]ueblo rights were not enforced to the detriment of others in the community. . . . [T]he only supportable conclusion is that no municipal entity, Indian or non-Indian, had a right to enlarge its claim to water without consideration of the legitimate needs of other users, individuals or communities. . . . Absolute water rights were inconsistent with Spanish thinking and inappropriate.[28]

It is clear that Spanish and Mexican municipalities did enjoy a strong set of water rights, but they were not based on prior rights and they were anything but paramount. One searches the decrees, the corpus of legislation, and the contemporary case law in vain for a phrase such as *derecho superior, derecho supremo,* or *derecho preeminente* as a description or categorization of municipal water rights. On giving municipalities such an extravagant water monopoly, the so-called Pueblo Rights Doctrine grossly distorted the corpus of Hispanic law and the existing documentary record. Individual water rights enjoyed many

27. "le resstante [el concejo] se señale el tierras de labor de que se hagan suertes en la cantidad que se ofreciere de manera que sean tantas como los solares que puede auver en la poblacion, y si ouiere tierras de regadio se haga dellas suertes y se repartan en la misma proporcion a los primeros pobladores por sus suertes y los demas queden para nos, para que hagamos mrd a los que despues fueren a poblar." Real Ordenanzas para Nuevas Poblaciones, July 3, 1573, Article 130. Nuttall, "Royal Ordinances," p. 748.
28. Tyler, *The Mythical Pueblo Rights Doctrine,* pp. 44–45.

protections. The Pueblo Rights Doctrine, one must conclude, was invented by the California and New Mexico courts, superimposed on the Hispanic water tradition, and ultimately accepted by historians unfamiliar with the pertinent primary documentation.

If our knowledge of groundwater law and municipal water rights was rather limited a decade ago, our understanding of how water was administered in the rural areas of northern New Spain was grossly deficient. Our present appreciation of this topic stems largely from research undertaken for pending litigation in the Taos valley of northern New Mexico.[29]

Settlement patterns in northern New Spain did not always find migrants moving to recently established communities. New Mexico offers a telling example. From the beginning of the Spanish colonization efforts in New Mexico, the rural agricultural cluster proved to be a viable alternative to town life. By the time of the Pueblo Rebellion of 1680, the majority of the Hispanic population did not live in formal towns but in dispersed ranchos and hamlets.[30] The trend continued after the Spanish Reconquest of New Mexico by Diego de Vargas.

The rural agricultural cluster emerged in one of several ways. A *poblador principal* could receive a land grant if he promised to recruit a few families and agreed not to settle within ten leagues (approximately twenty-six miles) of an established town. Unlike the community grants—also sometimes initiated by a poblador principal—there was no expectation that these private grants would ultimately result in the establishment of a formal town with an ayuntamiento and a full array of other governmental accoutrements.[31] The recruiting efforts generally focused on extended families, former neighbors, and groups tied by *compadrazgo*.[32] A second pattern often yielded the same result. A single individual could receive a private land grant and, after fulfilling all the accompanying obligations, was free to sell portions in subdivision. It is clear that at least some land petitioners had just this kind of

29. *State of New Mexico v Abeyta* pits three water competitors in the Taos valley: the town of Taos, the Indian Pueblo of Taos, and the Hispanic irrigators of the Taos Valley. For a lengthy research report prepared for this case, see Meyer, "The Water Regimen of New Mexico in 1848," passim.

30. Marc Simmons, "Settlement Patterns and Village Plans in Colonial New Mexico," *Journal of the West* 8 (January, 1969), 10.

31. The distinction between private grants and community grants is not always crystal clear in the New Mexico documentation as *pobladores principales* were sometimes used in both. An important clue, however, is that the community grants, unlike the private grants, set aside common land for the town. This distinction is nicely developed in Malcolm Ebright, *The Tierra Amarilla Grant: A History of Chicanery* (Santa Fe: Center for Land Grant Studies, 1980), pp. 4–8.

32. Roxanne Dunbar Ortiz, *Roots of Resistance: Land Tenure in New Mexico, 1680–1980* (Los Angeles: UCLA Chicano Studies Research Center, 1980), pp. 48–50.

real estate speculation in mind from the outset.[33] Inheritance by children of the poblador principal, or by the children of those to whom he sold individual plots, led to further subdivision.

The resulting small agricultural clusters were almost always found on small alluvial floodplains. It was impractical, if not impossible, for each small landowner along a watercourse to build and maintain an acequia, which often required construction and upkeep of a stone and brush *atarque* (a weir or diversion dam) on the water source.[34] In addition, the water might have to be channeled from the source across a neighbor's land, not a rare occurrence; some evidence even suggests that in certain areas it was actually the rule rather than the exception.[35] Beginning with the medieval fueros of the thirteenth century, Hispanic legal tradition, through a special kind of easement, or right-of-way (the *servidumbre de aquaductos*),[36] did permit this activity, but the possibilities for resulting conflict were never very far away.[37] Moreover, it was necessary to articulate mechanisms and implement enforcement procedures to protect the always beleaguered downstream irrigators on the water source. Provisions had to be made for late arrivals who wanted to add themselves and their families to the clusters. Because not everyone could always have all the water he or she wanted, schemes for sharing had to be devised. In the complete absence of an ayuntamiento, or any other formal governmental structure in these small agricultural assemblages, mutual need begot a unique and effective cooperative effort. Political theorists would classify it as an example of democratic collectivism motivated by self-interest.

Through the process of *mancomunicación*, the community of rural irrigators, the *parciantes* (called *parcioneros* in some areas of New Spain

33. On this point see Victor Westphall, *Mercedes Reales: Hispanic Land Grants in the Upper Rio Grande Valley* (Albuquerque: University of New Mexico Press, 1983), pp. 126–129.

34. Atarques were not uncommon, especially in New Mexico's Rio Arriba. See, for example, El C. Pedro Honario Gallegos, Alcalde Constitucional del Pueblo de Sto Tomas el Apostol de Abiquiu y Presidente del Ylustre Ayuntamiento, July 17, 1832, MANM, Reel 15. Some of the problems inherent in constructing and maintaining atarques can be gleaned from Richard Flint, Shirley Flint, and Pedro V. Gallegos, "Una Atarque Duradera," *New Mexico Historical Review* 63 (October, 1988), 357–372.

35. ". . . todas las acequias que estan fundadas antiguamente hasta la epoca presente ban rompiendo tierras de diferentes duenos y ninguna toma de agua se aya ubicada en terreno propio." Certification of Pedro Ignacio Gallegos, July 17, 1832, MANM, Reel 15.

36. Sánchez, *Libro de los Fueros de Castilla*, p. 77; Galván Rivera, *Ordenanzas de Tierras y Aguas*, p. 14.

37. Not all New Mexico officials understood the concept of the *servidumbre de aquaductos*. One *alcalde de agua* authorized Maria Antonia Lucero to continue in possession of land that belonged to neighboring Indians because her acequia was located on part of that land. He should have simply awarded her the right-of-way. Francisco Xavier Bernal to Gobernador Fernando de la Concha, SANM, I, 1264.

and *aparceros* in others), voluntarily formed associations (*mancomuni-dades*) to build, maintain, and administer the ditches as well as to re-solve future disputes.[38] The agreements, in part modeled after the mu-nicipal water systems, were much more likely to be oral than written and were passed down from generation to generation of irrigators. There is no indication in the surviving documentary record that they required ratification from any nearby municipal or provincial author-ity.[39] For each ditch they devised water sharing plans on an informal basis. The type of agreements were similar, but not identical, from one acequia to another on the same watershed. Most were simple, as each parciante's rights were of equal dignity, but some encompassed a more complicated nexus of priorities, rotations, and water relationships. While the mechanism of self-restraint was enshrined and cooperation anticipated, compliance was not taken for granted. Some form of pro-tection was needed, and the rural irrigators opted for administration without government. This, they believed, was a better instrument of equity than subjugation to a bureaucracy that could easily develop competitive, or even hostile, interests.

The parciantes of each ditch elected a ditch supervisor and em-powered him to enforce the agreements and manage ditch affairs. On occasion the supervisor was even elected prior to the digging of the acequia so that he could both supervise the planning and organize the work force needed to build the original ditch.[40] While in Valencia, these ditch managers were termed *cequiers*, the titles changed on the northern frontier of New Spain. In some areas, primarily in California, they were called *zanjeros* and in other areas, primarily in Texas, *acequieros*. Occasionally, the contemporary documentation uses the term *repartidor de aguas*.[41] The most common designation in northern New Mexico was *mayordomo*, but no matter what the specific designa-

38. The dictionary of the Royal Spanish Academy defines the verb *mancomunicar* as "unir personas, fuerzas o caudales para un fin," "to join together persons, forces, or fortunes for a given purpose." The mancomunidad is the result of that joining together. *Diccionario de la Lengua Española*, p. 834. The term *parcionero*, referring to an irrigating partner, is found in a number of early nineteenth-century New Mexican documents. For example, "todos los par-cioneros de las acequias" Proceedings of the Ayuntamiento of Santa Fe, April 12, 1832, MANM, Reel 14, and "los parcioneros del terreno contiguo a las margenes del rio," Antonio Matias Ortiz to Señor Prefecto del 1er Distrito, April 30, 1840, MANM, Reel 28. The term *parciante* is more common in the late nineteenth and twentieth centuries.

39. This type of relative autonomy in private irrigation agreements is consistent with practice in eastern Spain and in the Canary Islands, Spain's first important overseas possession. See Glick, *The Old World Background of the Irrigation System of San Antonio, Texas*, p. 23.

40. This was the case at the time of the construction of the Upper Labor Ditch in San Antonio in 1776. See Edwin P. Arneson, "Early Irrigation in Texas," *Southwestern Historical Quarterly* 25 (October, 1921), 127.

41. Governor's Letter Book, Santa Fe, August 13, 1825, MANM, Reel 4.

tion, this official constituted the only semblance of government for generations of rural Hispanic New Mexicans.[42]

Most of these rural acequias, supervised by mayordomos, were named, but they are generically designated in the contemporary documentation as *asequias de común*.[43] They were generally small in size, perhaps a mile or a mile and a half in length, but because they were totally dependent upon gravity flow, they were sometimes as long as five miles. If they crossed arroyos, as they often did, log flumes (*canoas*) were put in place. Because of the limitations of existing hydraulic technology, more often than not they drew water from small streams rather than major waterways such as the Rio Grande. They proliferated in New Mexico, especially in the late eighteenth century. By the time Mexico struck out for independence from Spain, these small community acequias greatly outnumbered the often larger community acequias governed by the ayuntamientos. In a preliminary study of community acequias in New Mexico, Wells Hutchinson found that by 1820 approximately 175 community acequias had been built.[44] Since there were only a handful of corporate communities with functioning ayuntamientos in New Mexico at that time, the vast majority of these were private community acequias under the supervision of mayordomos elected locally by the parciantes.[45] They were the primary institution for allocating and managing the water used for agricultural purposes and as such were the fundamental instrument for production in the countryside.

---

42. In its Mexican context, the term *mayordomo* is generally understood to refer to the resident supervisor who was in charge of the work force on a hacienda. But it is also a generic term encompassing any type of supervisor. See Francisco J. Santamaría, *Diccionario de Mejicanismos* (Mexico: Editorial Porrua, S.A., 1978), p. 708. For use of the term *mayordomo* to refer to the ditch supervisor in rural agricultural communities, see Antonio de Armenta to Governor Manrique, July 7, 1813, SANM, II, 2503; Lorenzo Gutierrez to Governor Manrique, August 6, 1813, SANM, II, 2503; and Antonio Manuel Vigil to Governor Melgares, September 13, 1819, SANM, II, 2846.

43. See, for example, *Precentacion de Franco Antonio Chaves y Bartolome Montoya contra Dn Diego Antonio Chaves sobre daños y linderos, Año de 1786*, Court of Private Land Claims, Case 45, Roll 37; and Petition of Jose Miguel Aragón, July 9, 1827, MANM, Reel 7.

44. Wells A. Hutchins, "The Community Acequia: Its Origin and Development," *Southwestern Historical Quarterly* 31 (January, 1928), 277–278. It is clear that Hutchins was able to identify only those acequias that for one reason or another had made their way into the historical record by 1820. In reality, many more acequias were irrigating New Mexico cropland in that year.

45. In 1812 the Spanish Cortes enacted legislation requiring all towns with a population in excess of one thousand to have ayuntamientos. A census taken in 1821 indicates that New Mexico counted fifteen towns larger than one thousand, but only four of these towns (Santa Fe, Santa Cruz de la Cañada, Albuquerque, and El Paso) definitely had ayuntamientos. See White, Koch, Kelley and McCarthy, *Land Title Study* (Santa Fe: State Planning Office, 1971), p. 19.

Acequias constructed and maintained by extended families or other small groups of irrigators figured prominently in the water history of Spanish and Mexican New Mexico. They enjoyed legal status; that is, they had a *persona jurídica* and thus had the full protection of Hispanic law. The fact that they enjoyed legal status was not an aberration in the Hispanic legal system. Under Roman law, voluntary associations enjoyed a juridical personality and could own property communally.[46] This condition continued in a number of Spanish kingdoms during the Middle Ages. By the time the first rural community acequias were being built in New Mexico, similar types of property-owning voluntary associations could be found in Spain. One example was the *encesas*, the voluntary communities of fishermen in the northeastern Catalonian port town of Cadaqués. The fishermen comprising the encesas owned their nets and other equipment communally and were even awarded communal rights to fish in specified coves in the Gulf of Rosas.[47]

In the enjoyment of their judicial personality, the irrigators in New Mexico's community acequias not only argued their own claims forcefully before the proper judicial authority but were also able to withstand the unwarranted claims that others might bring against them. In one 1741 water dispute on the Rio Chama, a frivolous water claim against a small group of parciantes resulted in a fifty-peso fine and a stern warning that such behavior would not be countenanced.[48] Construction and maintenance of these community acequias was also used in land disputes as an excellent example of effective agricultural use, a common requirement needed in the fulfillment of land grant obligations.[49]

Over time the mancomunidad, or acequia association, tended to assume an importance that transcended its original purpose. It grew from an instrument of physical survival to one of cultural survival. Just as the ditch tied the fields together, the association tied the rural neighborhood together, reinforcing *compadrazgo*, giving each village a distinct identity, and offering itself as a mechanism for mutual aid during crises or times of need. In essence it became a kind of secular *cofradía*, a sodality which formed the nucleus of rural life in Hispanic New Mexico.

46. Rafael Altamira y Crevea, *Historia de la Propiedad Comunal* (Madrid: J. López Camacho, 1890), p. 93.
47. Ibid., pp. 235–236.
48. "[P]ena de cincuenta pesos, se abstegna de ponder demandas injustas y de inquietar a los vecinos del partido," Auto en la Villa de Santa Fe, February 23, 1746, SANM, I, 847.
49. Juan de Rios Peña, March 4, 1818, SANM, I, 1292.

The mayordomos, elected and paid by the ditch users through an assessment known commonly as the *mayordomía*, enjoyed considerable autonomy in exercising the acequia's collective water right. More than most, they appreciated the value of water when wedded to the land. Not trained in the law, and not prone to learned theorizing, most of the mayordomos were irrigators themselves and had not only an excellent grasp of the specific agreements of their own ditch but also a decent understanding of those fundamental Hispanic water principles used for centuries to move water competitors in the direction of equity. They were not easily duped by the complexities of the Hispanic legal labyrinth and were able to infuse orderliness into an irrigation system that had inherent in it the potential for discord and even social violence.[50] Upon their best understanding and appreciation of legal traditions, customary law developed and was used in the resolution of future disputes. Custom in Hispanic jurisprudence made possible the periodic divorce between law as it was and law as it ought to have been.[51]

The activities of the mayordomos encompassed inspecting the rural acequias and assuring universal participation in the spring cleaning and repair. While cleaning and repair of the *sangrías, venas,* or *contra acequias* (laterals) was the responsibility of the individual user, everyone was expected to contribute to the necessary work on the main ditch. The mayordomo assigned individual tasks. The ditch had to be cleaned of unwanted growth, leaves, weeds, and silt, and on occasion weakened banks had to be reinforced lest they unexpectedly break, flooding fields and wasting water. Flumes had to be checked and cleaned, and often their girders had to be stabilized. The task was very significant culturally as it marked the beginning of a new agricultural cycle and brought the rural community together on a major project in which everyone had a direct stake.

The mayordomos also were charged with apportioning available water among the parciantes, guarding against violations of water law and custom, determining when excess water was sufficient to allow

50. While some water disputes threatened open community rebellion, others occasioned physical assaults and personal injuries. See, for example, Antonio de Armenta to Governor Manrique, July 7, 1813, SANM, II, 2503; and Antonio María Trujillo to Governor, September 13, 1819, SANM, II, 2846.

51. "Custom" in Spain's classic *Manual del Abogado* is defined as unwritten law introduced by usage, accepted by a greater part of the population over a substantial period of time, and in harmony with the common good. For more on this point, see William Hall, *Irrigation Development* (Sacramento: State Office, 1886), p. 386, and Daniel Tyler, "Underground Water in Hispanic New Mexico: A Brief Analysis of Laws, Customs and Disputes," *New Mexico Historical Review* 66 (July, 1991): 287–302.

sobrante rights to be exercised, and adjudicating disputes between feuding parciantes.[52] Moreover, working in concert with other mayordomos, they also sought to mediate disputes between different acequias sharing the same watershed. Most important in this regard was the need to protect acequias lower on the stream during periods of drought.[53] If local adjudication or mediation proved too elusive, the mayordomo, or several mayordomos, could take a dispute to a municipal or provincial authority for ultimate resolution, but in the interest of maintaining customary local autonomy, they preferred not to do so. Although mayordomos were responsible only to the parciantes, their activities fell under the scrutiny of the provincial government. In 1826, shortly after Mexican independence, a commission appointed by the ayuntamiento of Santa Fe had a statute enacted that provided for the fining of mayordomos who were derelict in their duties.[54] The goal, however, continued to be the resolution of disputes in the community of their origin.[55] The resilience of the system defies ready explanation. It continues to dominate the rural community complex of Hispanic New Mexico today.

Resistance to the continued application of Hispanic water law principles in contemporary United States courts is remarkable for it absence. Had the Hispanic water regimen, protected by the Treaty of Guadalupe-Hidalgo in 1848, been narrowly conceived, philosophically barren, or predicated on a constellation of narrow vested interests, it would have bequeathed the United States judiciary a virtually insoluble moral and legal conundrum. Fortunately for the courts that would be called upon to apply Hispanic water law in cases pitting water competitors against each other, the Hispanic water regimen rested on a rich philosophical foundation, one designed to serve broad individual and community goals and one which challenged judges to be guided by what was right and proper, *ex aequo et bono*.

52. Simmons, "Spanish Irrigation Practices in New Mexico," p. 141. The role of tradition, passed down orally from generation to generation, is still considered fundamental in the resolution of acequia disputes in the Taos valley. See Charlotte Benson Crossland, "Acequia Right in Law and Tradition," *Journal of the Southwest* 32 (Autumn, 1990), 278–287.

53. Acequia disputes between "los de arriba" and "los de abajo" are common in the surviving documentation. See, for example, José Manuel Aragón, July 9, 1827, MANM, Reel 7.

54. Lynn I. Perrigo, ed., "Revised Statutes of 1826," *New Mexico Historical Review* 27 (January, 1952), 72.

55. The Hispanic water system in no way confirms the famous Wittfogel thesis that irrigation societies led to despotic centralization of political power. Karl A. Wittfogel, *Oriental Despotism: A Comparative Study of Total Powers* (New Haven: Yale University Press, 1957).

Bibliography

ARCHIVES

A. L. Pinart Collection. Bancroft Library, PE-51. Berkeley, California.
Archivo General de Indias. Seville, Spain.
  Audiencia de Guadalajara
  Audiencia de México
  Indiferente General
Archivo General de la Nación. Mexico City.
  Ramo de Alhóndigas
  Ramo de Californias
  Ramo de Historia
  Ramo de Jesuitas
  Ramo de Justicia
  Ramo de Mercedes
  Ramo de Misiones
  Ramo de Provincias Internas
  Ramo de Tierras
Archivo Hidalgo de Parral. Microfilm Collection, University of
  Arizona.
Archivo Histórico de Baja California Sur. Microfilm Holdings. In-
  stituto de Investigaciones Históricas, Universidad Nacional Au-
  tónoma de México.
Archivo Histórico del Estado de Sonora. Microfilm copy. Arizona
  Historical Society. Tucson, Arizona.
Bexar Archives. University of Texas, Austin, Texas.
Bexar County Archives. Mission Records. San Antonio, Texas.

Mexican Archives of New Mexico. Santa Fe, New Mexico.
Seligman Collection. University of New Mexico, Albuquerque, New Mexico.
Spanish Archives of New Mexico. Santa Fe, New Mexico.
W. B. Stephenson Collection, Nettie Lee Benson Latin American Collection. University of Texas, Austin, Texas.

PUBLISHED DOCUMENTS

Adams, Eleanor (ed.). *Bishop Tamaron's Visitation of New Mexico, 1760.* Albuquerque: Historical Society of New Mexico, 1954.
Arteaga Garza, Beatriz, and Guadalupe Pérez San Vicente (eds.). *Cedulario cortesiano.* Mexico: Editorial Jus, 1949.
Beleña, Eusebio Bentura. *Recopilación sumaria de todos los autos acordados de la real audiencia y sala de crimen de esta Nueva España.* 2 vols. Mexico: Universidad Nacional Autónoma de México, 1981.
Bloom, Lansing B. (ed). *Antonio Barre o's Ojeada sobre Nuevo México.* Santa Fe: El Palacio Press, 1928.
Burrus, Ernest J., S. J. *Correspondencia del P. Kino con los generales de la Compañía de Jesús, 1682–1707.* Mexico: Editorial Jus, 1961.
"A Campaign Against the Moqui Pueblos Under Governor Phelix Martinez in 1716." *New Mexico Historical Review* 6 (April, 1931), 158–226.
The City of Los Angeles vs. the City of San Fernando. Court of Appeal Second Appellate District, State of California. Second Civil No. 33708.
Colección de decretos y ordenes dictados por el honorable Congreso Primero Constitucional de Chihuahua, en sus sesiones ordinarias desde 1° de julio hasta 30 de setiembre de 1827. Chihuahua: Imprenta del Gobierno del Estado, 1828.
Colección de documentos inéditos relativos al descubrimiento, conquista y organización de las antiguas posesiones de América y Oceanía. 42 vols. Madrid: n.p., 1864–1884.
Documentos de la historia de México. 7 vols. Mexico: Imprenta de Vicente García Torres, 1856–1857.
Encinas, Diego de. *Cedulario indiano.* 4 vols. Madrid: Ediciones Cultura Hispánica, 1945–1946.
Escriche, Joaquín. *Diccionario razonado de legislación civil, penal, comercial y forense.* Madrid: Calleja e Hijos, 1842.
———. *Elementos de derecho español.* Paris: Librería de D. Vincente Salvá, 1840.
"Estado actual de las misiones de la provincia de Coahuila y Río Grande de la misma jurisdición, año de 1786." In *Estudios de historia del noreste.* Monterrey: Editorial Alfonso Reyes, 1972, pp. 126–145.

Fernández y Somera, Blas. "Diario del viage que se hizo en la provincia de California . . . 1776." In *Noticias y documentos acerca de las Californias, 1764–1795*. Madrid: José Porrua Turanzas, 1959.

Galván Rivera, Mariano. *Ordenanzas de tierras y aguas: O sea formulario geometrico-judicial*. Mexico: n.p., 1849.

García Icazbalceta, Joaquín. *Colección de documentos para la historia de México*. 2 vols. Mexico: Librería de J. M. Andrade, 1858–1866.

Gregg, Josiah. *Commerce of the Prairies.* New York: Bobbs-Merrill, 1970.

Hamilton, Leonidas. *Mexican Law: A Compilation of Mexican Legislation*. San Francisco: n.p., 1882.

Hammond, George P., and Agapito Rey (eds.). *The Rediscovery of New Mexico, 1580–1594*. Albuquerque: University of New Mexico Press, 1966.

Lange, Charles H., et al. (eds.). *The Southwestern Journals of Adolph Bandelier, 1885–1888*. Albuquerque: University of New Mexico Press, 1975.

Matson, Daniel S., and Bernard L. Fontana (eds.). *Friar Bringas Reports to the King: Methods of Indoctrination on the Frontier of New Spain, 1796–1797.* Tucson: University of Arizona Press, 1977.

McCarty, Kieran. *Desert Documentary*. Tucson: Arizona Historical Society, 1976.

"Misiones del Colegio de Pachuca en 1793." *In Estudios de historia del noreste*. Monterrey: Editorial Alfonso Reyes, 1972.

Muro Orejón, Antonio. *Cedulario americano del siglo XVIII: Colección de disposiciones legales indígenas desde 1680 a 1800 contenidas en los cedularios del Archivo General de Indias*. Sevilla: Escuela de Estudios Americanos de Sevilla, 1969.

Nentvig, Juan. *Rudo Ensayo: A Description of Sonora and Arizona in 1764*. Tucson: University of Arizona Press, 1980.

Novísima recopilación de los leyes de España. 6 vols. Mexico: Galván, 1831.

Nuttall, Zelia. "Royal Ordinances Concerning the Laying Out of New Towns." *Hispanic American Historical Review* 4 (November, 1921), 743–753.

Och, Joseph, S.J. *Missionary in Sonora*. San Francisco: California Historical Society, 1965.

Porrua Turanzas, José (ed.). *Documentos para la historia eclesiástica y civil de la Provincia de Texas, o de Nuevas Filipinas, 1720–1779*. Madrid: Ediciones José Porrua Turanzas, 1961.

Quijada, Armando (ed.). *Documentos para la historia de Sonora*. Hermosillo: Gobierno del Estado, 1979.

Recopilación de leyes de los reynos de las Indias. 4 vols. Madrid: Ediciones Cultura Hispánica, 1973.

Relaciones del siglo XVIII relativas a Chihuahua. Mexico: Biblioteca de Historiadores Mexicanos, 1950.

Rodríguez de San Miguel, Juan N. *Pandectas hispano-mexicanas*. 3 vols. México: Universidad Nacional Autónoma de México, 1980.

Las siete partidas del sabio rey don Alfonso. 4 vols. Madrid: n.p., 1789.

Simmons, Marc (ed.). "An Alcalde's Proclamation: A Rare New Mexico Document." *El Palacio* 75 (Summer, 1968), 5–9.

Solórzano Pereira, Juan de. *Política indiana.* 5 vols. Madrid: Compañía Ibero-Americana de Publicaciones, 1930.

Tamarón y Romeral, Pedro. *Demostración del vatísimo obispado de la Nueva Vizcaya, 1765.* Mexico: Antigua Librería Robredo, 1937.

"Ynstrucción a Peralta por Vi-Rey, March 30, 1709." *New Mexico Historical Review* 4 (April, 1929), p. 180.

SECONDARY WORKS

Aguilar y Santillón, Rafael. *Bibliografía geológica y minera de la República Mexicana.* Mexico: Secretaría de Fomento, 1898.

Alba, Carlos H. *Estudio comparado entre el derecho azteco y el derecho positivo mexicano.* Mexico: Instituto Indigenista Interamericano, 1944.

Alessio Robles, Vito. *Francisco de Urdiñola y el norte de Nueva España.* Mexico: Imprenta Mundial, 1931.

Almada, Francisco R. *Resumen de historia del estado de Chihuahua.* Mexico: Libros Mexicanos, 1955.

Altamira y Crevea, Rafael. *Diccionario castellano de palabras jurídicas y técnicas tomadas de la legislación indiana.* Mexico: Instituto Panamericano de Geografía e Historia, 1951.

Altamira y Crevea, Rafael, et al. *Contribuciones a la historia municipal de América.* Mexico: Instituto Panamericano de Geografía e Historia, 1951.

Arana Cervantes, Marcos. *Agua para todos.* Guadalajara: Gobierno del Estado de Jalisco, 1980.

Baker, T. Lindsay, Steven R. Rae et al. *Water for the Southwest: Historical Survey and Guide to Historic Sites.* New York: ASCE Historical Publications, 1973.

Bancroft, Hubert Howe. *History of California.* 7 vols. San Francisco: A. L. Bancroft and Company, 1884–1890.

Barrett, Ward J. *The Sugar Hacienda of the Marques del Valle.* Minneapolis: University of Minnesota Press, 1970.

Bazant, Jan. *Cinco haciendas mexicanas: Tres siglos de vida rural en San Luis Potosí.* Mexico: El Colegio de México, 1975.

Beers, Henry Putney. *Spanish and Mexican Records of the American Southwest.* Tucson: University of Arizona Press, 1979.

Bolton, Herbert Eugene. *Coronado: Knight of Pueblo and Plains.* Albuquerque: University of New Mexico Press, 1964.

———. *Rim of Christendom: A Biography of Eusebio Francisco Kino, Pacific Coast Pioneer.* New York: Macmillan, 1936.

Brading, D. A. *Haciendas and Ranchos in the Mexican Bajío, 1700–1869.* New York: Cambridge University Press, 1970.

————. *Miners and Merchants in Bourbon Mexico, 1763–1810.* Cambridge: Cambridge University Press, 1971.

Campa, Arthur L. *Hispanic Culture in the Southwest.* Norman: University of Oklahoma Press, 1979.

Chevalier, François. *La Formation des grands domains au Mexique: Terre et Société aux XVIᵉ–XVIIIᵉ siècles.* Paris: Université de Paris, 1952.

————. *Land and Society in Colonial Mexico.* Berkeley: University of California Press, 1970.

Coe, Michael D. *Mexico: Ancient People and Places.* New York: Frederick A. Praeger, 1962.

Crumrine, N. Ross. *The Mayo Indians of Sonora: A People Who Refuse to Die.* Tucson: University of Arizona Press, 1977.

Day, A. Grove. *Coronado's Quest: The Discovery of the Southwestern States.* Berkeley: University of California Press, 1964.

Dean, Jeffrey S., and William J. Robinson. *Expanded Tree-Ring Chronologies for the Southwestern United States.* Tucson: Laboratory of Tree-Ring Research, 1978.

Dobkins, Betty Eakle. *The Spanish Element in Texas Water Law.* Austin: University of Texas Press, 1959.

Dobyns, Henry F. *From Fire to Flood: Historic Human Destruction of Sonoran Riverine Oases.* Socorro, New Mexico: Ballena Press, 1981.

————. *Spanish Colonial Tucson: A Demographic History.* Tucson: University of Arizona Press, 1976.

Dozier, Edward P. *The Pueblo Indians of North America.* New York: Holt, Rinehart and Winston, 1970.

Drew, Linda (ed.). *Tree-Ring Chronologies for Dendroclimatic Analysis.* Tucson: Laboratory of Tree-Ring Research, 1976.

————. *Tree-Ring Chronologies of North America.* Tucson: Laboratory of Tree-Ring Research, 1975.

Dunbier, Roger. *The Sonoran Desert: Its Geography, Economy and People.* : University of Arizona Press, 1970.

Dusenbery, William H. *The Mexican Mesta: The Administration of Ranching in Colonial Mexico.* Urbana: University of Illinois Press, 1963.

Dwinelle, John W. *Colonial History of the City of San Francisco.* San Francisco: Towne and Bacon Book and Job Publishers, 1863.

Engelhardt, Zephyrin. *The Missions ₁and Missionaries of California.* 4 vols. Palo Alto: N-P Publishers 1902–1915.

Filatti, Rosa. *Indicios de aridez en México.* Mexico: Talleres Gráficos de la Secretaría de Agricultura y Fomento, 1930.

Fireman, Janet R. *The Spanish Royal Corps of Engineers in the Western Borderlands: Instrument of Bourbon Reform, 1764–1815.* Glendale: Arthur H. Clark Company, 1977.

Florescano, Enrique. *Estructuras y problemas agrarias de México, 1500–1821.* Mexico: Sep Setentas, 1971.

————. (ed.). *Haciendas, latifundios y plantaciones en América Latina.* Mexico: Siglo Veintiuno Editores, 1975.

Floris Margadant S., Guillermo. *Introducción a la historia del derecho mexicano*. Mexico: Universidad Nacional Autónoma de México, 1971.

Fontana, Bernard L. *Of Earth and Little Rain: The Papago Indians*. Flagstaff, Arizona: Northland Press, 1981.

Frank, Andre Gunder. *Mexican Agriculture, 1521–1630. The Transformation of the Mode of Production*. New York: Cambridge University Press, 1979.

Fuentes Mares, José. *Monterrey: Una ciudad creadora y sus capitanes*. Mexico: Editorial Jus, 1976.

Gibson, Charles. *The Aztecs Under Spanish Rule: A History of the Indians of the Valley of Mexico*. Stanford: Stanford University Press, 1964.

Glick, Thomas F. *Irrigation and Society in Medieval Valencia*. Cambridge, Mass.: Harvard University Press, 1970.

———. *The Old World Background to the Irrigation System of San Antonio, Texas*. El Paso: Texas Western University Press, 1972.

Gongora, Mario. *Studies in the Colonial History of Spanish America*. Cambridge: Cambridge University Press, 1975.

González, María del Refugio. *Historia del derecho mexicano*. Mexico: Universidad Nacional Autónoma de México, in press.

Hall, William H. *Irrigation Development*. Sacramento: California State Office, 1886.

Harris, Charles, *A Mexican Family Empire: The Latifundio of the Sanchez-Navarros, 1766–1867*. Austin: University of Texas Press, 1976.

Hederra Donoso, Ana. *Comentarios al código de aguas*. Santiago: Editorial Jurídica de Chile, 1960.

Hernández Sánchez-Barba, Mario. *La última expansión española en América*. Madrid: Instituto de Estudios Políticos, 1957.

Hughes, Anne E. *The Beginnings of Spanish Settlement in the El Paso District*. Berkeley: University of California Press, 1914.

Irigoyen, Renan. *Bajo el signo de Chaac*. Merida: Editorial Zamna, 1970.

Keith, Robert G. (ed.). *Haciendas and Plantations in Latin American History*. New York: Holmes and Meier Publishers, 1977.

Kessell, John L. *Friars, Soldiers, and Reformers: Hispanic Reformers and the Sonora Mission Frontier, 1767–1856*. Tucson: University of Arizona Press, 1976.

Lister, Florence C., and Robert H. Lister. *Chihuahua: Storehouse of Storms*. Albuquerque: University of New Mexico Press, 1966.

López Miramontes, Alvaro. *Las minas de Nueva España en 1753*. Mexico: Instituto de Antropología e Historia, 1975.

Maclachlan, Colin. *Criminal Justice in Eighteenth-Century Mexico*. Berkeley: University of California Press, 1974.

Manzano y Manzano, Juan. *Historia de las recopilaciones de Indias*. 2 vols. Madrid: Ediciones Cultura Hispánica, 1956.

Martínez, Bernardo. *El Marquesado del Valle: Tres siglos del régimen señorial en Nueva España*. Mexico: El Colegio de México, 1969.

Martínez Ríos, Jorge. *Tenencia de la tierra y desarrollo agrario en México: Bibliografía selectiva y comentada, 1522–1968*. Mexico: Universidad Nacional Autónoma de México, 1970.

Montenegro, Julio Cesar. *Aspectos legales del problema de la tierra, época colonial*. Mexico: Academia Nacional de Historia y Geografía, 1978.

Moorhead, Max L. *The Presidio: Bastion of the Spanish Borderlands*. Norman: University of Oklahoma Press, 1975.

Moreno, Roberto. *Joaquín Velásquez de León y sus trabajos científicos sobre el valle de México, 1773–1775*. Mexico: Universidad Nacional Autónoma de México, 1977.

Murphy, James M. *The Spanish Legal Heritage in Arizona*. Tucson: Arizona Pioneers' Historical Society, 1966.

Navarro García, Luis. *José de Gálvez y la Comandancia General de las Provincias Internas*. Seville: Escuela de Estudios Hispano-Americanos, 1964.

———. *Sonora y Sinaloa en el siglo XVII*. Seville: Escuela de Estudios Hispano-Americanos, 1967.

Newcomb, W. W. *The Indians of Texas: From Pre-Hispanic to Modern Times*. Austin: University of Texas Press, 1961.

Ocaranza, Fernando. *Establecimientos franciscanos en el misterioso reino de Nuevo México*. Mexico: n.p., 1939.

Orive Alba, Adolfo. *La política de irrigación en México*. Mexico: Fondo de Cultura Económica, 1960.

Ots Capdequí, José M. *El régimen de la tierra en América Española durante el período colonial*. Ciudad Trujillo: Universidad de Santo Domingo, 1946.

Palerm, Angel, and Eric Wolf. *Agricultura y civilización en Mesoamérica*. Mexico: Sep Setentas, 1972.

Parry, J. H. *The Spanish Seaborne Empire*. New York: Alfred A. Knopf, 1967.

Pérez Hernández, José María. *Compendio de la geografía del territorio de la Baja California*. Mexico: Comercio, 1872.

Polzer, Charles W. *Rules and Precepts of the Jesuit Missions of Northwestern New Spain*. Tucson: University of Arizona Press, 1976.

Polzer, Charles; Thomas C. Barnes; and Thomas H. Naylor, comps. *The Documentary Relations of the Southwest: Project Manual*. Tucson: DRSW, 1977.

Randall, Robert W. *Real del Monte: A British Mining Venture in Mexico*. Austin: University of Texas Press, 1972.

Real Academia Española. *Diccionario de la lengua española*. 19th ed. Madrid: Editorial Espasa-Calpe, S.A., 1970.

Reeve, Frank. *New Mexico: Land of Many Cultures*. Boulder, Colorado: Pruitt Publishing Company, 1969.

Riley, G. Micheal. *Fernando Cortes and the Marquesado in Morelos, 1522–1547: A Case Study in Socioeconomic Development of Sixteenth Century Mexico*. Albuquerque: University of New Mexico Press, 1973.

Ruibal Corella, Juan Antonio. *Memoria: Festejos conmemorativos del ses-quicentenario de Hermosillo como ciudad.* Mexico: Editorial Libros de México, 1979.

San Antonio in the Eighteenth Century. San Antonio: San Antonio Bicentennial Heritage Committee, 1976.

Sando, Joe S. *The Pueblo Indians.* San Francisco: The Indian Historical Press, 1976.

Schäfer, Ernst. *El Consejo Real y Supremo de las Indias.* 2 vols. Sevilla: Imp. M. Carmona, 1935.

Scholes, France V. *Church and State in New Mexico, 1610–1650.* Albuquerque: University of New Mexico Press, 1937.

———. *Troublous Times in New Mexico, 1654–1670.* Albuquerque: University of New Mexico Press, 1942.

Sheridan, Thomas E., and Thomas H. Naylor (eds.). *Rarámuri: A Tarahumara Colonial Chronicle, 1607–1791.* Flagstaff, Arizona: Northland Press, 1979.

Simmons, Marc. *Spanish Government in New Mexico.* Albuquerque: University of New Mexico Press, 1968.

Souchere, Elena de la. *An Explanation of Spain.* New York: Vantage Books, 1965.

Spicer, Edward H. *The Yaquis: A Cultural History.* Tucson: University of Arizona Press, 1978.

Stagg, Albert. *The Almadas of Alamos, 1782–1867.* Tucson: University of Arizona Press, 1978.

———. *The First Bishop of Sonora: Antonio de los Reyes, O.F.M.* Tucson: University of Arizona Press, 1980.

Taylor, William B. *Landlord and Peasant in Colonial Oaxaca.* Stanford: Stanford University Press, 1972.

Underhill, Ruth M. *Papago Indian Religion.* New York: Columbia University Press, 1946.

Vance, John T. *The Background of Mexican Laws, Circulars and Decrees in the Archives of Upper California.* San Francisco: O'Meara and Painter, 1858.

Vásquez, Genaro V. *Doctrinas y realidades en la legislación para los Indios.* Mexico: Departamento de Asuntos Indígenas, 1940.

Vlahos, Olivia. *New World Beginnings: Indian Cultures in the Americas.* New York: The Viking Press, 1970.

Weaver, Muriel Porter. *The Aztecs, Maya and Their Predecessors: Archaeology of Mesoamerica.* New York: Seminar Press, 1972.

Weber, David J. *The Mexican Frontier, 1821–1846: The American Southwest Under Mexico.* Albuquerque: University of New Mexico Press, 1982.

Whitecotton, Joseph W. *The Zapotecs: Princes, Priests and Peasants.* Norman: University of Oklahoma Press, 1977.

Wittfogel, Karl. *Oriental Despotism: Hydraulic Society.* New Haven: Yale University Press, 1957.

Wolf, Eric. *Sons of the Shaking Earth.* Chicago: University of Chicago Press, 1962.

Wormington, H. M. *Prehistoric Indians of the Southwest.* Denver: The Colorado Museum of National History, 1951.

ARTICLES AND CHAPTERS

Almada, Francisco. "El archivo de la Comandancia General de las Provincias Internas." *Boletín de la Sociedad Chihuahuense de Estudios Históricos* 1 (July, 1938), 71–73.

Archibald, Robert. "Canyon de Carnue: Settlement of a Grant." *New Mexico Historical Review* 51 (October, 1976), 313–328.

Arneson, Edwin P. "Early Irrigation in Texas." *Southwestern Historical Quarterly* 25 (October, 1921), 121–130.

Benedict, H. Bradley. "The Sale of the Hacienda of Tabaloapa: A Case Study of Jesuit Property Redistribution in Mexico, 1771–1781." *The Americas* 32 (October, 1975), 171–195.

Bloom, Lansing B. "Albuquerque and Galisteo: Certificate of Their Founding, 1706." *New Mexico Historical Review* 10 (January, 1935), 48–50.

Bunzel, Ruth L. "Introduction to Zuni Ceremonialism." In *Bureau of American Ethnology Report* 47 (1932), 474–487.

Burns, Robert Ignatius. "Irrigation Taxes in Early Mudejar Valencia: The Problems of the Alfarda." *Speculum* 44 (October, 1969), 560–567.

Carlson, Alvar W. "Long Lots in the Rio Arriba." *Annals of the Association of American Geographers* 65 (March, 1975), 48–57.

Carrera Stampa, Manuel. "The Evolution of Weights and Measures in New Spain." *Hispanic American Historical Review* 29 (February, 1949), 2–24.

Clagett, Helen L. "Las Siete Partidas." *The Quarterly Journal of the Library of Congress* 22 (October, 1965), 341–346.

Clark, Robert Emmet. "The Pueblo Rights Doctrine in New Mexico." *New Mexico Historical Review* 35 (October, 1960), 256–283.

Cline, Howard F. "Civil Congregation of the Indians of New Spain, 1598–1606." *Hispanic American Historical Review* 29 (August, 1949), 349–396.

Dozier, Edward P. "The Pueblos of the Southwestern United States." *The Journal of the Royal Anthropological Society of Great Britain and Ireland* 90 (1960), 146–160.

Dunham, Harold H. "Spanish and Mexican Land Policies in the Taos Pueblo Region." In *Pueblo Indians* (5 vols.), vol. 1, pp. 151–331. New York: Garland Publishers, Inc. 1974. I, 151–331.

Ebright, Malcolm. "Manuel Martínez Ditch Dispute: A Study in Mexican Period Custom and Justice." *New Mexico Historical Review* 54 (January, 1979), 21–34.

———. "The San Joaquín Grant: Who Owned the Common Lands? A Historical Legal Question." *New Mexico Historical Review* 57 (January, 1982), 5–26.

Florescano, Enrique. "Una historia olvidada: La sequía en México." *Nexos* 32 (August, 1980), 9–18.

Foscue, Edwin J. "Agricultural History of the Lower Río Grande Valley Region." *Agricultural History* 8 (1934), 124–136.

Garr, Daniel. "Villa de Branciforte: Innovation and Adaptation on the Frontier." *The Americas* 35 (July, 1978), 95–109.

Greenleaf, Richard E. "Atrisco and Las Ciruelas, 1722–1769." *New Mexico Historical Review* 42 (January, 1967), 5–25.

———. "Land and Water in Mexico and New Mexico, 1700–1821." *New Mexico Historical Review* 47 (April, 1972), 85–112.

Hackenberg, Robert A. "Ecosystemic Channeling: Cultural Ecology for the Viewpoint of Aerial Photography." In Evon Z. Vogt (ed.), *Aerial Photography in Anthropological Field Research*, 28–39. Cambridge: Harvard University Press, 1974.

Haury, Emil W. "Arizona's Ancient Irrigation Builders." *Natural History* 54 (September, 1945), 300–310.

Hodge, F. W. "Pre-historic Irrigation in Arizona." *American Anthropologist* 6 (July, 1893), 323–330.

Hutchins, Wells A. "The Community Acequia: Its Origins and Development." *Southwestern Historical Review* 31 (January, 1928), 261–284.

Jenkins, Myra E. "The Baltasar Baca Grant." *El Palacio* 68 (Spring, 1961), 47–64.

———. "Spanish Land Grants in the Tewa Area." *New Mexico Historical Review* 47 (April, 1972), 113–134.

Keleher, William A. "Law of the New Mexico Land Grant." *New Mexico Historical Review* 4 (October, 1929), 350–371.

León, Nicolás. "Bibliografía mexicana del siglo XVIII." *Boletín del Instituto Bibliográfico Mexicana* 4 (1903), 28–29.

Linton, Ralph M. "Land Tenure in Aboriginal America." In Oliver La Farge (ed.), *The Changing Indian*. Norman: University of Oklahoma Press, 1942.

Lockhart, James. "Encomienda and Hacienda: The Evolution of the Great Estate in the Spanish Indies." *Hispanic American Historical Review* 49 (August, 1969), 411–479.

MacMillan, Esther. "The Cabildo and the People, 1731–1784." In *San Antonio in the Eighteenth Century.* San Antonio: San Antonio Bicentennial Heritage Committee, 1976.

Manrique, Jorge A. "Una colección importante para la historiografía del noreste." *Historia Mexicana* 16 (April–June, 1967), 636–643.

Mintz, Sidney. "The Role of Water in Julian Steward's Cultural Ecology." *Journal of the Steward Anthropological Society* 11 (Fall, 1979), 17–32.

Muro Orejón, Antonio. "La igualdad entre indios y españoles." In *Estudios sobre la política indigenista española en América*, 366–386. Valladolid: Universidad de Valladolid, 1975.

Nicholson, H. B. "Los principales dioses Meso-americanas." In Centro de Investigaciones Antropológicas de México. *Esplendor del México antiguo* (2 vols.), v. 1, pp. 161–78. Editorial del Valle de México, 1976.

Perrigo, Lynn I. (ed.). "Revised Statutes of 1826." *New Mexico Historical Review* 27 (January, 1952), 69–72.

Plog, Fred. "The Keresan Bridge: An Ecological and Archaeological Account." In Charles L. Redman, Mary Jane Berman, et al. (eds.), *Social Archaeology: Beyond Subsistence and Dating,* 349–372. New York: Academic Press, 1978.

Radding de Murrieta, Cynthia. "The Functions of the Market in Changing Economic Structures in the Mission Communities of Pimeria Alta, 1768–1821." *The Americas,* 34 (October, 1977), 155–169.

Ressler, John Q. "Indian and Spanish Water Control on New Spain's Northwest Frontier." *Journal of the West* 7 (January, 1968), 10–17.

Rohn, Arthur H. "Prehistoric Soil and Water Conservation on Chapin Mesa, Southwestern Colorado." *American Antiquity* 28 (April, 1963) 441–446.

Schuetz, Mardith K. "Excavation of a Section of the Acequia Madre in Bexar County, Texas." Texas Historical Survey Committee, *Archaeological Report Number* 19 (July, 1970), 1–17.

Simmons, Marc. "Spanish Irrigation Practices in New Mexico." *New Mexico Historical Review* 47 (April, 1972), 135–150.

Sunseri, Alvin. "Agricultural Techniques in New Mexico at the Time of the Anglo-American Conquest." *Agricultural History* 47 (October, 1973), 329–337.

Taylor, William B. "Land and Water Rights in the Viceroyalty of New Spain." *New Mexico Historical Review* 50 (July, 1975), 189–212.

Tittman, Edward D. "The First Irrigation Lawsuit." *New Mexico Historical Review* 2 (October, 1927), 363–368.

Toulouse, Joseph H., Jr. "Early Water Systems at Gran Quivira National Monument." *American Antiquity* 10 (April, 1945), 362–372.

Tyler, Daniel. "Mexican Indian Policy in New Mexico." *New Mexico Historical Review* 55 (April, 1980), 101–120.

Vassberg, David E. "Concerning Pigs, the Pizarros and the Agro-Pastoral Background of the Conquerors of Peru." *Latin American Research Review* 13 (1980), 47–61.

Vivian, R. Gwinn. "Conservation and Diversion: Water Control Systems in the Anasazi Southwest." In Theodore E. Downing and McGuire Gibson (eds.). *Irrigation's Impact on Society,* 95–112. Tucson: University of Arizona Press, 1974.

Walker, Billy D. "Copper Genesis: The Early Years of Santa Rita del Cobre." *New Mexico Historical Review* 54 (January, 1979), 5–20.

Weber, Francis J. "Jesuit Missions in Baja California." *The Americas* 23 (April, 1967), 408–422.

Weniger, Del. "Wilderness, Farm, and Ranch." In *San Antonio in the Eighteenth Century.* San Antonio: San Antonio Bicentennial Heritage Committee, 1976.

Willey, Richard R. "La Canoa: A Spanish Land Grand Lost and Found." *The Smoke Signal* 38 (Fall, 1979), 154–171.

Wittfogel, Karl A. and Esther S. Goldfrank. "Some Aspects of Pueblo Mythology and Society." *Journal of American Folklore* 56 (January–March, 1943), 17–30.

Woodbury, Richard B. and John Q. Ressler. "Effects of Environmental and Cultural Limitations Upon Hohokam Agriculture, Southern Arizona." *University of Utah Anthropological Papers* 62 (December, 1962), 41–45.

UNPUBLISHED WORKS

Dobkins, Betty Eakle. "Indian Water Rights Under Hispanic Law: A Historical Perspective." (Unpublished manuscript prepared for *State of New Mexico vs. R. Lee Aamodt et al.*, 1974).

Jenkins, Myra Ellen. "The Río Hondo Settlement." (Unpublished manuscript, 1974).

———. "Spanish Administration of Indian Affairs during the Sixteenth Century." (Unpublished manuscript).

McKnight, Joseph W. "The Spanish Heritage in Texas Law." (Address presented to the Dallas Historical Society, May 6, 1970.)

Meyer, Michael C., and Susan M. Deeds. "Land, Water, and Equity in Spanish Colonial and Mexican Law: Historical Evidence for the Court in the Case of the State of New Mexico vs. R. Lee Aamodt." (Unpublished manuscript, August, 1979).

Schuetz, Mardith K. "The Indians of the San Antonio Missions, 1718–1821." University of Texas dissertation, 1980.

Taylor, William. "Colonial Land and Water Rights of New Mexico Indian Pueblos." (Unpublished manuscript prepared for the *State of New Mexico vs. R. Lee Aamodt et al.*, n.d.).

Vlasich, James Anthony. "Pueblo Indian Agriculture, Irrigation and Water Rights." University of Utah dissertation, 1980.

Index